Your Breakthroughs

Advice and Instructions from The 400 Year Project (1995-2015)

Donald Mitchell

Author of *Adventures of an Optimist,*
2,000 Percent Living, and *Excellent Solutions*
Coauthor of *The 2,000 Percent Solution*

400 Year Project Press
Weston, Massachusetts
United States of America

Other 400 Year Project Books by Donald Mitchell

2,000 Percent Living
Help Wanted

Excellent Solutions (For-Profit and Nonprofit Editions)
Excellent Leadership

The 2,000 Percent Nation

Witnessing Made Easy (with Bishop Dale Combs, Lisa Combs, Jim Barbarossa, and Carla Barbarossa)
Ways You Can Witness (with Cherie Hill, Roger de Brabant, Drew Dickens, Gael Torcise, Wendy Lobos, Herpha Jane Obod, and Gisele Umugiraneza)

The 2,000 Percent Solution (with Carol Coles and Robert Metz)
The Portable 2,000 Percent Solution (with Carol Coles)
The 2,000 Percent Solution Workbook (with Carol Coles)
The 2,000 Percent Squared Solution (with Carol Coles)

The Irresistible Growth Enterprise (with Carol Coles)
The Ultimate Competitive Advantage (with Carol Coles)

Business Basics

Advanced Business
Advanced Business for Innovation
Advanced Business for Social Benefits

Adventures of an Optimist

Your Breakthroughs
Advice and Lessons from The 400 Year Project (1995-2015)

ISBN: 978-0692520239
0692520236

For information, contact:

Donald W. Mitchell
400 Year Project Press
P.O. Box 302
Weston, Massachusetts 02493
781-647-4211

Published in the United States of America

This book is dedicated to:

Innovators of breakthrough solutions
who apply The 400 Year Project's methods

May quickly and easily making breakthroughs
always be ahead of them!

And their spouses, their children and grandchildren,
and their descendants

May this book help them to always focus
on the Lord and doing His will!

Contents

Acknowledgments

Oh, give thanks to the LORD!
Call upon His name;
Make known His deeds among the peoples!

— 1 Chronicles 16:8 (NKJV)

I thank Almighty God, our Heavenly Father, for creating the universe and all the people on the Earth; our Lord and Savior, Jesus Christ, for providing the way for us to gain Salvation; and the Holy Spirit for guiding our daily paths towards repentance and righteousness. I also humbly acknowledge the perfect guidance I received from God through the Holy Spirit and His Word to write this book.

I feel deeply honored by Carol Bruckner Coles' writing in the book's excellent foreword. Carol coauthored the first six of The 400 Year Project's books with me. Her contributions to the early days of developing the project added many valuable perspectives and practices that continue to be prized. I was particularly pleased by her observations in the foreword about how important it is that the lessons of the project be applied in more areas, especially those that most profoundly affect the quality of life. Carol also cofounded Mitchell and Company, the management consulting firm that formed many of the most valuable precursors for The 400 Year Project's methods. I am most grateful to have had her as a remarkable colleague for so many years.

I am grateful to Peter Drucker for encouraging me to write about 2,000 percent solutions (ways of accomplishing 20 times more with the same or less time, effort, and resources) and to seek ever-simpler ways to help people learn to employ them. His faith in this method for solving problems caused me to take much more seriously the opportunity to share what I had been doing.

I appreciate all those who have permitted me to share with them 2,000 percent solution methods and the output of The 400 Year Project in improving far beyond these methods. I thank those who have applied what they learned for all the insights I have gained from observing their wonderful work.

I can never thank my family enough for allowing me the time and peace to work on such a huge and awe-inspiring project for God. They made many sacrifices without complaining and have been a continual inspiration.

I appreciate my many clients who held off on their demands for my help so that this project could receive the attention it required. Their financial support also made it possible for me to give this time to the Lord and to make this book available.

Finally, I am most appreciative of the many fine improvements that my editor, Bernice Pettinato, made in the text. This is the nineteenth book where she has helped me to make the messages clearer and more pleasant to read. As always, she was a delight to work with. Her kindness made the writing much easier. I value all she has taught me about writing. I look forward to learning new lessons from her during future books.

I accept sole responsibility for any remaining errors and apologize to my readers for any difficulties and inconvenience that they encounter as a consequence.

Foreword

This program [The 400 Year Project] began twenty years ago to try to find ways to accelerate by 20 times the performance of all aspects of human improvement by 2015. The initial applications came in business through writing *The 2,000 Percent Solution*. The project's simple message is to work smarter [stop being stalled] and do something differently [eight steps of effectiveness]. Totally separate from one's religious beliefs, *Your Breakthroughs* offers practical thinking for small and large for-profit companies, nonprofits, and governments to help expand their productivity.

Although manufacturing and service industries were first to accept these ideas, there is a crying need in government, especially in health care, to use new approaches to ensure that all people have the care they need in living and in dying. As a rabbi and hospice chaplain, I am continually astonished and ashamed at the poor level of education and understanding in our healthcare system and in all branches of governments about caring for our elderly and ill at such difficult times in their lives. It has been proven that palliative and hospice care saves vast quantities of money while improving the quality of life. Palliative and hospice service can neither shorten nor lengthen life; that is up to God. However, enjoyment and meaning of life for individuals and their families are the work of humans. One or a combination of the twenty-six lessons of this book can be used to make this objective a reality through practical and rational steps.

Twenty years ago I had the honor and joy of working on the beginning of this project with Don Mitchell and so many other smart and dedicated people. Don has relentlessly pursued this work for two decades with students and professionals in America, Asia, Africa, and Europe. Even with 19 books written for this project, there is still so much to do.

There are simple ideas for beginners in this work like overcoming stalls, or habitual ways of thinking that impede progress. Why do you do something the way you do? Because that's the way it was always done! This is the *tradition stall*. Remember the story of the granddaughter who cut off the ends of the meat before roasting it because that's how her mother and grandmother did it. And why? Because her grandmother did not have a big enough pan, so she sliced off expensive food to fit in her pan, and the part of the roast some people like the best! What are you doing the same way for years? What would you like to improve? The first level of methods discussed in *Your Breakthroughs* will help you learn how to develop and apply a solution to accomplish 20 times more with the same or less time, money, and effort. The book will also show you how to combine more than one of these solutions so that the benefits will multiply. Beyond that you can also make one set of changes that can yield as much as ten complementary 2,000 percent solutions.

Pirke Avot (*The Ethics of Our Fathers*) teaches that the world depends on three things: Torah (the laws and commandments of the Bible), Avodah (work or service to God) and G'milut Chasadim (acts of loving kindness). May we all pursue this work together, and may the work of The 400 Year Project provide ideas to improve humanity and the human condition.

Carol Bruckner Coles
Weston, Massachusetts

August 2015

Introduction

*... (as I have briefly written already,
by which, when you read, you may understand
my knowledge in the mystery of Christ) ....*

— Ephesians 3:3-4 (NKJV)

Summarize 20 years of work by many highly talented people who were led by the Holy Spirit. It's easy to write such a sentence, but it's much harder to accomplish what the sentence says.

At one level, such a summary could be simply stated: The 400 Year Project set audacious goals and with God's help far exceeded the goals. However, such a summary wouldn't teach you how to benefit from what the project accomplished. You wouldn't even know what the goals were. So let me begin with the project's goals. The goals were two:

1. Identify ways that all forms of human improvement could be accelerated by 20 times so that 400 years of normal improvement could occur from 2015 through 2035. (I'm sure the project's name makes a bit more sense to you now.)
2. Conduct demonstrations to identify the most practical ways to accelerate such improvements.

You are probably a little more interested now in what I have to say. After all, if you could accomplish 20 times more or the same things 20 times faster, your life could be much improved. You could live life much more fully, either by accomplishing more in what you are called or have to do, or by having much more free time to do what you like.

I want to honor any such interest by showing how you can be so much more effective. A lazy author might simply point to the list of the eighteen books produced so far by The 400 Year Project and say, "Go to it!"

However, I know that asking you to do such reading is not the most practical way to help. If you wanted to read all of those books, you would have already done so. I'm also aware that the average adult American reads just one book a year, usually a novel. So I need to boil matters down and make them appealing, or not as many people as could benefit will apply The 400 Year Project's lessons.

Let me go further back in time. A story from my youth will help you understand how I am going to provide the advice and instructions you need. As a youngster, I liked nothing better than to read books, magazines, newspapers. My mother sponsored a weekly trip to the library to borrow books, and our family subscribed to the local newspaper, the *San Bernardino Sun-Telegram*. Magazines were a problem, however. Subscriptions were expensive, and buying individual copies was even more costly. To fill the gap, my parents subscribed to the *Reader's Digest*. If you don't know this publication, let me explain how it is prepared. The editors browse many different sources to find the most timely and interesting articles. Other editors then rewrite the articles to make them shorter, simpler, and easier to understand. The result saves readers much time, money, and effort in finding powerful kernels of knowledge, wisdom, and inspiration. My world was greatly expanded and enriched by reading these articles.

To encourage subscribing, the magazine offered contests from time to time. Simply for entering the contest (even if nothing was purchased), you had a chance to receive a prize. At the age of 16, I was one of the lucky winners. I received a beautiful stereo and a set of records containing what someone considered to be the greatest classical music pieces of all time. I was overwhelmed to receive this gift, which launched my lifelong interest in such music. I was also impressed by how repeatedly playing these recordings helped me hear more details and better understand the composers' intentions.

From these two experiences, I learned the value of simplifying, concentrating, and repeating important material. While I doubt if I am nearly as effective in doing so in *Your Breakthroughs* as editors are for the *Reader's Digest*, I have certainly done my best.

While writing this book, I kept two kinds of readers in mind. The first reader was someone who has read none of the project's books. For such a reader, this present volume is complete, accurate, and detailed enough to apply. The second reader is someone who has read at least one of the prior project texts. For this reader, I have built bridges to connect what has already been learned to understanding and applying the related lessons.

Let me explain now about the book's contents and its organization. After much prayer and listening to the Holy Spirit's directions, I summarized the most important lessons The 400 Year Project has learned and accomplished into this one book. In doing so, I restructured the information to emphasize the logical and practical connections, rather than the historical sequence of development, publication, and application. Hopefully, this new structure will be clearer, and easier to grasp and apply. In addition, the structure may make it easier for you to locate information when you revisit the book. (By the way, if you would like to know more background about The 400 Year Project, I've included a brief summary in Appendix B. If you have questions beyond what's there, e-mail me at donmitchell@fastforward400.com/ or read *Adventures of an Optimist* [Mitchell and Company Press, 2007] for the early history.)

In Part One, I describe how your life can be 20 times more fruitful in all dimensions, from the spiritual to the day-to-day. Lesson One focuses on enhancing your personal abilities and effectiveness. Lesson Two addresses accomplishing more at work by bringing the enhanced capabilities developed through Lesson One's practices to the tasks you undertake with others: whether for a paying job, helping your family at home, or as a volunteer serving others. Lesson Three looks specifically at contributing more at your church. As a Christian, I apply my faith's perspective in this lesson. (If you want to learn more about how I became a Christian and how that decision has improved my life, read Appendix A, which contains my testimony.) Lesson Four examines how to greatly enhance your neighborhood and community. Finally, in Lesson Five, we consider how to assist in transforming your nation in the most positive ways.

In Part Two, you will learn how to develop and apply a solution to accomplish 20 times more with the same or less time, money, and effort (something the project calls a "2,000 percent solution"). I begin by describing this method because it has been the easiest one developed by the project for most people to learn and apply. In Lesson Six, we look at a broad range of bad thinking habits that waste time, create frustrations, and steal productivity, what the project calls "stalls," and how to overcome and replace those habits with "stall-busters." In Lesson Seven, I spell out the eight-step process for developing, applying, and improving on a 2,000 percent solution.

In Part Three, we explore ways of combining more than one 2,000 percent solution in complementary ways so that the benefits of each one fully multiply the benefits of all the other ones. In doing so, you can gain 400 times the benefits with two such "complementary" solutions, rather than 40 times greater benefits with two 2,000 percent solutions that aren't complementary. With enough of such complementary solutions, overall benefits can be expanded to mind-boggling dimensions (from 20 with one, to 400 with two, to 8,000 with three, to 160,000 with four, to 3.2 million with five, to 64 million with six, to 1.28 billion with seven, to 25.6 billion with eight, to 512 billion with nine, and to over 10 trillion times with ten such solutions). In Lesson Eight, we look at the proper sequencing of complementary 2,000 percent solutions for those seeking to multiply benefits provided by nonprofit organizations. In Lesson Nine, we do the same for those seeking profits while expanding benefits. In Lesson Ten, we focus on how all organizations can become more effective by frequently improving several dimensions of their business models (the "who," "what," "when," "why," "where," "how," and "how much" of their activities for serving others). Lesson Eleven describes how to always gain advantages from trends, including those that are seemingly adverse or that unexpectedly reverse directions.

With Lesson Twelve, we begin a series of eight lessons addressing 2,000 percent solutions that can easily be made complementary to one another. This lesson looks at how benefits can be greatly multiplied for an organization's stakeholders (all who are significantly affected by what the organization does). In doing so, we focus mostly on beneficiaries, end users, and customers. In Lesson Thirteen, we explore cost cutting. Lesson Fourteen describes ways to reduce investments. In Lesson Fifteen, our investigation considers making current benefits more valuable while supplementing them with still more valuable benefits. Lesson Sixteen details how to accelerate innovation. In Lesson Seventeen, we explore profitable ways to serve pressing social needs. Lesson Eighteen shows ways to help people who are unemployed or underemployed become effective contributors to a breakthrough solution. In Lesson Nineteen, we examine how to best upgrade the effectiveness of stakeholders in ways that will enhance benefits for one and all.

In Part Four, we learn about how to create excellent solutions, the most powerful output so far of The 400 Year Project — a process for making one set of changes to expand benefits by 10 trillion or more times with the same or less time, money, and effort. Lesson Twenty helps you identify your role in such an activity. Lesson Twenty-One then explains the two master processes that can be used to design and implement an excellent solution. Lesson Twenty-Two describes how to identify what benefits to provide. Lesson Twenty-Three discusses ways to launch an unstoppable chain reaction that will speed and increase the benefits the excellent solution delivers.

In Part Five, we focus on applying the first four parts of the book. Lesson Twenty-Four describes how to set more appropriate personal goals. If you find it difficult to conceptualize the details of what improvements to seek, this lesson will be helpful to you. In Lesson Twenty-Five, I explain what kind of help you should seek in making any breakthrough and where you might find such help. Lesson Twenty-Six concludes the book by explaining the importance of keeping up-to-date on future developments in making breakthroughs and how to do so.

Finally, Appendix A relates how I became a Christian and the ways that this decision has improved my life. Appendix B contains a brief history of The 400 Year Project from its inception in 1995.

Part One

2,000 Percent Living

Wisdom is *the principal thing;*
Therefore *get wisdom.*
And in all your getting,
get understanding.

Take firm hold of instruction,
do not let go;
Keep her, for she is *your life.*

— Proverbs 4:7, 13 (NKJV)

What is wisdom? It is doing God's will through abiding in Christ and being fruitful for God's Kingdom, as Jesus described:

"I am the true vine, and My Father is the vinedresser. Every branch in Me that does not bear fruit He takes away; and every *branch* that bears fruit He prunes, that it may bear more fruit. You are already clean because of the word which I have spoken to you. Abide in Me, and I in you. As the branch cannot bear fruit of itself, unless it abides in the vine, neither can you, unless you abide in Me. I am the vine, you *are* the branches. He who abides in Me, and I in him, bears much fruit; for without Me you can do nothing. If anyone does not abide in Me, he is cast out as a branch and is withered; and they gather them and throw *them*

1

into the fire, and they are burned. If you abide in Me, and My words abide in you, you will ask what you desire, and it shall be done for you. By this My Father is glorified, that you bear much fruit; so you will be My disciples." (John 15:1-8, NKJV)

This is a book about fruitfulness, accomplishing more of what God intends. When you follow His directions, you will play a role in creating valuable results that He wants. For your willing contributions to those fruitful results, He will reward you in heaven. In some cases, your life on Earth will also be improved, but remember that exercising faith may, instead, require suffering on Earth:

Others were tortured, not accepting deliverance, that they might obtain a better resurrection. Still others had trial of mockings and scourgings, yes, and of chains and imprisonment. They were stoned, they were sawn in two, were tempted, were slain with the sword. They wandered about in sheepskins and goatskins, being destitute, afflicted, tormented — of whom the world was not worthy. They wandered in deserts and mountains, *in* dens and caves of the earth. And all these, having obtained a good testimony through faith, did not receive the promise, God having provided something better for us, that they should not be made perfect apart from us. (Hebrews 11:35-40, NKJV)

In any case, Jesus promised that all your Earthly needs will be met if you focus on God's Kingdom:

"But seek first the kingdom of God and His righteousness, and all these things shall be added to you." (Matthew 6:33, NKJV)

Understanding Godly ways has led some Christians to enjoy life more, to accomplish so much that they amazed themselves, to have much free time, to be with loved ones more often, and to earn a living in less time and with less effort. When it is God's will, these are some of the potential benefits that 2,000 percent living may offer you.

And while you may or may not gain Earthly benefits, remember that you will certainly gain heavenly ones:

> "Do not lay up for yourselves treasures on earth, where moth and rust destroy and where thieves break in and steal; but lay up for yourselves treasures in heaven, where neither moth nor rust destroys and where thieves do not break in and steal." (Matthew 6:19-20, NKJV)

To gain such benefits, you'll have to make some changes: Stop doing what is harmful and unproductive, and start doing what is greatly beneficial. In doing so, with God's help you will bring Him glory, and gain joy and peace for yourself and those you love.

How do I know what's possible and what's involved? By drawing on God's guidance through reading the Bible, praying, and listening to what I believe is His Holy Spirit, I've been helping people make such improvements for many years in ways that demonstrate the opportunity for everyone on Earth to make improvements at 20 times or more the usual rate. In addition, through the Lord's grace I have gained benefits from 2,000 percent living for myself here on Earth.

Are you ready to start? Lesson One tells you what to do to greatly increase personal effectiveness. Lessons two through five demonstrate how to increase the fruitfulness of God's Kingdom by influencing others.

Lesson One

Personal Effectiveness

Therefore, leaving the discussion of
the elementary principles *of Christ,*
let us go on to perfection ...

— Hebrews 6:1 (NKJV)

This lesson helps you build a foundation for being much more effective, more than 20 times greater, in every important thing you do. Such results can be better than if you could clone yourself 20 times, since that approach complicates communications and coordination.

This lesson identifies fourteen fruitful practices. If you decide that you would like more details about how to apply any of these practices, read the relevant lessons in *2,000 Percent Living* (Salvation Press, 2010).

Practice One: **Accept Salvation by repenting of your sins; believe Jesus is God's Son and in His resurrection from the dead; and give your life to Jesus Christ to do His will, not yours (or rededicate your life to Him if you have accepted Salvation but have not been walking with Him). Start every day by praising and thanking the Lord; praying for what is righteous that you want done in the name of Jesus; and studying the Bible. Attend church whenever possible; make a weekly written commitment of added ways to follow His direction; and continually witness to others** about your faith, seeking to help lead at least 20 people to whom you have been speaking to choose to accept Salvation.

Doing these things will help you to better hear and understand the Holy Spirit's directions for taking the most productive actions on Earth. He may magnify your efforts with supernatural support to make greater performance breakthroughs. As a result, you will have all the wisdom and power you need to do any righteous thing you want that is in God's will. When you respond as directed, you can also earn eternal rewards that will be enjoyed in heaven. How awesome is that?

Practice Two: **Cleanse your mind of distractions, accusations, worries, fears, and annoyances through twice-daily meditation.**

Most people have trouble accomplishing breakthroughs because their minds are full of idle, distracting chatter. Private, peaceful meditation on Bible verses can reduce the volume of irrelevant, useless mental chatter by at least 96 percent, enabling you to hear the Holy Spirit better and focus more on the worthy things that you want to do with your life. As a result, you'll redirect much mental focus to work on opportunities that you've been ignoring or not pursuing actively enough.

Practice Three: **Pick better life objectives through prayer and consultation with your family and friends.**

Many people are working long and hard to achieve results that won't please God, won't be very productive and satisfying for their own lives, and will not improve their relationships with family and friends. For example, one parent may be working long hours and traveling to the ends of the Earth seeking career progress so the family can have more possessions and experiences; but the effect may simply be to undermine the family and its spiritual life by not providing enough time to be together in loving ways doing Godly activities. Talk to the people who know and care about you to get their ideas for better objectives, pray about what you hear, read what the

Bible has to say on the subject, listen to the Holy Spirit, and redirect your energies into far more fruitful paths for doing His will.

Practice Four: **Increase by at least a factor of 20 how much time you spend on your most important goals in serving the Lord.**

What's most important deserves top priority and more than enough time and attention. Instead, most people spend the bulk of their time attending to what others demand be done immediately. By reorganizing and redirecting how you spend your time, you will soon have the ability to focus enough more attention and action to make breakthrough gains by following the Holy Spirit's guidance.

Practice Five: **Expand your ability to read, comprehend, and remember by at least 20 times.**

In order to make breakthroughs, you need to acquire and understand a great deal of new information. Reading is very helpful as one source for such learning. No matter how well or how poorly you read now, you can make great improvements in permanently capturing valuable information through reading more effectively. Doing so can include learning to read without "verbalizing" the words in your mind, looking at more than one word at a time, shifting your eyes more quickly across the material, asking piercing questions about what the writer intended and did as you go, and making notes about what you learn that you can easily access. With the Holy Spirit guiding your reading, you'll then be led to appreciate what new things to do and how to better accomplish worthwhile things you already do.

Practice Six: **Select reading materials that will help you identify and understand the future best practices (the best ways anyone in the world will do that or any similar activity in the next five years) and the ideal best practices (the best ways anyone can ever hope to do that or any similar activity by using technology that** will be available in the next five years) in those areas where you want breakthrough results.

You'll learn more about future and ideal best practices in Lesson Seven. Make a note now to review this principle after reading that lesson. One reason most people accomplish far less than their potential is due to their ignorance about what more effective people already accomplish. It's far more productive to make improvements after first understanding the best knowledge and most effective experiences that are available. With such understanding, the Holy Spirit will show you how to make valuable breakthroughs that serve God.

Practice Seven: **Learn how to identify stalls (bad thinking habits), to eliminate and replace stalls with good thinking habits (stall-busters), and to design and implement 2,000 percent solutions to serve others on God's behalf by producing your first one.**

Lesson Six will teach you about some of the most common stalls and how to overcome them. Make a note now to review this principle after you read that lesson. Most people can develop their first 2,000 percent solution with between 60 and 120 hours of reading, study, and work under the Holy Spirit's direction. If the improvement is an important one, the increased performance gained from the solution will easily repay the time, money, and effort that were invested. You can learn more about how to identify your bad thinking habits and replace them with good ones and to develop 2,000 percent solutions by reading and answering the questions in *The 2,000 Percent Solution* (AMACOM, 1999) and *The 2,000 Percent Solution Workbook* (iUniverse, 2005). Many of the key questions from the workbook are contained in Lesson Eight.

Practice Eight: **Teach someone else how to identify and eliminate stalls and to design and implement 2,000 percent solutions that are attuned to the Holy Spirit.**

The only thing better than creating your own 2,000 percent solutions for God is having others create them without you. When you teach someone the 2,000 percent solution process, you gain the potential to create more Godly benefits from their work. At the same time, the Holy Spirit will help you deepen your understanding of the process. If you ask those you teach to teach others, you create the potential to enjoy a family, a circle of friends, and an organization that's so wonderfully productive for God that most important tasks require little time, attention, or expense. Some people even decide to undertake such teaching as a major activity. If you are interested, *Help Wanted* (2,000 Percent Living Press, 2011) provides much more information about how to conduct such an activity.

Practice Nine: **Apply the 2,000 percent solution process each year to one additional important activity that the Holy Spirit inspires you to improve.**

By doing so, you will become more effective in designing and implementing solutions and surround yourself with the benefits of having many more solutions. Otherwise, you could fall back into your old habits of using far too much time, money, and effort to accomplish what's needed, wasting your life and resources while not fulfilling God's purposes for you.

Practice Ten: **Repeat the 2,000 percent solution process annually to enhance benefits from the solutions you developed by at least an additional twenty times.**

Despite the 2,000 percent solution process calling for continually repeating the first seven steps, most people never do. Since the gains from the first repetition will be 20 times larger than the initial gains, that's a big mistake. And the gains from the second repetition will be 400 times greater than the initial improvement. And so on. In addition, repeating the process in the same solution area usually takes much less time than on the preceding occasion. Further, if the benefits from such a solution can help other solutions to be more fruitful, the potential gain is even greater.

Practice Eleven: **Link together at least seven complementary 2,000 percent solutions to create multiplied, exponential Godly results, or establish an excellent solution.**

We discuss which complementary solutions to combine in Part Three. When you complete the lessons in that part, make a note to return to this principle. This approach is a 2,000 percent solution for making 2,000 percent solutions, increasing the gain achieved from each solution by at least 3,200,000 times. How's that for increased fruitfulness on God's behalf? The Holy Spirit will be essential to helping you pick the right complementary solutions to develop. An excellent solution can be even more productive and should take less time, money, and effort than putting together seven complementary 2,000 percent solutions. Part Four describes how to determine if you are called to play a role with excellent solutions and how to do so.

Practice Twelve: **Increase the benefits from what you do by 20 times to assist some of those who cannot help you.**

Many people take the easy way out when it comes to providing for the poor and helpless, not heeding the Holy Spirit's directions to serve others. As a result, they may simply write a check to help with the symptom of the person's problems (such as buying a meal for a hungry person) while not helping to eliminate the source of the problem (which might be the lack of reading skills needed to be hired for a good job). By using your 2,000 percent solution skills under the Holy Spirit's direction to serve those who cannot help you, you can improve the quality of your life by purifying your heart through becoming more humble and self-sacrificing. Otherwise, all your success with 2,000 percent and excellent solutions could make you prideful, spoiling your relationship with God, the Father; the Lord, Jesus Christ; and the Holy Spirit.

Practice Thirteen: **Approach others with fresh interest, warm gratitude, and a deep desire to draw 20 times closer to them.**

If you don't take steps, your successes may isolate you from many people God wants you to contact. Begin by seeking the Holy Spirit's help to become well acquainted with everyone who is near you (family, friends, neighbors, fellow churchgoers, coworkers, anyone who serves you, people you travel with, and those you see on the street). Then, find out how they look at life. Be delighted when those views are different from yours. Encourage them to also regularly look for views that are different from what they share with you. Delight in sharing differences and learning to understand them. Appreciate each person whenever you see or think of them. Seek opportunities to be with them and to talk with them more often. Pray for them daily. Ask the Holy Spirit what else you should be doing with them.

Practice Fourteen: **Examine your conduct before acting to see if it will be pleasing to God.**

Throughout the day, look at your choices through His eyes before acting and ask the Holy Spirit to direct you. When you find that you've made a mistake, immediately repent and ask His forgiveness and seek to correct the error with those who are affected. Pray for guidance in how to do better next time. In addition, pray several times a day for a pure heart and to be acting in His will. The mistakes you avoid will save you from acting in rebellion to God's will and wasting time, money, and effort. In addition, fixing whatever mistakes you do make right away will limit the damage so that you won't have to do as much later and can, instead, be following the Holy Spirit to the next Godly task you are intended to do.

Are you excited about the possibilities of what I've just described? I hope so. I know that I'm excited for you. These practices are so powerful that when you apply them all your fruitfulness for God's Kingdom won't go up by only 20 times. Rather, you'll see your fruitfulness expand by an exponential factor of 20.

While it's fun to contemplate such a result, it's more important to begin achieving it. Your assignments are listed below to help you do so.

Lesson One Assignments

1. Establish a list of dates by which you will begin to apply each practice in this lesson.

2. Keep a journal of how you spend your time during the next two weeks, noting how you spend every waking moment. Summarize the results by types of activity. Determine what you could eliminate, reduce, or delegate to free up at least 10 hours a week to work on applying these fourteen practices.

3. The day before you are scheduled to begin applying a practice, make a plan for what you will do each day to learn about, gain experience in, or expand your use of the practice until it becomes an ingrained, effective habit.

4. Pray daily for the Holy Spirit to refill you with His presence so that you can be more fruitful in these activities.

5. Write down and report your daily progress to a loved one or friend who shares your interest in increasing fruitfulness. Ask that person to encourage you and to hold you accountable for your commitments to learn and apply these practices.

Lesson Two

Work Accomplishments

For no other foundation can anyone lay
than that which is laid, which is Jesus Christ.
Now if anyone builds on this foundation with
gold, silver, precious stones, wood, hay, straw,
each one's work will become clear;
for the Day will declare it, because it will be revealed by fire;
and the fire will test each one's work, of what sort it is.
If anyone's work which he has built on it endures,
he will receive a reward.
If anyone's work is burned, he will suffer loss;
but he himself will be saved, yet so as through fire.

— 1 Corinthians 3:11-15 (NKJV)

In these verses from 1 Corinthians 3 (NKJV), the Apostle Paul is referring to the work of sharing the Gospel. However, I believe that the same points apply to all of our work: Our efforts either build on the foundation of what Jesus has taught us to do, or the results of our efforts will be fruitless. While much work we do, such as handling paperwork, paying personal bills, washing clothes, or stuffing envelopes for a charity, would seem to have little spiritual significance, we should keep in mind that doing these activities with love, in faith, and with kindness can set good examples for causing others to wonder what we, as believers, have that they do not. Someone might eventually gain Salvation after beginning with such wondering.

The choice of what work we do, as well, makes a difference. While our activities on behalf of serving our families may be somewhat unavoidable due to their necessity, the kind of work we do for pay, for friends and neighbors, and for those who are strangers to us can often be chosen to be more helpful for expanding God's Kingdom. We each have different spiritual gifts, and those gifts can be employed in many different contexts. Let's imagine someone with the gift of hospitality. A young person with this gift might work in a service job, whether as a food server, as a cleaner, or in taking orders for various offerings. While such seemingly low-skill jobs might at first seem to be unrelated to God's Kingdom, they can, instead, be employed in places where the Kingdom is served. The work might be done at a Salvation Army homeless shelter, or even at a swank restaurant. While the latter will pay better, the former is probably going to contribute more to the Kingdom. Such choices are even clearer when we consider volunteer activities. Some are going to be relatively unrelated to the Kingdom, other than providing opportunities to meet unbelievers, while other volunteer tasks are going to inspire believers and unbelievers alike to serve the Kingdom. In this regard, consider the difference between volunteering for a secular charity and working for a child evangelism ministry.

After incorporating Lesson One into your life, you face a new challenge: carrying your newly developed skills for being more fruitful into the places where you work and influencing believing and unbelieving family, friends, neighbors, volunteers, and coworkers to acquire and apply such skills. While that challenge may seem like an easy one, you will probably meet at least some resistance.

Let me explain. It's human nature to feel confident about the purposes you have chosen to advance and the ways that these purposes are being advanced. After all, a lot of thought goes into making most of your life decisions, including choice of work.

The same confidence is felt by those in authority. Consider that someone who has a leadership role in any sort of work has probably put his or her personal stamp on how that work is conducted and feels that doing so in that way is most appropriate. When such a perspective exists, any suggestion of doing something different can feel to the leader like being personally criticized or even repudiated. Naturally, such a feeling means that someone might dig in her or his heels and resist the beneficial changes you propose. In fact, the more well-meaning and righteous the person is, the more confidence such a person may bring in resisting. Unless the individual is truly humble, the pathway to greater fruitfulness can be blocked.

In this lesson, I introduce you to some of the ways of thinking that can serve as such blockages, what I call *stalls*. I'll also introduce *stallbusters*, ways of overcoming such stalls, whether in yourself or someone else.

We begin with the *Tradition stall*, the unquestioning assumption that the ways things have and are being done do not need to be changed. While you may not think that you and your colleagues are subject to this limitation, consider this version of an often-told story about resistance to change as related in *The 2,000 Percent Solution* (AMACOM, 1999):

Imagine a cage containing five apes. In the cage, hang a banana on a string and put stairs under it. Before long, so the story goes, an ape will go to the stairs and start to climb toward the banana. As soon as it touches the stairs, spray all the apes with cold water. After a while, another ape makes an attempt with the same result: All the apes are sprayed with cold water.

Do this repeatedly and then just watch when another ape later tries to climb the stairs. The other apes will try to prevent it even though no water sprays them.

Now, remove one ape from the cage and replace it with a new one. The new ape sees the banana and wants to climb the stairs. To its horror, all of the other apes attack. After another attempt and attack, it knows that if it tries to climb the stairs, it will be assaulted. Next, remove another of the original five apes and replace it with a new one. The newcomer goes to the stairs and is attacked. The previous newcomer takes part in the punishment with enthusiasm although it has no idea why it was not permitted to climb the stairs.

After replacing the third, fourth, and fifth original apes, all the apes that had been sprayed with cold water have been replaced. Nevertheless, no ape ever again approaches the stairs. Why not? "Because that's the way it's always been around here." Sound familiar?

To overcome such faulty thinking requires making each person conscious of decisions to keep things the way they are and what the consequences of those decisions are. Here are four key questions that can help:

1. What traditions slow down or increase the cost of accomplishing important results?
2. What benefits do these traditions provide?
3. What values were intended to be served by the traditions?
4. What problems are created by the traditions?

Having identified these answers, it's time to consider if the traditions need to be amended or be totally replaced by more fruitful traditions that are consistent with the values involved. Naturally, if you are dealing with believers, you can draw on Biblical examples to encourage shifts. Otherwise, you'll have to ask for permission to experiment with new methods in ways that are consistent with the values of those involved.

Next, we look at the *Disbelief stall*, discounting the accuracy or usefulness of new information. In taking this approach, someone is saying that she or he knows all: No one else could possibly improve on this knowledge and understanding. Here are two famous examples:

One hundred years ago, Alexander Graham Bell supposedly offered his ailing telephone business to the then king of communications, Western Union, for $100,000. Western Union's leader scoffed at the idea, disparaging Bell with the words, "What use could our company make of an electrical toy?"

The usefulness of electronic computers, created during World War II, was suspect even to their most avid supporter. Thomas J. Watson, Sr., who was to build the massive IBM upon mainframe computers, was quoted in 1943 as saying there was probably a world market for only five of the machines.

Improving matters means putting the burden of proof on the current ways of thinking, as well as on the new information. Here are four useful questions to ask:

1. What are others doing that produces better results?
2. What are people talking about that you are ignoring?
3. What complaints have you been ignoring?
4. What is the minimum evidence needed about the new information to require taking action?

Let's look now at the *Misconception stall*, misinterpreting information and then drawing the wrong conclusions. Here is a deadly example:

The fate of the *Titanic* illustrates the misconception stall at work overtime. It was a monumental misconception to believe that the ship was unsinkable and not to provide sufficient lifeboats to save all passengers in case of an accident.

The ship's designers created a ship that could survive any head-on collision. They didn't think about the possibility of the side of the ship being gashed by a passing iceberg so that many of the watertight compartments would be breached.

Having "known" that the ship could not sink, why would the owners bother to put a full complement of lifeboats on board? As a result of their misconception, 1,503 people lost their lives.

Digging into interpretations of information can help. Here are nine questions for doing such digging:

1. What is being assumed about what will almost always work?
2. What is being assumed about what will hardly ever work?
3. What is assumed will happen?
4. What is assumed will never happen?
5. On what beliefs and evidence are these assumptions based?
6. Have these beliefs and evidence been checked lately for accuracy?
7. Are the beliefs and evidence still true?
8. Which incorrect assumptions are most harmful?
9. What assumptions should replace the most harmful ones?

We consider next what I call the *Unattractiveness stall*. Think of the fairy tale, *The Ugly Duckling*, in which a duck family raises a swan chick, which is considered to be a most unattractive duckling until becoming a gorgeous swan that is much admired. Could some avoidance of what seems to be unattractive be keeping you from seeing remarkable potential? Here are eight questions to help avoid missing opportunities due to seeming unattractiveness:

1. What places are seldom visited?
2. What can be learned by visiting these places?
3. What individuals and organizations are never contacted?
4. How can more be learned about these people and places in open-minded ways?
5. Who already sees these people and places as desirable?
6. How could these people and places provide great opportunities?
7. Who could help with identifying the potential?
8. How can ideas for change be easily and quickly tested?

We turn now to the *Communications stall*, assuming that others know and understand what we want. Here's a probably apocryphal Hollywood story that humorously demonstrates the point:

Film director Cecil B. DeMille spared no expense to part the Red Sea for his epic *The Ten Commandments*. Actors, film crew, engineers, horses, and assorted other animals were everywhere. The dust, heat, and noise were ferocious. Finally, everyone was ready to go and DeMille called out, "Roll the cameras."

After the scene was shot, DeMille called to a cameraman on a high cliff to check how that part of the shooting had gone.

The cameraman reportedly yelled back, "Ready when you are, C. B.!"

Here are seven questions designed to improve your communications:

1. Which communications have worked best?
2. Why were these communications more successful?
3. How can these lessons be carried over into other communications?
4. How can the same results be achieved more easily and efficiently?
5. What was missing from the most problematic communications?

6. What do great communicators do differently?
7. What aspects of the great communicators' methods can be applied?

Our next subject is the *Bureaucratic stall*, which you can probably appreciate simply by thinking about its name. Just in case you didn't get the point, here's a joke that may help:

How many bureaucrats does it take to change a lightbulb?

We'll get back to you on that.

Bureaucracy can cause an organization to experience delays, make more mistakes, be misunderstood, have higher costs, and be ineffective in important activities. Here are four questions designed to help clear away such effects:

1. How can problem areas that need improving be identified?
2. How can fragmented processes be streamlined?
3. How can what's unnecessary be eliminated?
4. What are appropriate improvement goals?

Finally, we look at a personal nemesis for many people: the *Procrastination stall*. As the name implies, some people put off doing what should be done sooner. In an organization, procrastination by one person can lead to important work being delayed and done less well. Such problems are especially likely when the boss is a procrastinator. Here are three questions that can help with learning how to hesitate to procrastinate:

1. When and where is delay usually harmful?
2. How can a bias for action be established in such circumstances?
3. What rules might help to establish an appropriate bias for action?

While there are many other stalls, I think mastering these particular stalls with stallbusters for those you work with should enable you to accomplish much more. Be sure to also read and apply Lesson Six, which describes several more stalls and their stallbusters that may affect you as well as others.

Lesson Two Assignments

1. How can your choice of work become more fruitful for God's Kingdom?

2. How can you work in ways that will draw nonbelievers to be interested in learning about Salvation?

3. Which stalls are limiting your use of the newly developed skills in Lesson One?

4. How can answering the questions related to overcoming stalls be made more fruitful for advancing God's Kingdom?

Lesson Three

Church Contributions

Paul went in to him and prayed, and
he laid his hands on him and healed him.
So when this was done, the rest of those on the island
who had diseases also came and were healed.
They also honored us in many ways;
and when we departed,
they provided such things as were necessary.

— Acts 28:8-10 (NKJV)

Mention church contributions, and many people first think about putting tithes and offerings onto a plate that's passed during a service. While that's certainly one way that a believer can contribute to a church, in this lesson we look at church contributions in a broader sense, as partially captured by Acts 28:8-10 (NKJV). In these verses, the Apostle Paul uses his spiritual gift of healing through the Holy Spirit to bear witness to the truth of the Gospel. In doing so, Paul added new believers to the Body of Christ, the universal church. The newly healed, in turn, then provided for the material needs of the shipwrecked travelers. Consider these events as a partial picture of how each person should contribute in her or his unique ways so that the needs of all others can be met.

Unless you are the senior pastor of a congregation, chances are that you haven't given much thought to what the key activities of a church should be. Take a moment now to explore this subject with me. As a result of better understanding these purposes for helping to expand God's Kingdom, you'll be able to identify more ways that you can contribute. If learning about these potential contributions interests you, you can find more information in Chapter 3 of *The 2,000 Percent Nation* (400 Year Project Press, 2012).

To greatly increase fruitfulness for the Lord, many churches will need to expand the breadth of what they do and improve performance in some of what they do now. Before explaining what I mean by the prior sentence and describing what churches should concentrate on, let me note that we should always remember that Christ leads the church. Let me also observe that human leadership is unusually important for a congregation to serve God in the most fruitful ways.

In setting their agendas, congregations are led in a variety of ways in addition to what the Holy Spirit and the Bible direct: some by higher human authorities, some by pastors and ministers, and some by the congregation or lay leaders of it. While I am sure that the Holy Spirit and the Bible are perfect sources of Godly wisdom, in dealing with humans there are bound to be misunderstandings and errors. God knows that and forgives when we repent. However, His grace in this regard should not draw us away from seeking more of His wisdom so that we can do better.

In sharing my observations in this lesson, I pray that I have been faithful and accurate in expressing God's will. I apologize to God and to all my readers for any errors. In addition, I am in no way judging what any churches or their leaders are doing now. Leaders should simply pray about this lesson's information to receive guidance from the Holy Spirit and the Bible, should study what the Bible has to say on the subject, and should take action according to that Divine guidance.

Many Christians would agree that a church should provide for at least the following needs:

- Treat all with love. It's commanded by Jesus in the Bible. Some may not be receiving love from other people.
- Teach Scripture to the young and adults who lack knowledge about the Bible's contents, especially concerning what God's Word says about receiving the free gift of Salvation.
- Encourage of-age congregants and visitors to repent their sins, believe in the risen Savior, and follow Jesus as Lord so they will obtain the free gift of Salvation.
- Nudge congregants to invite and bring their families, friends, neighbors, and coworkers to church.
- Tend to the spiritual needs of the congregation and visitors.
- Approve of living in ways commanded by the Bible.
- Rebuke saved people who are stuck in some repeated sins.
- Provide opportunities for fellowship with saved people.
- Serve the physical needs of the congregation and its poorest and most vulnerable neighbors.
- Support foreign missions through prayer, working visits, and gifts of needed items and funds.

However, if a church limits its official activities to this list, there's a problem: Most people in the congregation won't be as fruitful for the Lord as they could be. Let me begin explaining why I say that by quoting Jesus, as He commented on what the parable of the sower means:

"The sower sows the word. And these are the ones by the wayside where the word is sown. When they hear, Satan comes immediately and takes away the word that was sown in their hearts. These likewise are the ones sown on stony ground who, when they hear the word, immediately receive it with gladness; and they have no root in themselves, and so endure only for a time. Afterward, when tribulation or persecution arises for the word's sake, immediately they stumble. Now these are the ones sown among thorns; *they are* the ones who hear the word, and the

25

cares of this world, the deceitfulness of riches, and the desires for other things entering in choke the word, and it becomes unfruitful. But these are the ones sown on good ground, those who hear the word, accept *it,* and bear fruit: some thirty fold, some sixty, and some a hundred." (Mark 4:14-20, NKJV)

While Jesus clearly told us that many people who learn about the Bible and Salvation aren't going to make good use of that knowledge, He also told us that some Christians can be exponentially fruitful for Him in sharing the Good News. Building on His observation, it seems that churches have substantial opportunities to help people learn the Gospel, become saved, fulfill their Godly callings, and use their efforts to exponentially increase His influence. Such potential for extraordinary fruitfulness lies within us all.

Churches have marvelous opportunities to focus on increasing fruitfulness. One such opportunity that might not occur to some church leaders is helping individuals learn and apply the practices described in Lesson One. Increased witnessing and effectiveness in doing so will be among the benefits. Here are some church activities that can make such learning even more fruitful:

- Spend at least five minutes teaching and encouraging witnessing with in-congregation evangelists during each church activity, class, and service.
- Add these six other fruitful dimensions of teaching and encouraging witnessing:

    (1) Ask Christians to make increased written commitments to witnessing activities.
    (2) Establish low-cost Christian radio networks and stations providing music and programs that appeal to unsaved people where little or no programming exists for sharing the Gospel. If a church's locale has enough of such sta-

tions, a church should support this activity where such stations are needed.

(3) Make available at all times and to all people witnesses who are well equipped to discuss accepting Salvation.

(4) Ask for more kinds of help to expand witnessing from more people in more ways.

(5) Serve pressing physical and emotional needs of more unsaved people and seek opportunities to witness after aiding them.

(6) Seek out and witness to more unsaved people with secret sins that deeply embarrass them.

- Establish each necessary congregational ministry and develop three complementary 2,000 percent solutions that make each ministry at least 8,000 times more fruitful, especially in developing disciples.
- Advance the congregation's effective knowledge of the Christian faith by greatly increasing how many saved people know:

(1) the essential elements of what the Bible says about receiving Christ's free gift of Salvation

(2) how to deepen and strengthen their relationships with Jesus Christ after accepting Salvation

(3) the difference between sinning and not sinning in their typical daily activities

(4) why and how to repent when they sin

(5) what the Bible says they should pray for and what they should not pray for

(6) what the Bible tells us about how to relate to people who aren't Christians

(7) what the Bible tells us about how to behave toward a fellow Christian who is observed to be sinning

(8) how to accurately apply their Biblical knowledge with joyful and loving hearts to the seven prior measurement areas in this part of the list

At the present time, few churches are stretching themselves to do as much as possible in these dimensions. In this regard, a church that focuses on and becomes more fruitful in accomplishing these purposes can also be an example to other churches. Such a church should also be sharing its experiences with other churches and helping those churches that want to be more fruitful to do so more effectively.

Naturally, you might be feeling a little overwhelmed by thinking about such large changes. Take some time to reread the prior part of this lesson now and pray about what God is calling you to do in these regards. Also, realize that not all such changes can be made at the same time. I'm sure you will find peace about what role God has planned for you.

Let me suggest a few possible roles to help start your thinking. First, you could simply share this lesson with others in your church. I suggest doing so in a spirit of friendly inquiry to learn their reactions, rather than in a spirit of inflexible advocacy. Churches need to be united in Christ, and any ideas for change contain within them the potential to stir harmful division rather than to increase unity.

Second, a church may be engaged in some of these activities, but simply lacks enough resources to be able to accomplish as much as would be desirable. In such a circumstance, your willingness to volunteer or to add resources can make a huge difference.

Third, you could volunteer to assist in establishing some of these activities. Since the process for doing so varies from church to church, I can't precisely tell you how to go about that. However, there is probably someone on the church staff who has responsibility for what you want to improve. Chances are good that person would also like to improve, but he or she hasn't yet found a way to do so that fits with existing resources. Your willingness to accomplish more without drawing down existing resources will probably be appreciated. Doing so may mean attracting new volunteers or encouraging those with access to resources to share more of them.

Fourth, your church might be so overwhelmed with needs compared to the available staff, volunteer time, and financial resources that remedying such difficulties would have to precede making the kinds of changes described in this lesson. You might be called to dig in to help out with your own time, attracting other volunteers, and assisting with attracting more financial resources to deal with those pressing needs.

Lesson Three Assignments

1. What role has God called you to play in helping your church become more fruitful?

2. How can you help your church to become much more fruitful?

3. How can you do so in a way that will increase the congregation's unity in Christ?

Lesson Four

Community Enhancement

"And do not seek what you should eat
or what you should drink,
nor have an anxious mind.
For all these things
the nations of the world seek after,
and your Father knows
that you need these things.
But seek the kingdom of God, and
all these things shall be added to you.
Do not fear, little flock,
for it is your Father's good pleasure
to give you the kingdom."

— Luke 12:29-32 (NKJV)

These verses from Luke 12 (NKJV) remind us that God will provide for the needs of those who follow Him in seeking to advance His Kingdom. Clearly, one opportunity for which many individuals and companies have not done enough is in supporting Christian ministries, organizations, and activities in the communities where they work and live. Here is an area where setting a good example can make a difference. Those who want to be well regarded in a community often emulate whatever the most respected people do. When such individuals are actively leading and serving in fruitful Christian ministries, organizations, and activities, many others will do the same.

Let's look first at the role of Christian ministries so we can best appreciate how to assist their activities. Tasks for creating an enhanced community that require support from a large number of believers can almost always be better accomplished by independent Christian ministries than by a single church. Here are some of the typical reasons why having greater size and independence can permit accomplishing more and better serving God's will:

- Greater visibility of a ministry and its task makes it easier to recruit volunteers and any needed resources.
- Tasks can be better studied and simplified so that more people can succeed as helpful volunteers and increase how much each person can accomplish.
- Volunteers can be more easily focused on learning more about how to perform and gain joy from doing their activities.
- Scale effects offer opportunities to lower the time and costs of performing an activity or delivering a benefit so that volunteer efforts and financial resources can be stretched to serve more beneficiaries.
- Recipient benefits can be greatly increased by combining many more dimensions of exponential breakthroughs.
- Larger and more difficult projects can be accomplished.
- Credibility from providing excellent benefits at low cost helps attract more resources as well as greater interest in obtaining the benefits.

Despite the value and importance of improving as much as possible in performing activities that God wants us to do, most Christian ministries are only achieving a small percentage of their full performance potential. Those who are skilled in developing and helping others learn how to use exponential performance-improvement methods can assist any such ministries to close any gaps between their full potential and the Godly fruit they currently provide.

Each Christian ministry's opportunities for accomplishing more are somewhat different, but I believe that many have in common five important performance-improvement opportunities that should usually be attended to in the following sequence:

1. Ensure that the ministry is optimally focused on accomplishing the right results for God.
2. Determine the tasks needed to accomplish the right results.
3. Make the benefit-producing tasks irresistibly appealing.
4. Find ways to serve needs in extraordinarily low-cost, effective ways that require few physical resources and little volunteer time.
5. Obtain enough resources to provide for *all* needs.

By contrast, many Christian ministries focus first on obtaining more resources, less often search for more effective ways of serving needs, rarely look to improve the appeal of performing any required tasks, haven't considered in decades what results should be accomplished, and don't ever think about what tasks are required for producing the right results. Because few donors are excited about providing resources for organizations that inefficiently deliver benefits and have trouble attracting enough volunteers, focusing first on obtaining greater resources often works poorly. In addition, the resources that are received don't help much due to inefficiencies in the ways that benefits are supplied. Volunteers see and are discouraged by any waste, don't enjoy the work very much, complain about their experiences to potential volunteers and donors, and are reluctant to continue. When potential donors learn about the volunteers' reservations, they become less willing to provide financial and physical resources.

Exponential improvements in serving needs are developed faster and better by doing more to engage the attention and enthusiastic support of as many dedicated people as possible. When you design from the beginning any tasks for providing benefits to be the ones God wants done and to make those tasks irresistibly appealing, you will attract the kind and size of interest that can lead to rapid, substantial improvements in a Christian ministry's activities. How individuals can assist Christian nonprofit organizations to accomplish such a shift in focus is described in Chapter Three of *Help Wanted* (2,000 Percent Living Press, 2011), and those lessons also apply to assisting Christian ministries.

Some Christian ministries have a fundamental improvement opportunity that should precede identifying and making performance enhancements: evaluating how well they are focusing on accomplishing God's purposes. If the intended purposes being acted on are incomplete or mistaken, then the activity's focus will be misdirected for increasing fruitfulness, as well. Other nonprofit organizations, as well as for-profit companies, may have similar opportunities to redirect their purposes to become more fruitful. Let's turn now to looking at the ways that fruitfulness of all such other organizations and companies can be increased. Since for-profit companies are a bigger part of most communities than all other organizations, we'll mostly talk about them.

Enhancing communities is an activity where there is often a lot more organizational lip service (such as informally promising benefits) than practical results. Instead, organizations with jobs that can be brought into or taken away from a community are always being aggressively pursued by government authorities with offers of large subsidized loans, tax forgiveness, and legal exceptions the value of which almost always vastly exceed the value of what the companies ultimately bring to the community. In some cases, taking advantage of a community is unintentional on the company's part. In some other cases, it's a deliberate part of the company's way of doing business.

While at one time leaders and respected people were usually committed to being community improvers, such activities are more often sought today primarily for ego gratification. The closest some companies come to making an investment in some communities where they operate is through sponsorship of a professional sporting event (such as a golf tournament) or buying the naming rights to a local sports stadium.

In addition, many companies also operate in ways that harm the value of neighbors' properties and activities, affecting a portion of the local community. Classic examples in the United States have occurred where companies dumped toxic materials for decades into groundwater, rivers, and streams. Some of these sites will take decades to clean up. The local land is valueless until the remediation is complete. In the meantime, those who come near often have increased risk of becoming ill and then dying prematurely.

Even the most well-meaning leaders often think much more in terms of their responsibilities to shareholders, customers, and lenders than they do to the communities in which they operate. That's often true, in part, because the highly paid leaders reside in different towns that are unaffected by their operations. With such employees leaving behind at 5 p.m. problems that the company has created, the communities in which they operate predictably decline.

Let me contrast such examples with one that I observed in White Plains, New York, part of high-income Westchester County located just north of New York City. For many years, one of the largest employers in the community was General Foods Corporation, then one of the largest companies in the world. Just after World War II, General Foods decided to build a new headquarters on a very visible, prime location near downtown White Plains.

While many companies only build such facilities to serve themselves, the leaders of General Foods were concerned about the effect on the neighborhood and what would happen when the company outgrew the building. As one example, with the site being located across the street from the largest hospital in the area, the company leaders spent time with the hospital's leaders determining how their new corporate headquarters might be later converted into expansion space for the hospital. Although that eventuality hasn't yet happened,

General Foods set a standard followed by many other companies that later came into the community. As a result, large employers are often located on sites that more resemble public parks than commercial facilities, with access to major roads that minimizes the effects on local traffic for those who live and work nearby. Go only a quarter mile from many of these locations, and you would never know that there are high-density commercial uses in the vicinity.

So, companies can be sources of and magnets for improvement rather than introducers of decay and death. That's what General Foods did. When that happens, the value of the company's land and buildings is higher, employees better enjoy their work, more people may decide to live nearby (cutting down on commuting time), and the community will have a larger tax base.

If enough companies do this, the community may see its ability to provide public services increase more rapidly than new demands are made for such services. This is especially true if the company makes improvements in ways that provide benefits for others in the community. For instance, a company going into a town lacking sewage treatment facilities might build such facilities large enough to provide service for other businesses, homeowners, and the local government.

Adding value isn't limited to making surroundings more attractive and providing new classes of services. Benefits can also relate to upgrading the kind of public services that have a large impact on the value of real estate in local communities, such as schools. A company is likely to be filled with employees whose knowledge and skills can be tremendous resources for the local community when such employees volunteer their time. Companies can increase volunteering by encouraging it. Some companies even pay employees to spend part of their work weeks in public service.

In recent years, Professor Michael E. Porter of Harvard Business School has been one of several researchers looking at the importance of developing vibrant local communities to provide talent, knowledge, resources, and infrastructure to allow everyone in an industry to prosper. One of his favorite examples is the international flower market located in the Netherlands. This market is so well organized and effectively operated that European, Middle Eastern, and North American suppliers bring flowers there to sell even when likely customers may be located in their own country. The advantages of this specialized community outweigh the transportation costs. You see similar benefits occurring in diamond-cutting.

Let me also describe what a successful company leader can do by citing the example of Tom Golisano, founder of Paychex, based in Rochester, New York. As a result of Golisano's success in building Paychex from a three-person operation to a multibillion-dollar-value enterprise, he became a billionaire. Looking closely at Rochester, he realized that there wasn't a sufficient base in IT education to keep his company strong if it stayed there.

While many companies would simply pick up and move, Tom Golisano felt that Rochester was a good place for Paychex to be located. He often jokingly referred to how bad the weather is there as one reason why Paychex employees often worked so long and hard: There's nothing better to do on most days. Choosing to make a local commitment, he donated hundreds of millions of his own money to upgrade the local high schools and colleges so that IT talent would improve and be more abundant. It's an example that could be followed by any company's leaders who succeed in creating substantial wealth for themselves and their stakeholders.

I believe that Kingdom-improving companies will study such examples and seek to exceed best practices in these and other dimensions of performance so that they can enjoy a sounder local foundation for their success: a much more vibrant, desirable, and valuable community in which to operate.

Although the benefits of such changes will often show up more visibly in terms of economic effects than in spiritual ones, I believe that even greater blessings will be enjoyed in terms of personal satisfaction from seeing people enjoy better lives and fulfill much more of their potential for God's Kingdom.

Lesson Four Assignments

1. What has God called you to do for enhancing your community's fruitfulness?

2. Who can teach you how to become a great example of enhancing your community through individual activities?

3. What can you learn from such people?

4. Who can teach you how to become a great example of enhancing your community through your leadership roles?

5. What can you learn from such people?

6. Who can teach you how to become highly effective in improving the fruitfulness of Christian ministries, organizations, and activities, as well as those of nonprofit organizations and for-profit firms?

7. What can you learn from such people?

8. What are the best ways you can contribute to enhancing the fruitfulness of your community?

Lesson Five

National Breakthroughs

*"You did not choose Me, but I chose you and appointed you
that you should go and bear fruit,
and that your fruit should remain,
that whatever you ask the Father in My name
He may give you."*

— John 15:16 (NKJV)

This lesson draws on Chapter 1 of *The 2,000 Percent Nation*. If you want to better understand these points, be sure to visit that chapter. Additionally, realize that what is described here can also be applied to governmental units both smaller and larger than a nation.

If you are like I was before writing that book, you may not have given much thought about how God might measure the fruitfulness of a nation for His Kingdom. While He knows exactly how things are going, we usually don't. We cannot hope to match His perfect knowledge, but we can certainly reduce our ignorance.

To help you make a faster start in appreciating what national breakthroughs are needed, I summarize here five possible dimensions and related measurements of national fruitfulness from God's perspective that are drawn from the aforementioned chapter:

1. Spiritual

   a. Number of saved people
   b. How many saved people correctly apply the Bible while sharing the Gospel
   c. How often saved people correctly share the Gospel and with how many unsaved people

2. Moral

   a. Number of moral acts inspired by the Holy Spirit that are occurring as described in Galatians 5:16-26 (NKJV):

   I say then: Walk in the Spirit, and you shall not fulfill the lust of the flesh. For the flesh lusts against the Spirit, and the Spirit against the flesh; and these are contrary to one another, so that you do not do the things that you wish. But if you are led by the Spirit, you are not under the law.

   Now the works of the flesh are evident, which are: adultery, fornication, uncleanness, lewdness, idolatry, sorcery, hatred, contentions, jealousies, outbursts of wrath, selfish ambitions, dissensions, heresies, envy, murders, drunkenness, revelries, and the like; of which I tell you beforehand, just as I also told *you* in time past, that those who practice such things will not inherit the kingdom of God.

   But the fruit of the Spirit is love, joy, peace, longsuffering, kindness, goodness, faithfulness, gentleness, self-control. Against such there is no law. And those *who are* Christ's have crucified the flesh with its passions and desires. If we live in the Spirit, let us also walk in the Spirit. Let us not become conceited, provoking one another, envying one another.

    b. Number of immoral acts due to the lusts of the flesh that are occurring as described in Galatians 5:16-26 (NKJV)

3. Health

    a. Number of people whose health enables them to fulfill His callings for them

    b. How long these people have had sufficient good health to fulfill their callings

4. Emotional

    a. Number of people who are emotionally able to fulfill His callings for them

    b. Number of people who are able to lift the spirits of others to fulfill their callings if they are already believers, or to seek Him if they are not yet saved

    c. Number of actions taken to lift the spirits of others so that they fulfill their callings if they are already believers, or to seek Him if they are not yet saved

    d. Number of actions taken to fulfill His callings and to seek Him as a result of having received emotional encouragement from Christians

5. Physical

    a. Number of people who have enough resources to sustain a healthy, active life

    b. Number of Christians who have the resources they need to draw closer to God and to fulfill their callings for Him

I well remember my first exposure to this list when the Holy Spirit had revealed it to me. You may be experiencing some of those emotions. My initial reaction was to think that it would be overwhelming to figure out all of these things. Then, the Holy Spirit filled me with knowledge about how to do so. If you feel as I did and happen to be unfamiliar with ways to measure such dimensions of a nation, you may find it helpful to read a brief description of how that might be accomplished through national polls and surveys conducted with significant samples of randomly selected people:

1. Spiritual

   a. Explain to all people in a nation what it means to be saved and ask if they have repented of their sins, believed in their hearts that Jesus rose from the dead, and dedicated their lives aloud to following Jesus as Lord and Savior.
   b. Ask saved people about how their lives and behaviors have changed since accepting Salvation.
   c. Ask family members who know saved people well what changes they have observed in increased good behavior and decreased bad behavior as defined by the verses of Galatians 5:16-26 (NKJV).
   d. Ask nonfamily members who know saved people well what changes they have observed in increased good behavior and decreased bad behavior as defined by Galatians 5:16-26 (NKJV).
   e. Routinely ask national samples of saved people how and how often they have shared the Gospel message with unsaved people in their own families.
   f. Routinely ask national samples of saved people how and how often they have shared the Gospel message with unsaved people who are not in their own families.
   g. Routinely ask national samples of unsaved people how and how often someone has shared the Gospel message with them.

2. Moral

    a. Routinely ask randomly selected national samples of people how often they have observed or experienced a list of moral acts (as defined in Galatians 5:16-26, NKJV) done by others in the prior week.

    b. Routinely ask randomly selected national samples of people how often they have observed or experienced a list of immoral acts (as defined in Galatians 5:16-26, NKJV) done by others in the prior week.

    c. Routinely ask randomly selected local samples of people how often they have observed or experienced a list of moral acts (as defined in Galatians 5:16-26, NKJV) done by others in the prior week.

    d. Routinely ask randomly selected local samples of people how often they have observed or experienced a list of immoral acts (as defined in Galatians 5:16-26, NKJV) done by others in the prior week.

3. Health

    a. Track annual physical examinations supplemented by laboratory tests to measure factors that accurately describe the current and future level of full functioning, longevity, and ability to perform each person's calling from God.

    b. Develop information about what the measurements mean and how to improve the underlying circumstances that lead to the measured results.

    c. Measure national usage information about medications and therapies employed to ameliorate unhealthy medical conditions that limit full functioning, longevity, and the ability to perform each person's calling from God.

4. Emotional

    a. Routinely ask a randomly selected national sample about saved people's emotional ability to fulfill their personal callings from God to serve Him.

    b. Routinely ask a randomly selected national sample of unsaved people about the frequency of receiving emotional encouragement that led them to draw closer to God.

    c. Routinely ask a randomly selected national sample of believers about the frequency of receiving emotional encouragement from Christians that led them to take actions to fulfill their callings from God.

5. Physical

    a. Routinely ask each person about the availability of whatever she or he needs to sustain a healthy, productive life.

    b. Routinely ask each person about the personal habits that encourage or endanger physical fruitfulness.

    c. Routinely ask Christians about the availability of whatever he or she needs to draw closer to God and to fulfill God's callings.

After seeing that it was feasible to keep track of such dimensions by using these measurements, I was next feeling a little deflated by thinking about how my own actions would look in these terms. For instance, I probably miss a vast multiple of witnessing opportunities God provides relative to the number I act on.

That reaction soon subsided, to be replaced by a sense of excitement about how much more attention most Christians would probably pay to expanding God's Kingdom if they only had a sense of what actions would be most fruitful. This last reaction has been the one that's stayed with me, which is why I wanted to include this lesson in *Your Breakthroughs*.

Having gotten this far, you are probably wondering what it is that you should do to apply this lesson. Clearly, each of us can apply these measurements to our own lives through keeping a journal of what happens each day. We can also pray for encouragement and strength to do better along these dimensions.

Beyond that, you should look to what the Holy Spirit and your Bible reading direct. Do you feel called to share this information with others in your family, neighborhood, church, workplace, and other organizations? Do you, instead, feel called to encourage people to expand God's Kingdom using some or all of these dimensions and measures? There are obviously roles as large as you want to make them in contributing towards making your nation at least 20 times more fruitful for the Lord. Do any of those roles seem to be part of what God wants you to do? To share your answers and ask questions, send an e-mail to donmitchell@fastforward400.com/.

If you feel daunted about how to accomplish any of such things, keep reading. The rest of the book will teach you many useful things for serving the Lord more fruitfully. As you do, keep in mind how many of the great revivals of the past were started by the spontaneous obedience of a single person to take one sincere action on behalf of God's Kingdom.

Lesson Five Assignments

1. What has God called you to do in enhancing your nation's fruitfulness?

2. Who can teach you how to become a great example of increasing fruitfulness for the Lord in your nation by helping others understand the five dimensions in this lesson and how they can be measured?

3. What can you learn from such people?

4. Who can teach you how to become a great example of enhancing your nation's fruitfulness through various leadership roles that are available to you?

5. What can you learn from such people?

6. Who can teach you how to become highly effective in improving the fruitfulness of your nation's leaders?

7. What can you learn from such people?

8. What are the best ways you can contribute to enhancing the fruitfulness of your nation?

Part Two

2,000 Percent Solutions

But also for this very reason, giving all diligence,
add to your faith virtue, to virtue knowledge,
to knowledge self-control, to self-control perseverance,
to perseverance godliness, to godliness brotherly kindness,
and to brotherly kindness love.
For if these things are yours and abound,
you will be neither barren nor unfruitful
in the knowledge of our Lord Jesus Christ.

— 2 Peter 1:5-8 (NKJV)

Notice that the culmination of this list from 2 Peter 1: 5-8 (NKJV) is to move past brotherly kindness to embrace giving and receiving love. Yet, Peter tells us that we must abound as well in faith, virtue, knowledge, self-control, perseverance, and godliness before our knowledge of the Lord Jesus Christ will be fruitful. I read these verses as saying that there's knowledge to be gained about fruitfulness that goes beyond simply knowing about Jesus and the Gospel. As a boy, I often wondered what that knowledge might be.

While I certainly lack more knowledge than I have about how to be as fruitful as possible for the Lord, the Holy Spirit has taught me so many ways to be more fruitful in the last twenty years that my perspective on these verses has totally changed: I now realize that believers have to first grow in faith and virtue before they begin to make good use of the knowledge that God has revealed about how to be more fruitful. In coming to appreciate that point, I now realize how little faith many believers have. And without sufficient faith, it's easy for knowledge about fruitfulness to go unused. In addition, those with enough faith, but who lack adequate virtue, would simply attempt to use such knowledge for purposes unrelated to expanding God's Kingdom. Such an application of the knowledge won't work because the believer would be acting contrary to God's will.

Let me give you an example of why I make such observations. Having been healed as the result of prayer on many occasions, it's easy for me to have faith that I can again be healed in that manner and that others can be so healed, as well. Yet, if I have a conversation with other believers at my church, it's not unusual for everyone around the same round table to tell me that they don't believe that anyone can be healed by prayer. Without faith, such believers won't even try to be healed in this way.

Let's look at virtue now. The Bible makes it clear that the prayers of the righteous are powerful. So, if someone has faith, but isn't filled with enough virtue to be righteous while praying, the prayers may not work. Such righteousness can be gained through our Savior by simply confessing any sins, repenting, and asking forgiveness. With enough knowledge of the Bible about spiritual healing, the righteous believer would also call on the elders of the church and seek healing as described in James 5:14-16 (NKJV):

Is anyone among you sick? Let him call for the elders of the church, and let them pray over him, anointing him with oil in the name of the Lord. And the prayer of faith will save the sick, and the Lord will raise him up. And if he has committed sins, he will be forgiven. Confess *your* trespasses to one another, and pray for one another, that you may be healed. The effective, fervent prayer of a righteous man avails much.

Once having been healed in this way, any believer is going to tell others, serving to draw unbelievers to want to know more and believers to want to understand the lessons involved. In either case, greater fruitfulness for God's Kingdom will result.

Do you feel clearer now about the role of building faith and virtue for bringing effective knowledge to bear for fruitfulness? I hope so. Contact me at donmitchell@fastforward400.com with any questions and comments.

So what is a 2,000 percent solution? *It's any method of accomplishing what you or your organization does now with less than 1/21 the present time, resources, and effort; or accomplishing 20 times as much or more, while employing the same or less time, resources, and effort; or any combination of accomplishing more and using less time, resources, and effort that amounts to at least a 20-times increase in effectiveness.*

Okay, now you've got the official definition. What does it mean? Let's look at an example: Assume that you now spend 21 hours a week to do reading that's necessary for your work. Perhaps what you read are scientific or medical research articles, or updates on trends in your industry. A 2,000 percent solution would reduce your reading so that you could accomplish the same job results by only reading one hour a week. Such an improvement might be accomplished, as Lesson One describes, by improving reading speed, comprehension, and note taking. You might also delegate to others making preliminary scans of the material to focus you on just the most pertinent and valuable reading.

Keep these definitions in mind as you read the next two lessons. Some people mistakenly believe that these lessons apply to making the kind of small, gradual changes that they usually focus on. To avoid that tendency to think small, focus on something you would like to do 20 times more effectively and keep that activity in mind as you read these lessons.

Here's an example of a personal 2,000 percent solution that was also an organizational 2,000 percent solution. The chief financial officer of a leading company spent over 100 working days a year head-ing up the firm's budgeting process. By delegating all but 3 days of that process to the controller, the CFO added 97 days to work on untapped opportunities. In addition, he gained better working relations with the other company leaders by not being in the middle of budgetary conflicts. As a result, the CFO helped facilitate operating changes that added tens of millions of dollars to annual company profits.

If you want to create 2,000 percent solutions, you'll find it helpful to eliminate and delegate tasks that clog your schedule so you'll have time to work on this highly productive activity. Most 2,000 percent solutions can be developed with 60 to 120 hours of effort by one person. Split the effort across a team, and the individual time demands fall.

How available are 2,000 percent solutions? A corollary to Pareto's Law (referred to by many as the 80/20 principle, meaning that 80 percent of the results can be observed to come from 20 percent of the people doing an activity) states that 80 percent of the results of any economic activity come from 20 percent or fewer of the efforts. By examining an example of this corollary, the naturally high frequency of 2,000 percent solutions can be better understood.

Imagine that a business has 100 salespeople. Consistent with Pareto's Law, 20 of those salespeople produce total sales of 80,000 units per year while the remaining 80 salespeople produce total sales of only 20,000 units per year. The most productive 20 salespeople average 4,000 units per year while the 80 less productive average sales of 250 units per year. The 20 most productive salespeople create 16 times (4,000/250) the results of the average of the 80 remaining sales people. Thus, just matching what the most productive 20 salespeople accomplish is a 1,500 percent solution (accomplishing 15 times more).

Within the group of 20, some are more productive than the others. Let's assume that the most productive salesperson produces annual sales of 7,000 units. That amount is 28 times what the 80 less productive salespeople average. If the less productive people can increase to what the most productive salesperson achieves, that's a 2,700 percent solution.

Within the group of 80, some are less productive than others. Let's assume that the least productive salesperson who won't be fired sells merely 100 units per year. If that person could match the most productive salesperson, that would be a 6,900 percent solution.

The nature of which customers are served may have something to do with why the two salespeople vary so much in productivity. However, if the least productive salesperson can increase her or his performance to just over half that of the most productive group's average to 2,100 units, that result is still a 2,000 percent solution.

Let's also assume that the company has a more effective competitor where the most productive salespeople average selling 10,000 units per year. Within that group, let's also assume that the most productive person sells 18,000 units per year. If some of this success is based on selling methods that the least productive salesperson in the first company can emulate, that relatively low performing salesperson would only have to improve sales by 1/9 of the results of this competitor's most productive salesperson to achieve a 2,000 percent solution.

In addition, there are probably better performing salespeople in other industries who could also inform the lowest producing salesperson in the original company how to improve.

From the first company's management perspective, notice that the problem is different. Only if all the salespeople in total improve their productivity by 20 times does the company enjoy the benefits of a 2,000 percent solution. If the methods and personal qualities of the best few salespeople can be duplicated in the rest of the sales force, such a 2,000 percent solution can be achieved.

Pareto's Law also applies to every other activity that a person does in an organization: Twenty percent of the employees or volunteers will produce 80 percent of the results. By learning from the best inside and outside the company, the most productive employees and volunteers can improve further. Likewise, 20 percent of the customers will provide 80 percent of the earnings. So it's important to whom you sell as well as how efficiently you perform. Many organizations will find that their most effective salespeople are mostly bringing in business from relatively unprofitable customers. As a result, the best practice may be found among a so-called average performer who only produces high-margin sales. Cross-fertilize the methods of the high-volume salesperson with the high-margin one, and you should increase the profit-productivity of sales efforts by much more than 2,000 percent.

For a given organization, simply measuring to find out who is the most productive and what they do differently that may account for their success can be a very powerful tool for helping others to expand their effectiveness. That's why the few companies that do such benchmarking within a company are quick to find ways to make enormous improvements in their effectiveness.

Mitchell and Company measured a large number of companies that did the same activities to see how their effectiveness compared to others. Much like what Pareto's Law suggests, companies were highly effective compared to other firms in only a few areas ... usually fewer than 5 percent of their important functions. Companies were about as effective as the average firm in about 30 percent of their important activities. And these same companies were well below average in the remaining activities.

That measurement made us realize the enormous potential of outsourcing. If you have some activity where you are well below average throughout your organization, you may have the potential for a 2,000 percent solution by simply outsourcing that same activity to a top performing outside firm.

Let's start by looking in Lesson Six at what such Godly knowledge is like to understand more about how to drop bad thinking habits, or stalls, a topic we began considering in Lesson Two. From there, we'll look in Lesson Seven at the positive practices that need to replace what has been harming or delaying fruitfulness.

Lesson Six

Stalls and Stallbusting

And Elisha the prophet called one of the sons
of the prophets, and said to him,
"Get yourself ready, take this flask of oil in your hand,
and go to Ramoth Gilead.
Now when you arrive at that place,
look there for Jehu the son of Jehoshaphat, the son of Nimshi,
and go in and make him rise up from among his associates,
and take him to an inner room.
Then take the flask of oil, and pour it on his head, and say,
'Thus says the LORD: "I have anointed you king over Israel."'
Then open the door and flee, and do not delay."

— 2 Kings 9:1-3 (NKJV)

2 Kings 9:1-3 (NKJV) tells us how God directed Elisha to begin the actions that would wipe out the remaining evil influence connected to the deceased King Ahab. While preparing to send off a son of another prophet, Elisha carefully instructed him in how to anoint Jehu as the next king of Israel, and then told the son to flee without delay after the anointing. When the timing is right from God's perspective, He often wants us to act expeditiously. Yet we often tolerate what He doesn't want, stuck in being accustomed what has been and is happening. When we don't act immediately, we are stalled for some reason, much like a car that doesn't have any gasoline and oil

in it. However, in our case, the cause for stalling can almost always be found in the unexamined assumptions, beliefs, desires, and habits of those who delay or take too little action.

Here's a metaphor to help you understand this lesson's content: In our neighborhood, a house stood empty for several years and became an eyesore. The owner was satisfied to live elsewhere and let the house fall apart. He was a rich physician who didn't care enough about the money he could have gained by renting the house to bother with that option. As a result, the doctor was stuck with property he didn't need and had developed a habit of ignoring. That's what we call a "stall," a bad habit that delays progress.

Finally, a new owner bought the property, bulldozed the old house, and flattened the now-empty lot. He had cleared the way of the obstacles to making a lovely home and yard. That's what we call "stallbusting." The prior owner's habit could no longer affect this property.

With everything about the property now open for change, the new owner built a lovely home that took excellent advantage of the property's improved qualities. In the process, a home was created that could easily house a large family and provide enough room to entertain many guests at a party. By making the location suitable for enjoyable habitation, the new owner created a better way of using the lot. He had created a 100 percent solution by building a desirable home in the usual way.

If, instead, he had built that new home with 1/21 the time, effort, and resources of a usual home, he would have created a 2,000 percent solution for that part of his activities. Such a result might have been accomplished by acquiring a lovely home for a pittance because it was scheduled for immediate demolition to make way for a new highway, moving the home to the lot, and then making any needed repairs after the move.

In Lesson Two, we considered the stalls that are described in *The 2,000 Percent Solution* as possible sources for the kinds of opposition you might run into while encouraging others to employ Lesson

One's practices. As you read about the potentially harmful effects of the *Tradition, Disbelief, Misconception, Unattractiveness, Communications, Bureaucratic,* and *Procrastination stalls,* I'm sure you began to appreciate why increasing fruitfulness can be difficult. Of course, I am sure you were cheered by the information contained there about how to overcome these stalls with stallbusters.

Unfortunately, since there are many more than these seven stalls, we might encounter some more of the many stalls identified so far by The 400 Year Project. In fact, *The 2,000 Percent Solution* describes several other individual and organizational stalls that are quite harmful, including the *Complacency* (being happy with the status quo), *Easy-Path* (doing what takes the least thought and effort), *You-Can't-Get-There-from-Here* (assuming there is no solution without looking for one), *One-Dimensional-Thinking* (failing to develop a perspective from all relevant points of view), *No-Star-to-Guide-Me* (considering existing circumstances to be determinative, without looking for reasonably comparable examples of gaining success), *Monday-Go-to-Meeting* (always consulting everyone who might be affected or affronted before acting, whether helpful or not), *Accounting* (letting mistaken accounting conventions rule decisions, rather than common sense), *Forget-About-It* (failing to preserve and transmit useful knowledge to new employees), *Protocol* (following organizational channels rather than obtaining information directly), and *Gatekeeper* (being inaccessible to others when needed) *stalls.*

Let's look next at the stalls found in *The Irresistible Growth Enterprise* (Stylus, 2000) that keep individuals and organizations from harmoniously using the uncontrollable, powerful forces that they encounter. These stalls include:

- being so *directionless* that any pushes from irresistible forces are viewed with disinterest;
- employing *wishful thinking* about being able to accurately predict the future;

- experiencing *mental paralysis* when irresistible forces turn unexpectedly adverse;
- *fighting irresistible forces* rather than adjusting to gain benefits from them;
- choosing to be *too independent* in addressing new issues raised by irresistible forces, rather than seeking expert help;
- taking an *overly optimistic* view of the benefits from following the current direction;
- trying to *keep bad news secret* about being harmed by irresistible forces; and
- *underestimating the difficulty* of properly responding to volatile irresistible forces.

Rather than introduce even more stalls to you, let me mention that stalls can also be symptomatic of a nation or a culture. For example, Donald R. Kamdonyo, Ph.D., author of *Poverty by Choice* (A Contribution to The 400 Year Project, 2013), identified that entrepreneurs in his native Malawi are often afflicted by the *Debt* (borrowing to spend more than can be afforded on personal consumption), *Ignorance* (attempting important tasks without first learning how to do them), and *Subsistence* (engaging in business merely for the purpose of adding a little income to meet minimum survival needs) *stalls*.

My advice is to look for any situations where performance is slight and not improving. You'll find one or more stalls contributing to that stagnation. In doing so, be prepared to find stalls not listed here.

Of course, identifying stalls is only the first step for becoming more productive. We also have to eliminate stalls. Rather than list many stallbusters (ways of overcoming stalls) for various stalls, let me outline, instead, key questions that should help you to develop custom stallbusters to overcome your and your organization's stalls whenever the project's materials don't provide specific guidance. For such stalls, please answer and act on what you learn from the following questions to avoid, bust, or erase stalls:

1. What ways of thinking and acting slow down or increase the cost of accomplishing important results?
2. What benefits do these ways of thinking and acting provide?
3. What values are intended to be served by this thinking and acting?
4. What problems are created by such thoughts and actions?
5. What is being assumed or believed about what will almost always work?

6. What is being assumed or believed about what will hardly ever work?
7. What is assumed or believed will happen?
8. What is assumed or believed will never happen?
9. On what assumptions, beliefs, and evidence are these thoughts and actions based?
10. Have these assumptions, beliefs, and evidence been checked lately for accuracy?

11. Are the relied on assumptions, beliefs, and evidence still true?
12. Which incorrect thoughts and actions are most harmful?
13. What thoughts and actions should replace the most harmful ones?
14. How can a bias be created for having helpful thoughts and taking useful actions?
15. How can you monitor the relevant thoughts and actions?

If you find yourself stuck in answering any of these questions, please send an e-mail to donmitchell@fastforward400.com/, and I will be glad to help. I also encourage you to read Chapter 1 in *The Portable 2,000 Percent Solution* (Mitchell and Company Press, 2006), which supplies additional questions and suggestions for overcoming stalls.

Lesson Six Assignments

1. How can you accomplish more of your personal goals for expanding God's Kingdom sooner by changing your assumptions, beliefs, knowledge, and actions?

2. How can your organization accomplish more of its goals for expanding God's Kingdom sooner by changing your and your colleagues' assumptions, beliefs, knowledge, and actions?

3. What are any needed shifts by you and others that need to occur?

4. What can you do to influence or cause such shifts to take place?

Lesson Seven

Eight-Step Process

Now Thomas, called the Twin, one of the twelve,
was not with them when Jesus came.
The other disciples therefore said to him,
"We have seen the Lord."

So he said to them, "Unless I see in His hands
the print of the nails, and
put my finger into the print of the nails,
and put my hand into His side, I will not believe."

And after eight days His disciples were again inside,
and Thomas with them.

Jesus came, the doors being shut, and stood in the midst,
and said, "Peace to you!"

Then He said to Thomas,
"Reach your finger here, and look at My hands;
and reach your hand here, and put it into My side.
Do not be unbelieving, but believing."

And Thomas answered and said to Him,
"My Lord and my God!"

*Jesus said to him, "Thomas, because you have seen Me,
you have believed. Blessed are those who
have not seen and yet have believed."*

— John 20:24-29 (NKJV)

Accomplishing some things takes time and following the right steps. Thomas, one of Jesus' disciples, provides us with such an example in John 20:24-29 (NKJV). During the evening of His Resurrection on the first Easter, Jesus appeared to all but Thomas of His remaining 11 disciples. Upon being told this marvelous news, Thomas doubted that Jesus was alive and described all that would have to take place before he could believe in the Resurrection. Eight days passed and Jesus appeared again. This time Thomas was present. Knowing of his doubts, Jesus invited Thomas to apply the tests earlier described. In response to His words, Thomas simply acknowledged Jesus as Lord and God. Jesus then commented that while seeing is, indeed, believing, He also noted that blessings await those who can believe in the Resurrection without having seen Him. With these words, Jesus turned Thomas' doubt into an object lesson to help all of us have more faith in Him.

Similarly, we should not be surprised if time and passing through many proof steps will be required before we can determine with the help of the Holy Spirit the right ways to become much more fruitful for God's Kingdom. In this lesson, we consider the eight steps for producing 2,000 percent solutions:

1. Understand the importance of measuring performance.
2. Decide what to measure.
3. Identify the future best practice and measure it.
4. Implement beyond the future best practice.
5. Identify the ideal best practice.
6. Pursue the ideal best practice.
7. Select the right people and provide the right encouragement.
8. Repeat the first seven steps

Be sure to follow the steps in this order. I primarily draw from *The Portable 2,000 Percent Solution* to define and explain the process steps for application to an organization, since that's more complicated and potentially of higher value for God's Kingdom than improving something you do individually. However, the same process steps apply to individual 2,000 percent solutions, as to organizational ones.

We begin with *understanding the importance of measuring performance* (step 1). The losses caused by the stalls can be overcome by having measurements that your organization understands, pays attention to, and knows how to respond to. That observation is true because measurements help erase complacency.

Most people view the measuring process too narrowly. Here's an example: A corporate planner went to a seminar given by business strategist Peter Drucker. The planner asked Drucker to pick the best single measure of corporate performance. Drucker replied, "My dear sir, you obviously know nothing. There is no single measure of corporate performance that is any good. Use them all and try to develop new ones, and each will teach you something you need to know." Drucker's point was that measurements are highly subjective and imperfect. Would-be makers of 2,000 percent solutions are going to need lots of measures.

One CEO tells another Peter Drucker story about measurements that may fit you. Drucker had presented a seminar on personal improvement to the CEO's U.S. Air Force group years earlier. Each man was instructed to measure in great detail how he spent his time for a week. The CEO found this task to be a life-changing experience. The measurements revealed all of his bad habits and put the CEO on guard to avoid those bad habits in the future.

Unfortunately, this CEO's example is rarely followed. Few want to know how they spend their time or what their output is. Hopefully, you conducted the assignments in Lesson One that helped you identify how to increase the time by at least ten hours a week you spend on applying the fifteen practices described there. If you have not yet done so, perform this assignment now.

Let's look at the organizational implications of doing more measuring. Visitors to the finance and data processing staffs of a large company were astonished to note that each cubicle's walls were literally covered with performance measurements. The idea was to encourage more focus on expanding productivity. Almost all of the measurements had been developed by the workers for their own use. By looking at one another's measurements, staff members could see how well they were doing in comparison. People pitched in to help lower performers improve so that everyone could earn department-wide, performance-based bonuses.

How did they do? Personal productivity gains of 25 percent in a year were not unusual. Furthermore, corporate productivity in these same areas grew by a similar degree.

As we look at processes, finding causes to improve can be more difficult to accomplish. Here's an example: Management of a luxury hotel chain learned that guests were dissatisfied because it took too long for breakfast orders to arrive from room service. The chain jumped in to solve the problem. It added more room service waiters. It even added more kitchen staff. But the situation got worse, not better.

Finally, they looked at how long it took for a waiter to make a delivery and return to the kitchen. Wait! Here was something. The round trips took much too long. Management asked the room service waiters why. The bottleneck was quickly spotted. The waiters were delayed by as much as eight minutes by slow elevator arrivals at the kitchen and the guest room floors.

What was going on? Housekeepers were delivering a day's worth of clean sheets and towels at the same time. Since housekeepers had to unload large amounts of linen on each floor, they usually stopped the elevators while the unloading occurred.

After understanding the cause, linen deliveries were rescheduled. Room-service complaints dropped to near zero. With enough of the right measurements to find the causes of your underperformance, you'll soon be working on the right things, too.

You also may need to add some skills for measuring. After many American manufacturers found that their quality badly lagged non-American competitors in the 1980s, quality improvement became an obsession. Soon, many companies were bragging that they reduced errors to Six Sigma levels (hardly any errors per million activities).

Closer examination suggested that some of these companies had missed the boat. Some had only achieved being nearly perfect in delivering outmoded offerings. Motorola, for instance, the renowned Six Sigma innovator, saw its profits evaporate in the 1990s when the company fell behind Nokia and others in delivering new digital technologies to the market.

Some other companies didn't know how to measure their performance. They mistakenly broke down every process into hundreds of aspects. Each aspect was measured for performance. Sure enough, almost all aspects were done perfectly more than 99.9 percent of the time. Everyone was smiling ... except the customers. As measured by what customers cared about, deliveries were deficient almost half the time. What was going on? It turns out that those little errors across hundreds of aspects compound and can cumulatively hit the customer hard. The firm should have been primarily measuring its ultimate performance for customers and then looking selectively into detail to locate where large improvement strides could be made.

It's not enough to measure. You also have to learn from what the measurements tell you. Then, when you can access information that others lack, you can move ahead.

Let's get practical. Ask yourself the following questions to better allocate your time and efforts:

- How could I avoid having to do the least productive tasks at all and get better results?

- How else could I have gotten these tasks done with better results in less time?
- How could I delegate these tasks to others for better results?
- How could I inexpensively automate these tasks and meet my purposes?
- When was I effective?
- Why was I effective then?

- When was I ineffective?
- Why was I ineffective then?
- How much time am I wasting?
- How could I better spend the time I waste?
- What will be the benefits for me and others of spending my time in these more productive areas and activities?

After you have acted on the answers to your personal improvement questions, you will be prepared to be credible as a helpful coach to others, especially after answering the following questions:

- How can you interest other people in measurements?
- How can you help others set up and use helpful measurements?
- How can the message about the value of properly using measurements be spread even further?

We now shift to *deciding what to measure* (step 2). Measurement helps you achieve the most when focused on your organization's most important processes and most valuable opportunities. Here's an example of why such focus is important: A large consumer products company found that it lagged all of its competitors in measures of financial performance. Stung by this information into wanting to change, managers asked employees to suggest profitable improvements. Tens of thousands of suggestions were received.

Rather than treat all these ideas equally, management established a review team that included executives from every functional area.

The reviewers looked for ideas that offered enormous immediate and long-term benefits that were easy to implement right away.

Another team of fifteen executives was assigned to see that these top options got enough implementation attention. One percent of the ideas provided 95 percent of the cumulative improvement. As a result of this concentrated effort, three years later the organization was the number one performer in its industry by any kind of financial measurement.

Choosing to aggressively pursue those highest potential ideas was a good idea. You should do the same.

If you don't know what those highest potential opportunities are, here are some questions to help you find them. Begin by asking these questions to determine your most important processes:

- How long could your organization survive without using each process?
- How long could your organization prosper if each process were done poorly?
- How long will your organization last if it performs each of its processes less well than similar organizations?

After having gotten a sense of what your most critical processes are, ask these questions:

- If you did the process as well as you can imagine it, what would be the size of the benefit compared to how well you are doing today?
- If you did the process as well as you can imagine it, what other opportunities would open up?
- What would developing those opportunities be worth?

This is a good time to identify which measures are most available for comparisons outside of your organization. Be sure to check all your data to see how well they help you understand your performance. Once you've done that, begin eliminating some less helpful measurements while paying more attention to the more helpful ones. To make this shift, work with data until you can statistically identify causes and effects.

In deciding how much to spend to measure and analyze, keep in mind the size of the potential benefits. Some expensive measures are well worth the cost. One firm found that a single measure (which cost more than all of the other measures combined) provided almost all of the insights into improving an essential process. Had the company stopped looking because of the expense, the firm's sales would be less than half and profits below a quarter of the current level.

Knowing now what to measure, it's time to look at *identifying and measuring the future best practice* (step 3). Your next challenge is to identify what the best-in-the-world performance of that process will probably look like (in or out of your industry or type of activity) for the next five years with what the available technology and resources will probably be. We call that performance the "future best practice."

Chances are that your organization does not yet know how to find and select the improved practice elements that, when combined for the first time, will drive you well ahead of all others.

To do better than the best, you have to know what the best is and where that best performance will be in the future. Otherwise, you'll probably set an objective that's too low, and deny yourself what you could learn by studying the best.

Never assume you know the right answer before you seek to develop practices that exceed the best others will probably do. Unfortunately, many intelligent and experienced people do just that. They smugly pursue their own ideas without looking further. They forget that every activity is filled with bright, energetic people.

For every critical task within your organization, there will almost always be someone on the outside who does it better. In fact, the odds favor the future best practice lying outside your types of activities in reasonably similar areas. Here are useful steps to begin your search:

1. Look internally to find out who does it better than anyone else in your organization.
2. Identify why some operations perform better than others.
3. Ask around inside your organization to start learning who does something similar even better in other types of organizations.
4. Check out public sources of information on these subjects.
5. Contact those who may have something to offer.
6. Consider buying access to best-practice databases like those maintained by accounting firms and The American Productivity and Quality Center.
7. Interview experts and academics who may have applicable knowledge.
8. Ask those you contact for other leads.
9. Look globally.

Keep going. Determining the future best practice is a continuing task. Whether or not you notice it, the future best-performance bar is always being raised. Be circumspect about this work, however, lest you prematurely awaken a sleeping rival.

When you do your research into future best practices well, you will be able to identify:

- Several current best practices from outside your kind of organization that others of your type are not using
- The current best practices in your kind of organization
- Where both sets of current best practices will probably evolve as processes and to what performance levels over the next five years
- A new way to combine many of the current and future best practices to create performance that far exceeds the likely effectiveness of any other organization over the next five years

In doing this work, it is natural to assume that large, profitable industry leaders like Alphabet (formerly Google), Apple, Dell, Disney, GE, Intel, and Microsoft use only the current best practices. But that happy circumstance is usually not the case. The older and bigger the company is, the fewer future best practices it is likely to develop, apply, and improve. Oddly enough, marginal companies and organizations tend to be better sources for future-best-practice information. Why? Low-performing organizations face more cash-flow pressures and have little choice but to focus on efficiency in all of their endeavors. These organizations are also less likely to stand pat with existing procedures. They know that performance must improve or they won't be around for long.

Many people have misinterpreted what they see during visits to discern best practices. If you ask why things are done the way they are, you'll avoid that mistake. Henry Ford told buyers of his Model T automobile that they could have any color as long as it was black. Many people assume that Ford was either color-blind or had gotten a good price for black paint. In fact, black was the only color you could use for a consistent hue in those days. If other colors had looked good on the Model T, Ford would have offered them.

Likewise, visitors to Japanese factories usually marvel at how compact they are. Knowing that land is expensive in Japan, visitors assume they know the answer. And they are partly right, but even when land is relatively cheap such as in a corn field in Iowa, Japanese factories are compact. Why? Japanese executives know that compactness improves communications among workers. The closer together people work on a product, the better the quality. That's one reason why team-built products are usually better made than assembly-line offerings.

Here are questions designed to speed and ease your search for the future best practice:

• What online resources, periodicals, books, databases, seminars, services, and organizations are available to help you?

- Who are the favorite sources for the most knowledgeable authors and editors?
- What organizations have been described as being excellent in these areas?
- Who do experts say has the best operation that they've seen?
- Who do the best in the field pay attention to?

- Which organizations in the world could be using processes like yours?
- Who do the experts in these organizations think does these processes the best now or will do so in the future?
- Which experts in top-performing, noncompeting organizations will permit you to visit and observe, measure, and discuss their processes?

- What can be seen and learned during a personal visit?
- Can you gain more access to key people during a visit?
- Who should measure?
- What should they measure?

- What information do you need to estimate the best future performance over the next five years?
- What has been the rate of improvement?
- How is that rate of improvement likely to change?
- How can experts help you improve your estimate of improvement change?

Now that you have measured and know what the future best practice will be, it's time to *implement beyond the future best practice* (step 4). Successful leapfrogging the future best practice requires that your best change leaders unify efforts. These leaders must commit to this challenging objective and shift the organizational culture to do more to support them. Those working on the implementation must become masters of understanding the steps needed to successfully make the change.

Narrow your focus to a few areas of highest promise so that you do not water down your potential for achieving results. Begin by segmenting those aspects of exceeding future best practices into three categories that:

1. Can be implemented almost immediately with little effort.
2. Can be implemented within two years with effort and attention.
3. Can be implemented over more than two years.

In your triage agenda, you can probably do most things that fall into the first category easily, quickly, and with little help except where the activity stymies a high-priority item from the second category. The challenge comes in selecting what to implement from the second and third categories. Here's an important limitation to keep in mind: You probably cannot simultaneously make more than three or four changes involving several of the same people. You'll make the most progress when you pick the best balance of near- and intermediate-term benefits while placing the least strain on your people and resources. To that mix, add anything else you can do through aggressive use of outside resources that doesn't increase the internal burden. Within that agenda, give high priority to actions that will give you the most benefit over the next two years. Organize your efforts so that significant benefits will be realized every six months to keep everyone feeling motivated.

Since the thinking you will do during the next two steps will suggest other outstanding choices, beware of setting too many firm projects at this step. But if completing step six will take more than a few months, you should begin to implement some of what has been identified in step four. In this case, our recommendation is that you reserve some change capacity (such as time of key people, analytical resources, and budget) beginning around the time that you will have some new projects to add from your work in step six. This approach may mean that you will choose to mine category 1 from the triage list more heavily for now than category 2.

To estimate how long it will take you to put a new practice in place, look at the experience of those who preceded you in implementing these practice elements. Then consider whether your organization will be a faster or slower learner and integrator than they were. As you consider your choices, be open to having the company you studied or some of its former employees be an outsourcing provider to speed your progress. Simply because you want to employ a certain method doesn't mean that you need to become the world's expert in that area.

Beware of taking quantifications of likely benefits too literally. One project may appear to offer ten times the potential of a second project, but the former project may also be a hundred times more difficult. Instead, emphasize places where you can effectively concentrate your resources while facing little resistance from any stakeholder. Choose a project that seems to offer more benefits, however, when two competing projects present similar difficulty and degrees of opposition.

Organizations vary widely in their ability to exceed future best practices through using new combinations of best practices. Many overestimate how well they will do in bringing groundbreaking new directions to an industry. To avoid that mistake, ask yourself these questions:

- What significant attempts has your organization made to improve over the last five years?
- Which attempts achieved their purpose on budget and on schedule?
- Which attempts did not?
- What were the apparent causes for the two types of results based on discussions with those who worked on the attempts?
- How many of the successful implementations were key individuals able to work on at a time?

- What could you do in the future to improve your organization's effectiveness in such implementations?

Your ideas for projects to exceed the future best practice will usually come from research into what others are doing and planning to do. To test the direction you should take, check out what's involved by developing project plans based on the answers to the following questions:

- Which projects have a favorable cost-to-benefit ratio?
- Which projects have an affordable cost compared to your resources and limitations?
- Which projects have a reasonable likelihood of success?

Next, compare your plans to past results. Here are questions to help you do so:

- Which of these potential changes look like your past successes?
- Which potential changes look like your past misses and messes?
- Do the opportunities to use your strengths in implementing future-best-practice-exceeding changes provide you with enough benefit to exceed the future best practice?
- If not, what are the simplest, most effective ways to enhance your organization's ability to provide or absorb more valuable improvements?
- What are the risks of failing to succeed?

With thoughtful answers in hand to these questions, you are ready to *identify the ideal best practice* (step 5). The "ideal best practice" is simply the most effective process that can possibly be accomplished by anyone over the next five years. It will usually exceed the future best practice by a wide margin, and the ideal best practice reflects a performance level that might not normally be reached for decades.

Here's an example: In corporate communications, an ideal best practice would mean having all employees receive, understand, and act on a message in appropriate ways within a few seconds. We know that's possible because those seeing a fire, smelling smoke, and hearing a fire alarm in a building will respond appropriately in that amount of time.

By comparison, your organization's performance today represents a tiny fraction of what is possible. People perform nearly perfectly all the time in many different ways. Put those perfectly performing individuals into an organization, and it's often like removing 99 percent of their intelligence. That's the negative result that follows from employing poorly designed processes.

Before searching out the ideal best practice for your activity, let us observe that you are seeing the ideal best practices of near perfection all around you on a daily basis. But chances are that you don't notice the near perfection at all. Instead, your focus is probably on what isn't working well ... and you are becoming either frustrated or annoyed.

Here are questions that our students of 2,000 percent solutions have found to be mind-opening. Even if you don't answer any other questions in this lesson, be sure you answer these questions. They provide the key to exponential success for developing many breakthrough methods. Most people can do this exercise in less than an hour. But even if you spend more time, you'll be way ahead of those who never answer these questions. Keep in mind that adding understanding is more important than speed.

- What are 50 examples of how individuals perform near perfection on a regular basis?
- What are 50 examples of how people in groups perform near perfection on a regular basis?
- Why do these near-perfect performances occur?

• What's missing from your organization's approach to its most important tasks for your organization to improve to near-perfect performance?

Here's an example to get you started: Employees are very good at cashing their paychecks. Rarely do paychecks go uncashed. Why? Unless employees are very wealthy or extremely forgetful, they need to cash or deposit their paychecks in order to buy food, pay for shelter, and take care of the rest of their lives. For most people, not cashing a paycheck would be like trying to hold your breath for the rest of your life. It's an activity that cannot be sustained. Many examples of near-perfection draw on these elements: It's a natural thing to do; people enjoy doing it; the consequences of not doing it are severe; and people understand the consequences and know exactly what they have to do.

Most leaders will choose goals that are 30 to 50 percent likely to be reached. Setting more challenging goals can stimulate higher performance by making the tasks more interesting for employees and other stakeholders. But it's a bad idea to set high goals without providing a clear direction for how to succeed and helping employees gain confidence in the likelihood of reaching the goals.

Utilizing the ideal best practice focus provides a major improvement in goal setting by identifying both a higher standard and one that is achievable and credible to employees. In essence, you gain more stretch with the same degree of psychological comfort.

Let me now list five methods for using ideal best practices to go beyond your ideas on the subject of exceeding the future best practice and your first thoughts about applying ideal best practices:

1. Combine perspectives from similar ideal best practices for individuals in new ways.

Earlier in this lesson, we asked you to identify 50 examples of how individuals perform near perfection on a regular basis.

Take out your list. Examine it to see where two or more ideal best practices exemplify a general approach that could be used to create a breakthrough in something you do now. List at least five such general approaches.

Here's an example: School children leave their classrooms when the dismissal bell rings, and millions know it's New Year's Eve in the eastern United States when the ball drops in Times Square. The principle is that people use a signal to tell them it's time to move on to the next part of their plans.

Now let's apply that principle. Let's say that you want dinner guests to leave feeling happy at the time you want them to go. How might you create such a result? One possibility is to hold a formal ceremony that brings the evening to an end. This might be a prayer that thanks the guests for coming, a moment when you present them with little gifts to take home, or singing a good-bye song. For the ceremony to play its proper role, you'll have to tip your guests off in advance that you plan to end the evening on that note. The best time to provide your alert will be when you invite them. And be sure to mention your plans again during the evening. Otherwise, you may hold your ceremony and still have dinner guests hanging around after you wish them to leave.

2. Combine perspectives from dissimilar ideal best practices for individuals in compatible new ways.

Examine your list again to see places where two or more ideal best practices provide different principles that could be combined to create a breakthrough for you. List at least five different combination approaches.

Here's one example: You probably consume enough liquids to keep from becoming dehydrated. Why? Your body gives you a clue when it's time to drink more by having you feel thirsty. You probably also remember to get out of bed except on days when you are very sick. Why? You have plans that require leaving your bed, and those plans eventually encourage you to part from your comfortable cocoon.

Let's look for a possible application of those observations. Perhaps you want to do better at following through with plans to achieve your goals. How might the preceding observations help you?

Let's say that your goal is to learn to speak another language. You could tie your daily learning activities to when you drink liquids and to when you arise from bed. In this way, you use a reliable, stronger habit to build a new habit. For instance, on arising you might repeat all the words you learned yesterday and read through your list of new words for today. Then, each time you drink something, you could practice the new words for that day with flash cards you've made.

3. Combine perspectives from similar ideal best practices for organizations in new ways.

Turn your attention now to your 50 examples of how groups perform near perfection on a regular basis. Examine your list to see where two or more ideal best practices provide examples of a general approach that could be used to create a breakthrough in something your organization does now. Be sure to list at least five such general approaches.

Here's an example: Orchestras play complex pieces with amazing coordination and few errors. Military units march with impressive precision in keeping the same time and foot forward. These groups succeed because they have practiced a particular sequence until they can do it very easily and receive a signal (from a conductor or a drill instructor) that provides time and motion coordination. During practices, the signal giver tells people when they make mistakes and repeats those sequences until they are done correctly.

Now let's apply that method. Imagine that you want to launch a new product with a complex series of marketing and sales efforts. How might you create such a result? You need to start by playing the role that the musical composer does in writing down everything that needs to be done in the right order. That overall plan is like the score a conductor will use to coordinate everyone. The plan should include the speed, timing, and location of what needs to be done. Then the parts need to be copied out so that people know their roles and have instructions to follow. Finally, you need to practice the execution of that plan until it comes easily and perfectly.

By comparison, most organizations don't prepare such plans, have no practices, provide no feedback to those who make mistakes so they can improve, and don't have anyone playing the role of sending a central signal. Is it any wonder that such organizations don't coordinate their new product launches very well?

4. Combine perspectives from ideal best practices for organizations in new ways.

Examine your list once again to see places where two or more ideal best practices for groups provide different practices that could be combined to create a breakthrough for your organization. List at least five different combination approaches.

Here's an example to help you understand this process: Jazz combos improvise while playing music. No one knows exactly who will play next or exactly what they will play within a piece. The process works because the combo practices a lot and learns to closely observe what one another is doing so they smoothly adjust to each other. Postal services rarely fail to deliver mail that is entrusted to them. That's true both because postal workers understand the importance of the mail (they are customers, too) and roles are clearly defined in ways that reduce the risk of mail being lost.

Let's combine and apply these two practices. Assume that you want your organization to develop more flexibility by ensuring that each person learns how to do at least one other person's job who works in the same unit. In that way, if someone is out for a day, work proceeds smoothly. Using the jazz combo example, you might give workers the opportunity to choose what other job they learn. Only if some jobs were not going to be learned would you need to make assignments. To ensure that the learning takes place, you could set practice times when each person spends half the session helping someone else learn and the other half learning. To ensure that coordination did not break down, you could ask those who have the jobs to write out steps for the tasks so that the substitute would not forget an important step. To make that forgetfulness even less likely, you should set some time where each substitute spends a day on the receiving end of the work in order to appreciate (as postal employees do) what it's like to rely on what's done.

Such cross-training usually goes very slowly in most organizations. What's missing? Usually, the cross-training doesn't even begin until after a supervisor reviews an employee and decides to recommend cross-training. Regular opportunities to learn aren't scheduled in many organizations, so the training proceeds slowly. Because the employee may have no interest in learning the other job, the employee may avoid the learning opportunity altogether. It's even rarer to see the results of such a job as a customer either internally or externally. As a result, few have completed effective cross-training at any given time.

5. Combine perspectives from individual and organizational ideal best practices in new ways.

Of the five approaches to identifying ideal best practices, this fifth one is the most powerful because it allows you to build on individual strengths in nearing perfection to create new dimensions of group strengths. You'll be delighted with what this perspective can help you accomplish.

Here's an example to explain what we mean: Individuals are very good at remembering to put fuel into their vehicles. Rarely will you see a vehicle stranded for lack of fuel. Why? If you run out of fuel far away from a fueling station where there's no cellular telephone reception, you may have a long walk to fill and carry back a heavy container. The process may waste an hour or more. Also, if you run out of fuel when it's very cold, this exposure can be dangerous. Some people are probably worried about being robbed while going to and from the station. Most vehicles have fuel gauges that are reasonably accurate in letting drivers know when more fuel is needed. As a result of the measurements and concerns about safety and convenience, there is not much reason to run out of fuel.

Groups are exceptionally good about using up supplies that their organization provides. Why? There's no barrier. If you need it, you take it. There's no cost to you. However, groups may not be nearly as good about remembering to order more when supplies dwindle.

Let's assume now that you want to lower costs more rapidly in your organization. How might these two practices be combined? Let's start with the individual tendency to want to have enough. You might appeal to that instinct by tying salary and wage increases to achieving cost improvements above a certain target and letting everyone know on a daily basis how cost reductions are going. Those who want to be sure to have a decent income increase will be monitoring the information and taking action. There's a problem though. Many people may not feel like they have the knowledge or time to work on faster cost reductions. You could provide free breakfasts and lunches to those who were willing to attend training sessions to learn more about creating and implementing better cost reductions. Your organization could also provide a hotline people could call for help with developing cost reductions.

By comparison, most organizations disqualify almost everyone in the organization from being able to work on cost reductions. Only managers, supervisors, and engineers may be given the leeway. Yet the best ideas often come from outside those perspectives. Cost reduction is clearly one of those activities where more heads work better, but the task has to engage everyone in helpful ways.

For better results, you can combine even more near-perfection perspectives. You might use four individual and three organizational principles to identify the potential for an astonishing breakthrough practice.

To provide further opportunity, go back and add to your list of 50 individual and 50 group instances of near perfection. With experience, you'll locate even more helpful perspectives that can be applied.

Having now identified several ideal-best-practice opportunities, you should *pursue the ideal best practice* (step 6). Start by selecting one or more of those opportunities to implement. In making this choice, be sure to evaluate your organization's track record for successfully making similar changes and other ways you can reduce risk. You can use the analysis described concerning implementing beyond the future best practice to help you. *The 2,000 Percent Solution* and *The Portable 2,000 Percent Solution* provide additional cautions and directions.

Being now ready to pursue the ideal best practice, you should be sure to *select the right people and provide the right encouragement* (step 7). You must find people who are energized or excited by a change. Your ideal team members must see change as a challenge that will help them grow personally. Select team members who will feel that being chosen to work on approaching the ideal best practice is the most wonderful thing that ever happened to them.

Beyond enthusiasm, you need open-mindedness. Take a cue from Abraham Maslow and his concept of self-actualization: What a person can be, he or she must be (See *Motivation and Personality*, Harper, 1954). Among other characteristics, Maslow described the self-actualized as displaying higher levels of:

- Efficient perceptions of reality
- Comfort with reality
- Accepting oneself, others, and nature
- Spontaneity
- Simplicity

- Naturalness
- Focus on problems outside themselves
- Detachment
- Preference for privacy
- Autonomy and independence from culture and environment

- Freshness of appreciation and richness of feeling
- Transcendent experience
- Identification with all humanity
- Deep interpersonal relations
- Preference for democratic processes

- Ability to differentiate between means and ends
- Nonhostile humor
- Creativity, originality, or inventiveness

Maslow also spotted significant drawbacks among some of the self-actualized who could also be vain, irritating, cold, uncritical, and overgenerous. Obviously, you should choose team members with the fewest of these drawbacks ... even if you lose some creativity.

But don't be restricted to Maslow's concept. People who can adapt rapidly to unexpected problems are even more valuable because they point the group in a new direction when everyone else is stuck. You can spot these people by asking them how they solved seemingly impossible problems in the past.

Naturally, choosing the right team leader makes a big difference in your results. Look for a leader who shares the enthusiasm of each team member and knows how to direct that enthusiasm. In addition, you want someone who places the interests of the team and the organization ahead of any desire to exercise power as top dog.

Avoid borrowing leaders from another organization (whether they be consultants or outsourced service providers). Such outsiders will have a harder time reflecting the values of those they lead. If you cannot find an appropriate leader within your organization, be sure to hire someone who will sustain the excitement necessary to bring off major changes and who matches your company's values as closely as possible. Four leadership qualities determine success:

1. Shared values with the organization
2. Understanding the problems thoroughly before beginning the project
3. Ability to persuade others that the project will succeed
4. Skills relevant to the task

Sometimes the need for change is so daunting that the organization's leaders won't be able to cope. When that circumstance occurs, consider helping the organization by applying what we call "stealth" change. Rather than beginning by selling the people at the top and making great promises and proclamations, keep it all hush-hush. Recruit a few highly admired people who have the talent to lead the change by creating models of the new ways on the quiet. After setting the standard, loan talented teams who can install the better ways to a few more highly admired people who are in trouble with making their budgets. After succeeding, ask your bailed-out leaders to visit the rest of the organization to explain the successful change and to welcome visitors who want to learn more. Within six months, such stealth projects can often run circles around formally authorized teams with tons of resources.

Before finalizing your choice of team members and leader, let those you are considering know that there's risk involved. Team members will be betting their careers with this assignment. Team members and leaders who perform well will likely be asked to solve another problem or pursue a different opportunity — that's their career reward. If they don't execute the changes, they won't have jobs to go back to ... but you will help them locate a new position in another organization.

As you can imagine, knowing that you cannot retreat to your old job is unsettling, even demoralizing, information. People who have routinely exceeded the future best practices to approach the ideal best practice report that this up-or-out approach is necessary. Team members who like a challenge will thrive in this environment. But it's not for everyone. You are creating personal burning platforms that will make team members realize that the project's success is essential. Take on only those who are willing to accept the personal danger from this risk.

What about providing financial rewards? Incentives for a special project should in no way mirror the organization's existing financial incentives. Success should result in far larger than normal bonuses for team members at their given levels. Pick incentive levels that will *excite* exceptional and appropriate excellence. However, keep in mind that many organizations choose incentives that are too high. Larger financial incentives quickly fail to add greater excitement. Instead, financial incentives that are too large encourage people to play it safe to be sure to get a minimum reward from the overwhelming promise of largesse.

Having completed your first 2,000 percent solution, you come to the most important step of the eight: *Repeat the first seven steps.* "Practice makes perfect." We learned to walk by taking more and more tottering steps before we fell. We learned to write by copying each letter many, many times. Doing is the best way to learn. Imagine trying to read a book to learn how to ride a two-wheeled bicycle.

Achieving 20-times improvement also requires repetition. When you reexamine the same process and improvement opportunity, you will uncover new and better ideas with each repetition of the first seven steps of the eight-step 2,000 percent solution process.

The gains from such repetitions can be staggering because they usually multiply onto a higher performance base. Here's an example. Imagine that you just created a way to expand revenues by 20 times from the current level. On the next reexamination of that opportunity, you might find a way to increase revenues by an additional 200 percent from the 20-times improved base. That seemingly more modest increase would be equal to double the entire gain from the first 2,000 percent solution!

Many times, reexamination leads to larger absolute gains during the repetition than during the initial examination. Naturally, when a 2,000 percent solution is reached on top of the first 2,000 percent solution, you've turned a 20-times gain into a 400-times gain. Think of the opportunity to examine such an area for a third time.

If you have wisely chosen to work on your highest potential opportunity, this upside potential shouldn't surprise you. It's also unlikely that any other opportunity will be as large as reexamining what you just finished.

When people first create and implement a 2,000 percent solution, most will opt not to reexamine the same area for at least five years. That's a big mistake! In most cases, you can start reexamining the opportunities right away and come up with big gains. By looking for more opportunities sooner, you'll build on the momentum of what you learned in the first iteration as well as deepen your understanding of the opportunity.

There are valuable, related benefits from such repetition. Each success will increase commitment to creating 2,000 percent solutions while geometrically expanding the resources available to pursue new solutions. With practice, the 2,000 percent solution process becomes easier, more productive, and faster.

At some point, creating 2,000 percent solutions will become part of your organizational culture. As a result, you'll have even more good habits to help performance when you're not working on 2,000 percent solutions. You'll also notice and start working sooner on large opportunities.

When the 2,000 percent solution process has been accepted into your organization's culture, you will benefit from having a powerful common language, thought process, and capability for improvement.

To accomplish this desirable result, your organization's leader must create an expectation that creating 2,000 percent solutions is the new standard of what must be accomplished. With that focus, the leader's words will become beliefs throughout the organization. The beliefs will trigger thoughts. The thoughts will become ideas. The ideas will become actions. The actions will become new habits. The new habits will be reinforced and improved by experience and success. The new habits will upgrade the culture. Repetition will strengthen, deepen, and widen the impacts of each of these reinforcing mechanisms.

The main issue for you is reinforcing repetition of the eight-step process. Skip this step, and you will lose almost all of the potential benefit of using what you have learned in this book.

Here is your assignment for increasing the likelihood of frequent, effective repetitions of the 2,000 percent solution process:

- Make everyone aware that the eight-step process will be repeated in the same area, again and again.
- When the process is begun, set early dates to start repeating the process.
- Set dates to begin the eight steps in other important management processes.
- Set dates to begin repeating the eight steps in those other important management processes.

- Add to your organizational ability to use the eight-step process through improved capabilities such as:

  — More measurement capabilities to spot unperceived ways to improve
  — Better ability to identify cause and effect
  — Increased access to organizations with best practices you can use
  — Faster learning from other organizations
  — Improved forecasting of future practice improvements
  — Enhanced conceptualization of the ideal best practice
  — Effective planning for more quickly approaching the ideal best practice with contained costs, while moving rapidly into engaging new opportunities opened up by nearing the ideal best practice

Make a copy of this assignment and put it near your work computer so that you will see the assignment every time you use the computer and be reminded to take these critical actions.

Lesson Seven Assignments

1. Write down where your organization is performing well in relation to your needs for tomorrow.

2. Write down where your organization needs to improve now in light of tomorrow's potential.

3. Write down those areas where your organization must change in order to perform close to its future potential and set deadlines for when these changes need to occur.

4. Share what you have written with those who will have to make the changes. Give them this book and set dates for completing plans to meet these deadlines for change.

5. Help everyone in your organization learn to create many 2,000 percent solutions by employing the management process described in this lesson.

6. Put measurements in place within each key activity to track the rise and fall of complacency throughout your organization.

7. Check to be sure that the dates to begin repeating the eight-step process are being observed.

8. Reread this lesson annually.

Part Three

Complementary
2,000 Percent Solutions

Then He spoke a parable to them:
"No one puts a piece from a new garment on an old one;
otherwise the new makes a tear, and also
the piece that was taken *out of the new*
does not match the old."

— Luke 5:36 (NKJV)

In Luke 5:36 (NKJV), Jesus was teaching through this parable that when we have fruitful opportunities we need to engage in them with a new approach that reflects Him. In this part of *Your Breakthroughs*, we consider an extraordinarily effective way to be more fruitful for God's Kingdom. Be prepared to leave behind your old thinking as you do.

Let's start by asking a new question: What if 2,000 percent solutions could have multiplier effects on the size of benefits from other 2,000 percent solutions? Multiplying exponential improvements by developing complementary solutions that efficiently enhance each other's results provides the most feasible approach for everyone to enjoy 400 years of normal improvements in 20 years.

If you are like most people, you haven't yet created your first 2,000 percent solution. You won't get much benefit from this insight into multiplying exponential improvements until you do. By answering and acting on your answers to the questions in *The 2,000 Percent Solution*, *The 2,000 Percent Solution Workbook*, *The 2,000 Percent Squared Solution*, *Business Basics*, *Advanced Business*, *Advanced Business for Innovation*, and *Advanced Business for Social Benefits*, you will be able to develop as many 2,000 percent solutions as you like. Once you have become skilled and have enjoyed that experience, you'll begin to appreciate how critical your choice of improvements is for determining the magnitude of your accomplishments.

If you haven't yet produced a 2,000 percent solution, let me encourage you to do so by noting that the project's experience has been to find 2,000 percent solutions in a wide range of human endeavors. Those experiences suggest that the possibilities for such improvements are virtually universal. Reread the latter parts of the introduction to Part Two to appreciate why I say so.

When developing such solutions, what improvements should we concentrate on? That's a major focus for this part of *Your Breakthroughs*. The answer we found is simple, but profound: Start first by developing organizations (both for-profit and nonprofit) to do their work in astonishingly effective ways by using the 2,000 percent solution process.

That's a key direction because the most important improvements usually have to be accomplished by organizations rather than individuals working alone. Why? Almost all important tasks require the efforts of several people. Also, if people learned how to make these improvements in organizations, such learning would frequently provide the guidance they needed to make enormous progress as individuals. To make the concepts for what to do easier to follow in the rest of this Part Three Introduction, I focus on the right combinations of exponential improvements to multiply in for-profit enterprises that are initially constrained by a lack of growth opportunities.

What if you are totally disconnected from all organizations? You might find it valuable to become involved with at least one organization while you are learning to make exponential improvements. If that's not possible, think about what improvements you can make that would be helpful to you now and to organizations later.

Businesses lacking growth opportunities have three basic choices for overcoming that deficiency:

1. Expand the market's growth rate.
2. Gain market share.
3. Enter faster-growing markets.

Most businesses focus on the third opportunity. A few will try to do a little with the second opportunity. Hardly anyone will work aggressively on the first one. Typically, the most fruitful results, however, come from working in a different way by first greatly increasing the value of what customers and end users receive from whatever costs in time, effort, and resources they incur to obtain and use offerings. When such an improvement happens, the market expands, as does a company's market share.

Naturally, if value improvements are so helpful to a business, it would also be great to reduce costs to provide more ways to add value while still increasing profits. Thus, finding ways to drop the cost of providing an offering by 96 percent becomes an extremely useful complementary solution, multiplying the benefit of 20 times more revenues by such lower costs to enhance profits by 400 times.

My mother had an expression that she liked to use to explain why small businesses don't become bigger ones: As she rubbed her thumb and first two fingers together, she would say, "It takes money." What good does it do us to know how to become 400 times more profitable if we then cannot afford the expansion needed to create and build on that result to improve cash flow by 8,000 times?

What's the solution? I think it's to improve an organization's effective use of its invested money by 20 times. I define that improvement as increasing capital turnover by 20 times. What's that? Let me explain.

Capital turnover is the ratio of annual revenue (some people call this "sales") dollars divided by how many investment dollars are needed to produce the offerings for those revenues. Here's an example: A hypothetical mine requires $16 million to be dug and developed before any ore can be taken out of it. While the mine is being developed, the capital turnover ratio is zero because millions are being spent and there are no revenues (0/16). After development, the mine generates $4 million in ore that is sold each year. The capital turnover then would be 0.25 (4/16).

In contrast, a typical distribution operation looks a lot different from a mining operation in its capital turnover. A sales level of $4 million might be supported by as little as $120,000 in capital. The capital turnover of such a business is 33.33 (4.00/0.12). Why does a distribution business need so little capital? If the distribution business operates smoothly, it is paid by its customers before it has to pay its suppliers. The float (a continuing flow of cash received that doesn't yet have to be paid) helps offset whatever capital is required for warehouse space and trucks.

Some manufacturers achieve similar levels of efficiency by getting paid when orders are placed, keeping working capital and facilities needs to a minimum. Dell is a good example. That company's sparing use of cash to generate sales and profits allowed a multibillion-dollar firm to rapidly emerge from Michael Dell's dorm room at the University of Texas by drawing almost totally on its own cash flow, rather than by adding external capital.

So why is a 2,000 percent solution for using less capital to generate sales a good thing? It means you won't have to invest any more money than you have already in place to grow by another 20 times after already having increased by 20 times earlier. Does that sound good? When you reduce your capital intensity by this amount, your cash flow will expand by 8,000 times.

Surely you don't want to stop at gaining a mere 8,000 times more benefits. Wouldn't having 160,000 times more benefits be even better? To do so, let's reduce the cost of acquiring the initial and subsequent capital for your business by at least 96 percent. That solution will vastly increase the rate of return you'll earn on your capital, expand the amount of capital you can access, and boost the capital you can afford to spend for other purposes.

As a low-cost way to access capital, most companies fail to consider how they might turn customers and suppliers into low-cost sources of capital. Here's an example: An accounting firm might offer to hold its prices for two years for clients who are willing to pay annual retainers in advance. The accounting firm should do this if it can invest the unused retainer amounts to earn more than the cost of any foregone fee increases or to reduce debts that incur high interest and fee costs.

Why would clients want to do that? Many clients prefer the certainty of keeping expenses under control to the uncertainties of earning what near-term interest rates might provide.

This 160,000 times benefit-improvement level has another significant dimension: Multiply these four (sales increase, cost decrease, asset reduction, and lower cost of capital) complementary 2,000 percent solutions and you have created the equivalent of 400 years of normal improvements (assuming productivity gains of 3 percent a year for 400 years). That's pretty neat, don't you think?

That's not all. Benefits can actually reach millions of times the current levels. When that happens, it's like gaining the benefits of 8,000 years (over 100 lifetimes) worth of normal improvements. I don't know about you, but that prospect is pretty exciting to me.

What benefits am I talking about? While there are a number of complementary benefits that can be added, I suggest you now turn your attention to increasing the total benefits received by stakeholders who aren't customers or shareholders (such as end users, suppliers, lenders, distributors, employees, families of employees, and the communities in which you operate) to become at least 20 times more than what shareholders and customers gain. Why? Adding benefits for these people will help you sustain your success longer and give you a better foundation for new generations of 2,000 percent solutions. You can learn how to do this in *Advanced Business.*

Chances are this dimension for possible 2,000 percent solutions is new to you. Let me develop the concept so it's clearer. As a first step, consider who else can be helped and what might be done for those other stakeholders. Organizations affect those who are the end users of their offerings, even when those end users aren't customers. How can an end user be different from a customer? Here's an example: Hospitals purchase baby formula for mothers who aren't nursing to use for their newborns. The babies are the end users rather than the hospital customer. After moms and babies go home, the supermarket or discount merchandiser will be the customer, but the end user will always be that baby. Provide a better mix of nutrients in the baby formula than anyone else has ever developed, and the babies may gain valuable life-long advantages in physical, mental, and immune-system developments. Those benefits, in turn, can continue to help the whole community for decades. The company will also directly benefit if it becomes known that the babies are thriving better on those nutrients. More people will want to buy its offerings.

Suppliers are impacted by factors such as how much profit they gain from serving an account, the reputation they enjoy because of working with a given customer, skills they develop that translate into being applied to other opportunities, the increase in their ownership value from having the customer, and other revenues they are able to garner because of the customer relationship. If your improvements expand how much profitable business they do, suppliers will be greatly benefited as well.

You then repeat this thinking process for all other stakeholders, including customers, distributors, employees, employees' families, lenders, lessors, partners, owners, neighbors, and the communities in which the company operates, always seeking solutions that greatly expand benefits for all stakeholders.

Having expanded all such stakeholder benefits by 20 times more than the 20 times that owners receive, the total gain in benefits has reached at least 3.2 million times. Where do we go next to gain 64 million times more benefits? I suggest that we strive to increase innovation in your company and the industry. To do so, you should encourage copying.

Isn't it great that people are such copy cats? This virtually universal instinct can be relied on to help us create another 20-times boost in benefits: an increase in the number of people who apply the same improvements as do the most successful creators of benefit-multiplying 2,000 percent solutions.

Many people will be aghast at the suggestion. Why make it easier for others to copy you? Isn't it better to keep your best methods a secret? Well, that's not always the case. In many instances, an industry is being held back by the unprofessional way that some competitors operate. Improve the choices for customers, and more people will be willing to buy from an industry.

An unexpected benefit of giving away such valuable knowledge is to light a permanent fire under the company's own operations to improve. Those added improvements will, in turn, speed industry growth and provide for even more multiplied benefits. In most cases, there's not much to worry about concerning competitive advantage because organizations will be teaching management processes rather than revealing details of proprietary knowledge that is unique to their most valuable offerings. You can learn more about how to do so and gain more benefits by reading and applying *Advanced Business for Innovation*.

Isn't it fun to start thinking about creating over a billion times more benefits? Where shall we look next for a complementary 2,000 percent solution to gain that result? I know. Let's poke at some of those areas that economists like to complain no one pays any attention to.

What do I mean? Here's an example: The tragedy of the commons is a problem familiar to economists. Provide something for free to everyone, and the privilege will be abused until the common resource all but disappears. Such a problem today is the rapidly shrinking stock of fish in the world's oceans. Each fisherman makes the most by taking as many fish as possible until there are few fish left of a given species. The fishermen move on to another species, reducing the global food supply as fish stocks remain permanently depressed below what the oceans could support.

In studying these problems, scholars are usually quick to point out that while solving these problems has great value for everyone, there's not enough profit potential to encourage any individual or organization to be responsible for seeking the general good.

I have a little secret for you: Those scholars apparently don't know about 2,000 percent solutions. Centuries of pollution and waste have left the world filled with valuable opportunities to fix messes. A simple example can be found in the many new mining operations that don't dig up any ore at all; they simply reprocess the piles of tailings left over from earlier ores that were processed for a different mineral.

Profitably working on this solution is explained in detail by *Advanced Business for Social Benefits*. Why is providing this kind of benefit a good idea when you aren't directly helping your own customers? Let me partially explain by beginning with an economist's argument. If you make a profit by reducing global economic costs by 20 times your increased profits from this new activity, you've just expanded purchasing power that benefits everyone. Undoubtedly, some of the increased funds will flow back to your organization in the form of increased purchases.

There's also a terrific preference for doing business with companies that reduce harmful pollution and solve other expensive social problems. More customers will seek you as a result. For companies that directly serve consumers, that preference can be enough to turn you into an industry leader.

In addition, such companies have a much greater ability to attract top talent. Many people would like to work as employees for, be partners with, invest in, or be suppliers to those who are making important improvements. Many idealistic young people will only be drawn to larger companies for this reason, knowing that smaller organizations have potentially less impact when dealing with similar kinds of issues.

Naturally, there's individual self-interest in providing such benefits as well. Do you want to suffer some disease because others have done a poor job of containing harmful materials? I'm sure the answer to that question is no, so it helps you personally to create over a billion times more benefits in these ways.

You can then expand combined benefits by over 25 billion times by adding another complementary 2,000 percent solution. Consider that most of the world's people are desperately poor. Their lack of resources leads to permanent problems. Some babies don't properly develop their brains for lack of a few hundred dollars in nutrients. Lives are ravaged by diseases that are preventable with clean water, inexpensive vaccines, and easy-to-make medicines. Hundreds of millions of people with above-average intellect never receive enough education to develop their minds to anywhere near their full potential. Entrepreneurs capable of leading thousands to economically useful lives lack the investment capital to train and employ those thousands.

What's the root of the problem? It takes a long time and much investment in people before individuals can earn their keep and support others. Shortchange the most valuable parts of that time and investment, and the value of the lost potential is an enormous multiple of the resources that aren't expended in the near term.

Here's an example of what can be done: Research conducted by my students in Africa has shown that there are millions of partially able entrepreneurs who can become leaders in creating enormous economic and social progress. How could this potential be turned into a happy result? By establishing a new type of entrepreneurship — enterprises that will profitably employ hundreds of millions of people who now have few prospects for earning much of a living. *Adventures of an Optimist* explores many ways to do so.

Is that it for expanding benefits? I don't think so, but I fear that I may have reached the limit of your patience with and interest in multiplying my optimistic thinking into creating more benefits now than would normally occur in the next thousand years. You can read more of my ideas for multiplying benefits, if you want, in *Adventures of an Optimist*.

Are you feeling more confident about making 400 years of normal progress in only 20 years? I hope so. It's not that difficult a goal if enough people are sincerely interested in accomplishing more with their God-given potential.

The key to appreciating the potential for this rapid progress is to realize that no new knowledge or technologies need be developed. You just need to make better use of the time and resources you already have.

Having just explored a possible improvement path for a for-profit company that needs more growth opportunities, I am sure you'll enjoy the change of pace in Lesson Eight where we shift to looking at how nonprofit organizations should sequence the development of their complementary 2,000 percent solutions.

Lesson Eight

Nonprofit Sequence

*And Jesus, when He came out, saw a great multitude and
was moved with compassion for them,
because they were like sheep not having a shepherd.*

So He began to teach them many things.

*When the day was now far spent, His disciples came to Him and said,
"This is a deserted place, and already the hour is late.
Send them away, that they may go into the surrounding country and
villages and buy themselves bread; for they have nothing to eat."*

*But He answered and said to them,
"You give them something to eat."*

*And they said to Him, "Shall we go and buy two hundred denarii
worth of bread and give them something to eat?"*

But He said to them, "How many loaves do you have? Go and see."

And when they found out they said, "Five, and two fish."

*Then He commanded them to make them
all sit down in groups on the green grass.
So they sat down in ranks, in hundreds and in fifties.*

And when He had taken the five loaves and the two fish,
He looked up to heaven, blessed and broke the loaves, and
gave them *to His disciples to set before them;*
and the two fish He divided among them *all.*
So they all ate and were filled.
And they took up twelve baskets full of fragments and of the fish.

Now those who had eaten the loaves were about five thousand men.

— Mark 6:34-44 (NKJV)

Helping nonprofit organizations to become much more fruitful for God's Kingdom is a personal interest of mine. I think it's the best way to accomplish many important tasks. While some people urged me to make The 400 Year Project a profit-making activity, I felt called to operate as if it were legally a nonprofit. I didn't actually create such a legal structure because doing so would have taken time, effort, and funds that were much better spent in other ways. Also, I did not intend to seek funding from others. Although the project does charge for some of its materials, those funds are used to pay for providing free materials to those who are likely to make good use of them and cannot afford to purchase. The project has been blessed by many students and volunteers who have generously shared their time, talents, and treasure to establish demonstration projects and report their findings so that others could apply them.

In doing so, I'm sure that many of the students and volunteers were inspired by Jesus' example in miraculously feeding 5,000 men (and uncounted women and children, as well), as described in Mark 6:34-44 (NKJV) and other Bible books. Jesus appreciated that as valuable as good teaching is, He also needed to impress others by deeds that would help them to understand who He is and to learn what can be accomplished by drawing on Him and the resources of His Kingdom. Consider that Jesus did more than just feed thousands: He also created more leftovers than the original volume of food that He multiplied. In essence, he created an infinite percent solution by satisfying all of the needs and having a remainder that exceeded his initial resources.

While we cannot hope to use natural means to match His amazing accomplishment, we should always remember that God can decide to multiply the effectiveness of our efforts with His supernatural provision when we are serving His will. Through The 400 Year Project, God has also provided natural means for producing what would clearly be seen as miraculous results by many.

When I meet leaders of nonprofit organizations, such leaders invariably describe several major projects they would like to accomplish. Somewhere during that conversation, she or he will mention a lack of financial resources and begin to talk about attracting many more donations. Unfortunately, gaining donations isn't usually the best first focus for a nonprofit organization seeking to become vastly more fruitful for God's Kingdom.

If you are such a leader or work with one, you'll probably find some of what I have to say about the most productive nonprofit sequence for making complementary 2,000 percent solutions hard to understand. Please be patient as I do my best to describe the potential benefits of taking a different approach. If you still have questions or don't agree with what I share, I hope you will send an e-mail to me at donmitchell@fastforward400.com so that I can add more information and explanations for you.

The world is filled with nonprofit organizations pursuing noble purposes, many of which are directly related to expanding God's Kingdom. I was recently reminded of this fact while reading a travel book about Africa. Almost everyone the author met in hotels and restaurants during quite a long journey was connected to some nonprofit organization or other that was seeking to alleviate the many problems that can be found in Africa.

Because there are so many nonprofits, most of them have to compete fiercely for donations. Givers often feel inundated with the many different ways they can encourage or aid a given accomplishment. After comparing different nonprofits from the points of view of their effectiveness and efficiency, how many people are helped by how much for whatever amount has been spent, only a few nonprofit organizations stand out. The others will look woefully inadequate to anyone who does such a careful examination.

To escape the consequences of looking bad in such comparisons, some nonprofits primarily rely on attracting board members who will make large donations and use obligations developed in their personal relationships to influence others to give. A wealthy individual on a board might be donating to many causes after being solicited by friends. Such a board member might then ask such friends to reciprocate. In addition, a supplier's sense of appreciation for the purchases that an employee's business makes might lead to the supplier making a gift to that employee's favorite nonprofit organization. Why will people ask for gifts in such cases? Sometimes the donation solicitors aren't paying any attention to efficiency and effectiveness. In some other cases, the prestige gained from being recognized for raising a great deal of money can be appealing.

Instead of focusing first on obtaining more funding, I believe that most nonprofits would do better to initially locate ways to reduce the costs of supplying and using benefits by 96 percent. Think back to Jesus' example in Mark 6:34-44 (NKJV). If He had directed the disciples to buy the bread, instead, the solution would have pleased everyone. However, no one would have felt that he or she had to stay connected to Jesus ... unless He was going to provide food after every sermon. Such a solution wouldn't have done as much to advance the Kingdom, just filled more places on the grass whenever He spoke.

When I make this observation to nonprofit leaders, in most cases the reaction is negative. While few such leaders bother to explain their reactions, my guess is that they usually either feel that they cannot operate any less expensively or that they don't know how to lessen the costs. What they may not appreciate in either case is the substantial information available from The 400 Year Project for reducing organizational and beneficiary costs by 96 percent. However, someone will have to be committed enough to learn and apply this information. I have more to say on how to cut costs so dramatically in Lesson Thirteen. For now, just consider by how much total costs would decline if all the paid staff were replaced by unpaid volunteers. For many nonprofits, that shift would be sufficient to accomplish such a goal.

The nonprofit leader's next priority should be to increase benefit effectiveness. I see such an improvement coming from either making benefits more useful to those who need them or by adding complementary benefits. Lesson Fifteen contains more information about how to do so. Few organizations measure the effectiveness of the benefits they provide in accomplishing some valuable purpose. Making such measurements often opens the eyes to the advantages of providing current benefits differently as well as providing different benefits.

At this point, an organization will certainly be very appealing to potential donors. However, the need for most of such donations will have disappeared due to the increased efficiency and effectiveness in supplying benefits. Nevertheless, such a nonprofit will probably still need more volunteers. In this regard, more efficiency and effectiveness help by making volunteers feel that they are making a bigger difference through their efforts. It's also quite valuable to make volunteer work more desirable and motivating. Too many organizations treat volunteers as if they have no feelings about what they are asked to do and the conditions in which they are expected to do so. Instead, volunteer positions should be designed to be attractive to volunteers in terms of being interesting, providing opportunities to learn, meeting memorable people, and enhancing self-image. In addition, volunteers should be given an increased sense of what their work accomplishes through spending time with those who need assistance but aren't yet getting it, those who are receiving help and improving their circumstances, and those who have already "graduated" from needing assistance. Hopefully, many people in the last category will also be serving as volunteers, helping to make the experience more inspiring and relevant by sharing their stories. Please remember that *Advanced Business for Social Benefits* is a good resource for how to attract more volunteers and enable them to be much more effective.

Next, I suggest that the organization focus on ways to reduce by 96 percent the investments that are used to provide benefits. Doing so will eliminate the last major need for increased funds. Lesson Fourteen provides more information on how to make such reductions.

After that, nonprofits should add ways to make beneficiaries more productive in other aspects of their lives. Beneficiaries of nonprofits are normally operating at a tiny level of their full potential due to some difficulties and what they lack. After the first kind of benefits is provided, most such people will then have greater capability to use their potential. Unfortunately, many nonprofits are so narrowly focused that they fail to add new benefits for making the increased capability of their beneficiaries even more productive. Lessons eighteen and nineteen provide more information on this subject.

Obviously, there can and should be exceptions to the order of complementary 2,000 percent solutions that I have proposed in this lesson. For instance, one organization might be so much more hamstrung by high investment needs than by operating costs that the organization should reduce the investment needs first. To determine if you should engage in creating these solutions in a different order, I suggest that you begin by imagining that you have expanded your provision of benefits by 20 times. Then, spell out how much more you would need in terms of staff, volunteers, operating funds, investments, other resources, and skills to do so. Whatever aspects are hardest to increase are the ones where you should first increase efficiency and effectiveness.

So where does that leave an organization that has followed this route? The initial cost reduction meant that 20 times more benefits could be provided with existing resources. Improving benefit effectiveness means that beneficiaries don't need to receive benefits for as long, so that more people can be served with the same number of benefits over time. Adding a great number of volunteers who need few resources will mean that still more benefits can be provided and more people helped. Reducing investment needs will eliminate the last financial barrier to doing more. Making beneficiaries more effective will also reduce benefit needs and allow many more people to be served. Overall, a nonprofit may be doing thousands of times more good. How could such an organization hope to attract enough donations to come anywhere near to matching such an increase in expanding God's Kingdom by using current methods?

Let me share a personal perspective. My experience has shown that there are enough resources already being applied to supplying most benefits to meet *all* the world's needs. However, the resources are being used so inefficiently and ineffectively that only a tiny fraction of the most important needs are being served. Taking the approach that I've described can help to quickly narrow any such gaps. I look forward to hearing about your successes in adding evidence to support my observation. Please share all of your successes with me at donmitchell@fastforward400.com/.

Lesson Eight Assignments

1. How could your nonprofit organization increase the benefits it provides by 20 times without adding more financial resources?

2. To do so, what role should cost reductions play?

3. What role should increasing benefit effectiveness play?

4. How should the number of volunteers be most effectively increased?

5. What should be done to reduce the need for investments?

6. What other benefits should be provided to those who use the current ones most effectively?

Lesson Nine

For-Profit Sequence

*Now may He who supplies seed to the sower,
and bread for food, supply and multiply
the seed you have sown and
increase the fruits of your righteousness,
while you are enriched in everything
for all liberality, which causes thanksgiving
through us to God.*

— 2 Corinthians 9:10-11 (NKJV)

God intends to multiply all good things, whether they are the results of righteous actions or simply the harvests that He uses to feed us. Yet many people seldom notice such multiplication, despite the natural world abounding in it. For instance, just a handful of the right kind of seeds properly watered, fed, nurtured, harvested, and their seeds later planted, as well, with the process continuing from crop to crop, can feed large numbers of people for many decades. Although many people feel that such opportunities are few and far between, my experience has been that the potential to create such large multiplications is usually easier to achieve in our own lives than in the natural world. Why? Due to being informed and empowered by the Holy Spirit, we can pick better targets and move faster.

Despite the obvious advantages of being able to make such fruitfulness occur, few people feel that they need bother to learn how to accomplish such multiplication. It's as if they were hungry in the middle of a supermarket while holding a fistful of hundred-dollar bills. All they have to do is pick out the food, take it to the register, hand over some money, prepare the food, and eat.

While becoming competent in making 2,000 percent solutions requires more effort than buying and preparing food in the supermarket example, learning is minor compared to the size of the benefit. Few people require more than 80 hours for gaining the necessary skill. What's 80 hours compared to the potential to generate in a few months the equivalent of several centuries' worth of benefits produced in the same old ways?

Okay, let's talk about the role of 2,000 percent solutions in creating more value. *Perhaps the most important point to share with you is that 2,000 percent solutions with better goals create vastly more value than other such solutions do. If you care about improving value, pick the best solutions to work on and do so in the optimal order.*

I chose to take this perspective here because the introduction to this part and Lesson Eight do a good job of explaining how to increase benefits provided to customers and end users. Owners of for-profit companies are going to be quite interested in what they gain from multiplying complementary 2,000 percent solutions. If owners don't benefit, they will block any attempt to produce stakeholder benefits that are perceived as not providing value for them, as well.

Let me share seven points:

1. *Simply expanding revenues by 20 times will not, by itself, necessarily increase ownership value.* The exceptions to that observation mostly occur in the following circumstances:

   (a) You are in a new industry where no one is yet profitable and revenues are used as a surrogate for estimating future profits (such as how cellular telephone service providers and Internet-based businesses were valued in the 1990s).

(b) Your operation could be consolidated by a new owner into an existing one to make the revenues much more valuable in terms of profits, cash flow, and dividends.

(c) Your below-scale enterprise or operation leaps above the minimum scale to become much more attractive in terms of the percentage of revenues that provide profits, cash flow, and dividends. This shift will be true of many small businesses when they reach medium or large size.

(d) Your profits grow in line with the revenue increases, causing growth in profits rather than in revenues to account for your improvement.

2. *Decreasing costs by 96 percent to serve a customer or end user will usually yield a more than 20-times increase in ownership value:*

   (a) Such a change will normally increase profits, cash flow, and dividends by more than 20 times.

   (b) Some of the cost decreases can be applied either to attracting more customers who will be highly profitable or to adding revenues from existing, profitable customers.

3. *Decreasing the fixed assets and working capital needed to serve a customer or end user by 96 percent will usually yield a more than 20-times increase in ownership value:*

   (a) Such a change will normally increase cash flow and the ability to pay dividends by more than 20 times.

   (b) Some of the decreased investment intensity will permit faster growth, further accelerating profit, cash flow, and dividend expansion.

4. *Increasing value for noncustomer stakeholders by 20 times has no direct impact on the organization and value for its owners, unless*

those value improvements translate into changed behavior that expands the organization's profits, cash flow, and dividends.

5. *Increasing by 20 times the economic value received by customers and end users at the same or a lower price, cost, time, and effort may have a more positive impact on value for an organization and its stakeholders than any other 2,000 percent solution:*

   (a) This change potentially allows for rapid expansion in revenues, profits, cash flow, and dividends for all stakeholders, due to current and potential customers and end users greatly increasing their purchases and consumption at the current or lower price level.

   (b) If the market is above average in elasticity for increased economic value, the expansion in revenues, profits, cash flow, and dividends can be a large multiple of 20 times.

   (c) The increased performance experienced by other stakeholders is likely to create multiplied benefits for the organization and its stakeholders in terms of reduced costs, less investment intensity, lower cost of capital, and greater access to key people and critical physical resources.

6. *In most instances, the smaller the unit that is benefited by any particular 2,000 percent solution, the less the value impact will be on owners:*

   (a) The primary exception will be if the unit is engaged in activities that investors value much more highly than other units in the same company, organization, business, or operation.

   (b) A secondary exception will be when a smaller unit is more sensitive to the value aspects from the improvement than either the entire company is or some larger unit or subunit.

7. *Improvements that accelerate the rate of expanding earnings, cash flow, and dividends over more years will create a larger increase in ownership value.*

   (a) Potential investors will assume that the improvements will continue in the future and pay a premium for what hasn't happened yet.

   (b) The ultimate base that is created will usually be larger than what can be generated by a quick burst of improvements whose benefits don't continue to multiply.

From those seven observations, you can see that *the optimal order of 2,000 percent solutions may not be the same as first expanding revenues by 20 times, then reducing all costs to serve a customer or end user by 96 percent, followed by reducing investment intensity by 96 percent, and then making selected changes to increase value by 20 times.* Let's explore the question of the right order for engaging in 2,000 percent solutions that improve value through considering some hypothetical examples of various types of businesses.

For the first example, let's consider a typical investment-intensive manufacturing business. Such an organization needs $1 million in net assets for every $2 million in revenues. Obtaining the first million is going to be difficult for most start-ups. Growing by 20 times will then require adding another $10 million in investments. I'm sure you see the point. For such an enterprise, reducing investment intensity is probably the right first 2,000 percent solution. The investment needed in the beginning drops from $1 million to merely $40 thousand. To grow revenues by 20 times then requires only adding $800 thousand, a small amount compared to the cash flow that will be generated from adding the $20 million in revenues.

Let's look at a typical distribution business as the second example. Such organizations usually don't require much investment compared to revenues ($200 thousand in net investment might be sufficient for $2 million in revenues), but they usually have small margins (profits divided by revenues). If you start by reducing costs to serve a customer by 96 percent, you create enormous value improvements because profits, cash flow, and dividends grow so much and so rapidly. With such a healthier base, growing the business is very affordable, bringing more value to benefits.

As the third example, let's consider an organization that's very profitable, has a great cash flow, and pays enormous dividends ... but is very small. If this organization focuses on anything other than revenue growth, the value expansions will not be nearly as substantial.

The lesson I would like you to draw from these examples is that *each organization has to consider the value sensitivity of various 2,000 percent solutions for its organization and stakeholders in order to determine the optimal order for creating and implementing 2,000 percent solutions.* In doing so, it may also be the case that repeating a 2,000 percent solution (to create a 2,000 percent squared solution in the same activity) may be more valuable than moving on to make a complementary 2,000 percent solution in a different performance dimension. As a result, the most attractive 2,000 percent solutions to develop and the optimal order for expanding the value of an organization and its stakeholders will vary quite widely from one business to the next. One of the most important strategy decisions that an organization makes is selecting the right breakthroughs to work on and the best sequence for accomplishing them.

Keeping in mind that assets, businesses, and companies have varying valuations at different times, in alternate forms, when operated in other ways, financed from other kinds of sources, and with new owners, eleven selection methods can help in choosing the best 2,000 percent solutions for adding value:

1. Estimate the value of the asset, business, and company in its highest value forms, operated optimally to emphasize its appeal in each value form.

2. Use what you learn to assume combinations of value-improvement moves (such as selling some assets that investors who like the business don't care for but other investors who like the assets do).

3. Test sensitivities of your major 2,000 percent solution options for their effects on the highest value forms and potential value-improvement moves.

4. Consider how the order of implementing the more attractive 2,000 percent solutions affects the apparent values now, in a year, and beyond that.

5. Determine the time frame in which you want to optimize value.

6. Select the value-improvement moves you are willing to do.

7. Determine the easiest-to-accomplish 2,000 percent solutions to make in their proper order for apparent value enhancement during your time frame.

8. Write a description of what you plan to do and ask in a legally appropriate way those who could affect the value in your preferred form how they would evaluate the value of the plan you have put together now, after you have been doing it for a year, and after you succeed. Ask them also to tell you how confident they are of your success.

9. Adjust your plan based on the feedback you receive.

10. Begin implementation and adjust the plan to reflect the success you have with the 2,000 percent solutions.

11. Update what you did in step 8 and repeat steps 9 and 10 until you reach the valuation you want.

The lesson I would like you to draw from this process is that each organization has to consider the value sensitivity of various value forms, value-improvement methods, 2,000 percent solutions, and the order of 2,000 percent solutions for its organization and its stakeholders in terms of "theoretical impacts" as well as value influencers' reactions to what is planned in order to determine the optimal order for creating and implementing 2,000 percent solutions.

Company leaders and owners who would like to better understand the interaction of 2,000 percent solutions and value improvement for all stakeholders should read *Advanced Business* from which this lesson is taken.

Lesson Nine Assignments

1. What are the highest value forms for your company, businesses, activities, and assets?

2. What are the best value-improvement actions you can take for putting your company, businesses, activities, and assets in their highest value forms for all stakeholders?

3. How can 2,000 percent solutions make those results much more valuable?

4. What order of 2,000 percent solutions makes the most sense for the value-improvement time frame you have in mind?

5. Are there substantial value-improvement opportunities to repeat making breakthroughs in one area of performance before starting to work on a different performance improvement?

6. Can you create any 2,000 percent solutions that will expand multiple dimensions of value for your organization and its stakeholders without making additional breakthroughs?

7. How do those who can affect value in any of these forms assess what you have in mind in terms of value influences and credibility?

Lesson Ten

Business-Model Innovation

Therefore, if anyone is in Christ, he is a new creation;
old things have passed away;
behold, all things have become new.

— 2 Corinthians 5:17 (NKJV)

Becoming a believer in Christ causes a transformation into a new person, with the Holy Spirit in her or him. Similarly, new leadership can transform an organization into something better. Let me describe what I've learned in this regard.

When I started a tracking study of CEO best practices in 1992, I was interested in seeing which characteristics of successful leaders most often stood the test of time. That approach goes against the grain. Most people focus on what worked best last week, hoping to copy it for use this week and next. The typical short-term approach can be exciting because you are always charging off in a new direction. Many organizational leaders seem to be afflicted with some kind of adult ADD (attention deficit disorder) that causes them to flit from one thing to another almost as fast as a butterfly does. Organizations, meanwhile, have a hard time adjusting to change. Most of the flitting leads to action without consequences as last week's orders are countermanded by this week's new directives.

My study defined success in a very extreme way: You had to outperform virtually every other medium- and large-size company publicly traded in the United States in terms of stock-price growth over a three year period while you were CEO ... *and keep up that level of success for at least a decade.* Wall Street is notoriously fickle, so this was a tough test. In addition, such a high-profile success was bound to attract tough competitors who wanted to ride the same gravy train. To last for a long time at the top in such an environment would require leadership skills in overcoming competitors that few have.

My study was unique in my spending time with the executives while they achieved the success. CEOs told me what they were trying to do, what they expected to happen next, and later filled me in on how the results turned out differently than they expected. Every other study of CEOs' long-term effectiveness that I'm aware of was done after the fact, drawing on interviews of people who provided their opinions afterwards about what had happened. Those backward-looking studies were suspect because memory is selective and credit is often appropriated for things that were the result of chance or the actions of others.

Another great benefit of following these CEOs as they and their companies achieved was that I could measure more things. Surveys and in-depth questions probed both for what the CEOs thought worked for them as well as what else they were doing that they didn't normally talk about.

Publishing the results in *Chief Executive Magazine* helped me to get much better access to the CEOs. Almost all of the CEOs seemed to hope I would write a profile in the magazine about them. I let them know that to be considered for a profile, they had to fill out my latest survey and be available for an interview.

Where I sensed that something special might be going on in a company, I arranged for a personal visit to meet the CEO and his staff (all of the CEO top performers during those years were men). During those visits, unscheduled activities would often be more revealing than what was planned.

For instance, during one visit to Rochester, New York, to interview Tom Golisano, CEO of Paychex, I received an impromptu invitation to an employment anniversary party for one of the first three people in the company. During the party, I had a chance to talk to employees at all levels within Paychex about their relationships, how the company had evolved, and what they felt about Tom. The party was quite revealing in ways that I didn't expect about how Tom had gathered top people together to do hard tasks and helped everyone be eager to succeed.

By 2002, it was clear to me that the most adept CEOs shared one common element: They had prospered by repeatedly upgrading their business models (these seven elements of their commerce: who, what, when, why, where, how, and how much) every three to five years. With increased global competition, the correct frequency of such business-model innovations would undoubtedly increase. Since some types of business-model improvements can be much less disruptive than others (such as adding complementary offerings), I saw no obvious limit to such increased frequency.

This observation about continuing to make business-model innovations was also significant for The 400 Year Project. If organizations began to focus on rapid business-model innovations, performance could improve faster. Without this leadership capability, the sources of many potential benefits from The 400 Year Project might lie fallow, waiting for leaders to get around to working on them.

The real barrier to continuing business-model innovation was that most organizations did not have this most important task on their agendas. Instead, leaders and the rank and file focused on doing the old tasks better and better. The fact that these old tasks were obsolete didn't seem to occur to anyone (if it did, they kept quiet lest someone would shoot the messenger). The time had come to issue a clarion call to make continuing business-model innovation job one, which *The Ultimate Competitive Advantage* (Berrett-Koehler, 2003) does.

Our subsequent research caused us to look around the world and also more closely at the small businesses that we came into contact with every day. One-by-one, helpful examples were identified, explored, validated, and described. I spent weeks traveling around interviewing people and learning many great lessons. I was pleasantly surprised to find that one-person businesses provided some of the most powerful and helpful cases; anyone can relate to examples like these. Part of the advantage that one-person companies have is that the path from strategy development to implementation is just a few inches of grey matter apart in the brain. The differences in education and experience among the one-person businesses were quite impressive as well, ranging from a golf caddy who grew up on the Isle of Man to Peter Drucker.

Let me share three examples of the most effective types of business-model innovation breakthroughs found in *The Ultimate Competitive Advantage*:

Increase Value without Raising Prices or Costs.

Less than five miles from our home, we found a memorable inspiration for improving a business by adding value without increasing prices or costs at Jordan's Furniture, a discount retailer. Jordan's had first drawn customer attention by being open late on Saturday nights at its sole store in blue-collar Waltham, Massachusetts. Before or after the movies or a dinner out, you could shop for furniture while all the other stores were closed. The owners, Barry and Eliot Tatelman, kept the radio waves filled with humorous ads to remind everyone to come "where under-prices begin."

Eventually, the tiny company opened a sprawling store on a green field site in another suburb, Avon, Massachusetts. Something else was new besides size and location, an entertainment attraction. The appeal of this new store was so strong that the owners had to get on the air to ask customers *not* to come for a few days after the opening. In subsequent stores, the Tatelmans did more with entertainment, adding restaurants, IMAX theaters, Disney-type attractions, and entertaining shows. People came from hundreds of miles away to see the stores ... and some bought furniture. Soon, Jordan's became the most successful furniture retailer in the United States as measured by its sales per square foot. The secret was no secret: Its "shoppertainment" concept of providing free and reasonably priced entertainment to shoppers attracted buyers better than the traditional approach.

The entertainment appeal was so strong in attracting customers that costs to serve customers as measured by percentages of sales dollars decreased dramatically due to the investment in shoppertainment. For example, Jordan's could now commission special factory runs to meet its specifications at lower cost and spend much less than the national average on advertising as a percentage of sales. In the process, profits soared, the company grew from 15 to more than 1,000 employees in less than 25 years, and the owners sold out for a fortune in Berkshire Hathaway stock. Despite their wealth, the Tatelmans continued to run the company and looked to add even more value to customers without raising prices or costs.

Adjust Prices to Increase Sales Profitably.

For our next example, we turned to an amusement park that I have visited dozens of time since the age of nine. Disneyland in Anaheim, California, found that it could greatly increase attendance and profits on days when the park wasn't crowded by offering annual passes at a fixed price. While tourists might spend a fortune each day to visit while they were in the area, a low-income Californian who lived down the street could come almost every day for little more a year than the tourist spent for a three-day visit.

This was a great deal for families with young children. For the same cost as a walk in the park, the family could take an additional trip to Disneyland after paying the annual fee. Even if the family only bought some milk while inside, Disneyland's profits were higher than if the family did not attend that day. To the family, it seemed like an amazing bargain: The entry cost per visit could become less than a dollar a day.

What's more, Disney had a chance to expose the family to advertising for its many other offerings. In the Main Street stores and in kiosks throughout the park, Disney merchandise was on sale. Attractions featured tie-ins to ABC television programs (a Disney-owned company), the Disney Channel cable television programs, and promotions for upcoming movies. People were paying to see the advertising more frequently! What a deal for Disney.

Disney liked this approach so much that it built a second amusement park next to Disneyland: California Adventure. This additional park permitted Disney to sell a higher priced annual pass and attract annual pass holders to return even more often. If one park was jammed on a given day, there was always room at the other park. After the kids outgrew Disneyland's tamer rides, they could give themselves an adrenaline charge on the more daunting attractions at California Adventure. When grandchildren arrived, grandparents could take the youngsters to Disneyland. And the process continues thus through the generations of California's annual pass holders.

Eliminate Harmful Costs.

Many organizations act as though costs that customers and beneficiaries experience aren't real costs. Our dry cleaner, Marc Rosenthal, knew better. He was the first in his town to install a VIP service at no extra cost to customers. VIP customers could drop off their cleaning anytime by using a special key that provided access to a chute into which they could toss personally labeled laundry bags provided by Marc. When it was time to pick up the clothes and linens, you were served in a special line and you found that your credit card had already been charged. You could usually leave with your cleaning within three minutes of arriving. There was no extra charge for this service. Marc knew that VIP service also cut his costs: He was paid sooner, could serve his best customers in less time, and fill up slack time with handling the VIP orders. He probably lost fewer customers, too, to competitors with lower prices or who were open later at night.

Impressed by the example, we were floored to find out that the VIP service idea didn't originate with Marc. In fact, another friend of ours, Doug Ross, was the innovator. Doug was one of Marc's providers for dry cleaning supplies. Realizing that most of his customers could buy supplies less expensively from catalog vendors, Doug began developing all kinds of programs to make his dry cleaner customers more profitable by cutting their costs in other ways and attracting more dry cleaning customers. In the process, Doug saw his market share climb while he helped his customers and their customers eliminate harmful costs.

So what did we conclude about such successes? Some organizations are blessed with geniuses who can continue to find or occasionally inspire others to develop more successful business-model innovations. That blessing, however, turns into a curse if the genius or effective leader stops delivering or leaves. In the worst case, while one person does all the thinking, the others are daydreaming about what they will do after work rather than coming up with their own business-model innovations.

A better approach is to install a process that engages many people in proposing and testing potential business-model innovations. We found a few examples where continuing business-model innovation had been made into day-to-day work. Typically, however, when the leader left who had organized the innovation process, business-model innovation for that organization ended.

Naturally, we were thrilled to find a few companies where a second generation of management had improved on a business-model innovation process. From such examples, we proposed a process for doing this task across many generations of CEOs that you can read about in *The Ultimate Competitive Advantage.*

Since then, The 400 Year Project has developed more advanced concepts of how to perform continuing business-model innovation, as inspired by Isaiah 54:2 (NKJV):

> "Enlarge the place of your tent,
> And let them stretch out
> the curtains of your dwellings;
> Do not spare;
> Lengthen your cords,
> And strengthen your stakes."

This verse from Isaiah 54 (NKJV) is often cited as an example of what God wants each of his believers to do in preparation for increasing His Kingdom. A business model that's expandable in several dimensions provides opportunities for a corporate leader to accomplish something comparable for stakeholders.

An expandable dimension can be part of any of the seven business-model elements ("who," "what," "when," "where," "why," "how," and "how much" of serving customers and adding value for stakeholders), but the dimension has to enable a business to develop or improve an advantage versus competitors in accomplishing valuable new tasks for stakeholders. A business model can be greatly enhanced by improving performance in any one of the seven dimensions listed above. *However, an expandable business model innovation improves the performance of at least four of the seven dimensions.*

Here's an example to clarify these concepts. Sir Richard Branson has established more than 100 businesses under the Virgin brand, enterprises that range from bridal wear to cellular telephone service to an airline. His businesses have usually been reasonably successful.

Whenever he develops a new offering, Sir Richard changes "what" is provided from the standard to something that some customers or end users prefer. In most cases, the ways of providing the offering are different from prior ones, an adjustment of "how" a business is conducted. Many of the customers and other stakeholders are different, often affecting "who" is involved. Price points are different, usually lower, causing shifts in "how much" is charged. The geographic markets are sometimes different, affecting "where" the business is conducted. New and existing customers try the new offerings due to confidence built by having had good experiences with other Virgin offerings. Because of the overall brand strength and Sir Richard's reputation, this approach for expanding a business model into new dimensions can be continued for many more years.

Consider a different example. Amazon.com entered the book retailing business by putting book wholesalers' lists online, enabling the purchase of special-order books to seem almost like buying in-stock books. Based on the profits from this lucrative business, Amazon.com was able to expand into selling branded items in a large number of consumer-goods categories. From there, the company began to attract more visitors to its Web site by building an active online community, especially through reader "reviews." The company then became a book publisher for people who wanted to self-publish. To lower costs and improve service, the company used print-on-demand equipment in all of its warehouses, making these books immediately available to ship at a small additional production expense over mass printing. After that, the company developed the Kindle, an electronic format for reading that many people prefer to physical books, and Amazon.com became the world's largest publisher and retailer of e-books. Now, its book-related profits mostly come from selling e-books, which can be purchased for immediate download. Encouraged by this success, Amazon.com then sought to do the same thing with movies via streaming video. The company has clearly shown skill in converting physical businesses into electronic, online ones and building a huge, appreciative audience. Such a process can be repeated indefinitely, changing all seven elements of the business model by expanding into new dimensions. It shouldn't surprise us that the market capitalization for the firm at this writing is one of the largest in the world, with a price/earnings ratio at a stratospheric level.

To a casual observer, such a dimension-stretching strategy involving business models might only seem appropriate for market-expanding breakthroughs. While such strategies are certainly great for market expansion, I want you to realize that the approach is even more useful for developing and implementing solutions that greatly expand value for all stakeholders when they all have access to appreciation in the company's worth.

Let me explain. Investors pay very high prices when they believe that growth in revenues and profits can continue for a long time at a high rate. That's why some people bought private shares in the social networking site Facebook at an enterprise equity value of over $50 billion before the company went public.

An expandable business model that operates along several dimensions is ideal for encouraging such enthusiasm. Different investors will be persuaded by the various ways that the organization could grow, assigning much value for what the company isn't doing yet, but which it certainly can be counted on to accomplish. In the case of Facebook, the anticipated opportunity was selling substantial advertising to be displayed on mobile devices, something that wasn't accomplished for two years after being widely anticipated.

Establishing such an expandable business model requires developing some core business skills that relate to the opportunities, attracting an ever-increasing number of enthusiastic customers, and organizing innovative activities that can be accomplished simultaneously by many different people. If you want to see a contrast between an expandable business model with several dimensions and one that doesn't expand, just compare Apple with Microsoft as they were in 2010. I'm sure you'll agree that Steve Jobs had created an expandable business model then for Apple while Microsoft had not.

The latter's forays into other business models have almost always been flops.

Lesson Ten Assignments

1. Examine your business model to determine whether it is expandable or not, and, if it is, along what dimensions.

2. Consider how you could make your business model more expandable along more dimensions.

3. Evaluate how credible such expansions would be to potential investors and stakeholders.

4. Determine how you can increase effectiveness and credibility for expanding your business model along several dimensions.

5. Define a repeatable process for routinely making business-model innovations along expandable dimensions.

Lesson Eleven

Trend Riding

"The wind blows where it wishes,
and you hear the sound of it,
but cannot tell where it comes from and where it goes.
So is everyone who is born of the Spirit."

— John 3:8 (NKJV)

Then the sea arose because a great wind was blowing.

— John 6:18 (NKJV)

One of the most powerful metaphors in the Bible is the way that the wind was used by Jesus to explain what the Holy Spirit is like. Although we cannot see the wind, we are nevertheless strongly affected by it. Where I grew up, near hurricane-force winds caused seemingly unending dust storms and disastrous fires. On the sea, the wind can turn a placid body of water into a raging lion that threatens to devour whatever is on the surface. That's probably pretty close to how Jesus' disciples felt after rowing all night when they spotted Him walking across the water toward them in John 6 (NKJV).

I had been struck during my first projects at The Boston Consulting Group by the way clients were so very impressed when a strategic solution would take advantage of positive trends. Subsequently, I noticed how hard most people tried to get in step with whatever the latest trends were, unless poverty or infirmity made such adjustments impossible.

One source of that preference for aligning with trends was the increasing sense that leaders had less and less influence over their results. It's hard enough to keep balls in the air as you juggle them. Add strong winds, a powerful earthquake, and loud noises while standing on a tightrope, and juggling becomes much harder. The traditional response to stronger external influences had been to expect more of leaders: They needed to become ever more agile so that they could quickly switch themselves and their organizations into favorable orientations with whatever shifts affected their business. The description of a good leader increasingly sounded like that of Superman: "faster than a speeding bullet, more powerful than a locomotive, and able to leap tall buildings in a single bound." I didn't know any leaders who bore even the slightest resemblance to Superman. What could a mere mortal leader do instead?

I began reading broadly on the subject of how leaders can orient organizations to trends. My eye was caught by a book written by Arie de Geus, *The Living Company* (Harvard Business School Press, 1997), that argued persuasively for using biological metaphors for companies rather than inanimate ones. My understanding was also helped by something he said during a talk about his book at a forum of strategic thinkers: When people have no experience in an area, they draw a blank when they try to think about what to do. Fill in that blank with useful experience, and they will make rapid progress. Arie noted that working on simulated problems based on scenarios describing a challenging situation was very good for providing relevant experience. During a day together in London, he observed that scenario thinking had an unexpected benefit that everyone should pursue: Think about enough scenarios and you begin to see strategies and tactics that will leave you better off regardless of what comes next.

With that encouragement, we began looking for biological metaphors related to adaptability and found one in (you'll never guess what) ... the amazing survival abilities of cellular slime molds. Forgive me for introducing something that sounds obscure and possibly unpleasant. I think you'll be intrigued by what we learned. If you want more details, check out the article by John Tyler Bonner in the December 1984 issue of *Science 84*.

Cellular slime molds (a type of amoeba) live individually on the forest floor. The available food supply limits their growth as well as their survival, as it does for all amoebas. When the food is gone, stationary amoebas die out. But unlike stationary amoebas, cellular slime molds act in a most unusual way when food is scarce: The cellular slime mold amoebas clump themselves into a community that oozes along as slime until it reaches a spot where more food is present.

They have another trick for finding new homes as well. Clumps of the amoebas will undergo additional physical changes, creating a multicelled stalk holding a sac filled with dormant spores. When animals or people brush against the sacs, the spores attach themselves and are carried to new locations beyond the range that the clump could move to on its own.

As a result of these physical adaptations, it doesn't matter where the amoebas start out because they are designed to move themselves and their descendants to a better place. In essence, cellular slime molds are designed for adjusting to rapidly varying conditions ... much as early humans did by roving in hunting bands to where the game was.

Keep that metaphor in mind as we return to the wind, a more familiar subject. Wind has often been invoked as a metaphor for change. Having grown up in an area known for its Santa Ana winds, I was well aware of how the wind affects our moods and our daily tasks. Face into a howling desert wind and your eyes are soon filled with grit. At night, the same force drives cold drafts of air through the house and makes being indoors unpleasant. The sound of that force makes sleeping difficult. The trash that piles up in your yard from the wind clearly represents undesirable change. However, if you run a race with the wind at your back, you feel jet propelled. When the wind tapers off, everyone has a sense of new opportunities and optimism.

Think of wind as representing all of the irresistible forces outside of our control that have powerful impacts on us and our organizations. What are some of those forces? You should make your own list that's related to your business, but the most common irresistible forces described to us by CEOs are new technology, changing customer needs, fashion, government regulation, demographics, economic trends, and fluctuations in financial markets, the weather, and currency exchange rates.

The wind was also one of mankind's earliest sources of power for travel. Where winds were common, simple sails filled with the breeze pushed primitive vessels forward when the wind came from the right direction. Otherwise, oars were used for more sluggish propulsion. Later, shipbuilders learned to make adjustable sails and gear that would capture the wind's power from any direction other than straight ahead. By shifting course in a zigzag style, progress could be made even into a head wind.

On land, windmills were eventually employed for other kinds of work, from pumping water out of low-lying areas (as in Holland) to powering electrical generation in windy deserts. The biggest windmills originally had a serious drawback: Like the earliest sails, they only faced in one direction. If the wind came from another direction, little or no benefit was gained. Like the clever shipbuilders before them, windmill makers learned to adjust: They made propeller blades with vanes behind them that automatically pivot to optimally face the wind and generate power whenever there is wind. Think of such adjustable windmills as a metaphor for the kind of strategy and actions that individuals and organizations should take: Use an optimal strategy or action, and the irresistible forces are always creating power for you that allow more to be accomplished.

Creating an organizational equivalent of a pivoting windmill can appear to be more difficult and expensive than what is actually required. What's the basis of that misperception? Most people have never worked on the task and are sensitive to how tough it is to change any aspect of what an organization does. They incorrectly assume that all aspects of the organization need to become incredibly adaptable — a very difficult and expensive challenge. Contrary to that incorrect view, an organization with the equivalent of a weather vane continually pointing it in the right direction (the proper strategy) will need to adapt very little.

This common misperception taught us there must be stalls that make it especially difficult to take advantage of irresistible forces. I've listed for you near the end of Lesson Six what the most common stalls are. You may want to reread that material now.

Once you've taken care of any stalls, you'll be ready for the eight-step process for taking advantage of irresistible forces, which can be applied in conjunction with 2,000 percent solutions, complementary 2,000 percent solutions, and excellent solutions. In addition, your experiences in creating 2,000 percent solutions can be applied to these steps, which are quite similar. Here are the process steps:

1. Recognize how measurements can help your company identify and understand more about irresistible forces.
2. Use your own leading indicators to anticipate shifts in irresistible forces.
3. Determine the future best practices for locating, anticipating, and adapting to changes in irresistible forces.
4. Extend your vision to identify and apply best practices beyond anyone else in the future for locating, anticipating, and adapting to changes in irresistible forces.
5. Identify the ideal best practices for benefiting from changes in irresistible forces.
6. Determine how your organization should approach ideal best practices for benefiting from changes in irresistible forces.
7. Enhance your peoples' ability to achieve the benefits of irresistible force management.

8. Repeat steps one through seven for improved effectiveness in using irresistible force management.

You can learn more about this process by reading *The Irresistible Growth Enterprise* (Stylus, 2000). In addition, you can access book excerpts by registering at http://www.irresistiblegrowth.com/.

Lesson Eleven Assignments

1. What are the most important forces outside the control of you and your organization?

2. How well oriented are you and your organization to take advantage of these forces when they accelerate but keep going in the current direction?

3. How well oriented are you and your organization to benefit from these forces when they diminish in the current direction?

4. How well oriented are you and your organization to gain from these forces when they move in the opposite direction from the current one?

5. How well oriented are you and your organization to make faster progress with the help of these forces when they move in a more neutral direction than the current one?

6. What are the most effective ways you can adjust your business model, strategy, and operating plans to be like a pivoting windmill in being always positioned to benefit from any direction that irresistible forces happen to take?

Lesson Twelve

Expand Benefits for All Stakeholders

You have increased the nation, O LORD,
You have increased the nation;
You are glorified;
You have expanded
all the borders of the land.

— Isaiah 26:15 (NKJV)

In referring to stakeholders, I mean to include *all* those who substantially contribute to, benefit from, or are affected by a company and its actions: end users, customers, customers' customers, distributors, dealers, agents, suppliers, suppliers' suppliers, employees, employees' families, partners, shareholders, lenders, lessors, neighbors, communities in which the firm operates, and anyone else who is significantly impacted by what the company does. Although most of these stakeholders have no ownership in the company, be sure to consider how encouraging and facilitating such ownership could be an effective way to expand stakeholder value for many more people.

Let me also explain what I mean by "value." When academics refer to value for shareholders, this term has primarily come to mean having a higher current price for all of a company's shares. In ordinary language, of course, value also suggests acquiring something for less: a bargain. In contrast to the first two meanings, we often think of a value as describing what we esteem for guiding our lives, regardless of its current or potential financial worth. While this lesson often overtly focuses on value in financial terms, either owning something that increases in economic worth or acquiring offerings at less cost, the lesson also advances Biblical values by basing the advice on the perspective of what God values. While we may not know exactly how to measure value in God's terms, we should certainly not pay any less attention to advancing it.

For instance, consider Jesus' words in Matthew 6:24 (NKJV): "No one can serve two masters; for either he will hate the one and love the other, or else he will be loyal to the one and despise the other. You cannot serve God and mammon." (If you aren't familiar with the word *mammon*, it refers in this context to worshiping *riches*, as though they were personified as a god.) In relating ways to acquire more financial resources and pay less for what is needed, we should always keep in mind that any such benefits should be directed towards advancing God's Kingdom, rather than some selfish purpose of our own. Otherwise, we will simply be worshiping money rather than God, a great sin. We should see using any money developed in this context as simply a means for accomplishing that most important purpose, God's will.

I mention this point now because I have seen variations of some methods described in this lesson applied solely for selfish purposes. What's the lesson from such applications? I cannot recall seeing any lasting good come from such misdirected uses. So I hope you will apply this information to demonstrate God's greatness to the world and to use the resources He supplies through these methods to glorify Him while serving His purposes.

Other 400 Year Project books contain useful guidance for ways to use increased resources for God's purposes. If you aren't yet familiar with these books, I suggest that you read some or all of them before or while you read and apply this book. A good starting point is *2,000 Percent Living* (Salvation Press, 2010), which describes how to be 20 times more fruitful for the Lord. If you want to go deeper into the subject of being fruitful, I suggest *Help Wanted* (2,000 Percent Living Press, 2011). For those who want to focus on witnessing, I recommend *Witnessing Made Easy* (Jubilee Worship Center Step by Step Press, 2010) and *Ways You Can Witness* (Salvation Press, 2010). For anyone who wants to help make a whole nation more fruitful for the Lord, be sure to read and apply *The 2,000 Percent Nation* (400 Year Project Press, 2012).

Now that you know what I mean by the concept of stakeholder value, let me help you understand some specific examples of what might be provided. Here are a few of the possible stakeholder-value improvements:

- End users can gain knowledge and practical advantages that expand the types, quantities, and usefulness of the benefits they receive from the company's offerings. Readers who successfully apply the lessons in *Your Breakthroughs* will have received one such kind of substantial value improvement from this book.
- Similar effects can also occur for your customers and their customers, often in terms of their obtaining greater numbers of and more profitable customers for their own organizations, as well as knowledge and practical advantages that can be used to increase the value of what your customers provide to their own customers and end users.
- Distributors, dealers, and agents can gain from having more appealing offerings that provide much increased value for those they distribute to, deal with, and sell to, as well as for their own organizations.
- Suppliers and their suppliers can benefit from becoming vastly more effective, often gaining market share by selling more to your company, as well as to your competitors.
- Employees can see their lives improve through sharing in some of the company's success while enjoying better, more satisfying working conditions, career opportunities, and personal lives.

- Employees' families can experience better lives through any increased time they can spend with the employee, a better working environment for employees that facilitates improved family relationships, any company-provided family-enhancing benefits, and whatever increased income and wealth the employee obtains that is used for the family's benefit.
- Partners can gain wealth and knowledge to apply in their own businesses through ownership of and participation in joint ventures, as well as through investments in and with your company.
- Shareholders can be directly enriched through the expanded value of their equity ownership. The value growth from an initial investment of $10,000 in an advanced-business company that develops and applies complementary business-model innovations can be sufficient to support many future generations of the equity owner's family.
- Lenders will have less risk of not being repaid, as well as an opportunity to share in the expanded ownership value of your company whenever your company borrows money through debt instruments that are convertible into equity.
- Lessors can enjoy similar benefits to those gained by lenders, while also gaining the opportunity to do more business with your organization.
- Neighbors and the communities you serve can benefit from your company eliminating any problems it causes while these stakeholders can also receive new benefits designed to make it more attractive for the company, its employees, and neighbors to spend time in the vicinity of the company's activities.
- Anyone else substantially affected by your company can gain from any negative effects being eliminated, receiving more of any existing benefits, and gaining access to any new benefits.

Please note that effectively adding such stakeholder benefits can be done in ways that greatly expand profits, cash flow, and ownership value for your company. Such consequences follow because these sorts of stakeholder benefits also increase stakeholders' interest in, types of activities for, and effectiveness in usefully contributing to your company's success. Keep these connections in mind as you look for such ways to add to stakeholder value.

More potential benefits and how to supply them are described in *Advanced Business: Exponentially Increase Stakeholder Value* (400 Year Project Press, 2015). By applying the 50 lessons in *Advanced Business* in conjunction with the 50 lessons for expanding market growth, slashing costs, and eliminating unnecessary investments in *Business Basics* (400 Year Project Press, 2012), a company can increase total value for its stakeholders by 160,000 or more times. Two other volumes in the Advanced Business series (*Advanced Business for Innovation*, 400 Year Project Press, 2015, and *Advanced Business for Social Benefits*, 400 Year Project Press, 2015) demonstrate how to build stakeholder value from this level to 3.2 million or more times through encouraging competitors to innovate more as well as copy your innovations, and then by 64 million or more times through also profiting from serving important social needs. I have more to say about the subjects of these books in lessons sixteen and seventeen.

Lesson Twelve Assignments

1. Which stakeholders are benefiting most from the value expansion of your organization?

2. Which stakeholders are benefiting least from your organization's value expansions?

3. Which stakeholders are being harmed by your organization?

4. Why are such differential benefit effects occurring?

5. What would have to change about your organization's goals, business models, strategies, plans, operating methods, and practices to greatly increase stakeholder value for all?

Lesson Thirteen

Cut Costs

The LORD will be *awesome to them,*
For He will reduce to nothing all the gods of the earth;
People *shall worship Him,*
Each one from his place,
Indeed all the shores of the nations.

— Zephaniah 2:11 (NKJV)

If you have been following The 400 Year Project, you are well aware of the project's earlier writings about how to make substantial cost improvements such as are described in *The 2,000 Percent Solution's* examples; *The Ultimate Competitive Advantage's* cost-reducing business-model innovations; the methods in Part Two of *The 2,000 Percent Squared Solution*; and the lessons in *Business Basics*. In addition, you've probably been working on cost reductions throughout your career. You might be wondering, "What should I focus on differently from what I look at now?"

There's quite a lot that most people still need to learn, beginning with realizing which of their beliefs are harmful to reducing costs. You may be surprised by how much of what people do in the name of cost reduction is actually counterproductive. Let me explain by looking at a common flaw found in cost-reduction methods: taking a piecemeal approach.

What do I mean by that? Here are some bit-by-bit approaches that I've often seen applied:

- Cut all budgets by a certain percentage.
- Reduce personnel levels by a targeted number of jobs.
- Freeze, or reduce, salaries and benefits for a time.
- Reformulate a product to cut a certain percentage of costs.
- Stop providing aspects of a service to improve profit contribution as a percentage of sales.
- Apply Six Sigma methods to reduce errors in providing offerings to very low levels and thereby cut per-unit operating costs.
- Shift to lean-manufacturing or lean-service methods.
- Reduce the quantity provided to customers while maintaining the price per package.
- Provide a much smaller offering to reduce the price point while also erasing some costs for serving customers.

Why am I critical of such efforts? Based on my research I could make quite a long list of reasons, but I'll give just some of the more important evidence:

- Piecemeal cost reductions often substantially increase costs in areas not considered by the cost cutters. The result can be an overall cost increase.
- After making many such cost reductions, the appeal of offerings is eventually harmed in some fundamental way such that sales fall faster than costs decline and sales remain lower.
- Such approaches often discourage high-performing employees, who then look for and find jobs at other organizations.
- The productivity of those who remain after such efforts often declines.
- Even if costs decline, these solutions often make it harder to improve, adjust, and remodel offerings and processes to im-

prove performance for customers so that future sales and profits are reduced to well below their potential.

- Even if per-unit costs decline for the organization, the effects on customers and end users may be adverse ... often increasing their costs, causing sales to fall below what would have otherwise occurred.
- Social costs may increase as more harm is done to other people and to the environment, adding new opponents and incurring future costs for litigation and remediation.
- Efforts and funds that could have gone into making fundamental improvements to expand sales, profits, and cash flow are instead devoted to the piecemeal cost-reduction activities.

Such problems arise, in part, due to mistaken purposes for cost reductions. In many cases, a cost reduction is sought solely as a so-called quick fix to fill a temporary profit shortfall from the organization's budget. In such instances, the efforts may amount to no more than simply trying to score points with the boss. Is it any wonder that some of such ad hoc and ill-conceived cost-reducing efforts go wrong?

What accomplishments should a 96 percent cost reduction seek to provide for your organization and its stakeholders? While many people feel that they know, I believe that few actually do. Since few people have sought and achieved this objective, let me propose a set of goals for those engaging in this activity for the first time:

1. The organization's costs to serve a customer with an offering drop by 96 percent while the performance that a customer perceives that he or she receives from the offering stays the same or improves from the highest level ever experienced.
2. The customers' total costs to acquire and to use an offering go down by 96 percent.
3. End users' costs to apply or to employ the offering decline by 96 percent.

4. Social costs of an offering (net of social benefits) are reduced by 96 percent.

As a corollary to achieving such improved cost-performance levels, realize that 96 percent cost-reduction goals are also accomplished when tangible benefits received by customers, users, and society greatly increase such that they will pay more money and employ more efforts to receive the increased benefits, but the ratio of everyone's costs declines by 96 percent relative to the new level of price and benefits.

Here's an example of what I mean about cutting costs by providing higher value benefits at a higher price: If I provide at least 400 times more absolute value for you through this book as compared to *The 2,000 Percent Squared Solution* (such as by showing you many ways to gain at least 160,000 times, rather than 400 times, more cash flow than you have now), and the price I charge increases by sixteen times from the price for *The 2,000 Percent Squared Solution*; even at the higher price *Your Breakthroughs* delivers the equivalent of a 96 percent cost reduction compared to the benefits customers, users, and society have received in the past {100 [1 − (16/400)] = 96 percent}.

I know that if I proposed this cost-reduction objective and these goals in a meeting of executives, some of them would probably argue that such results are clearly impossible. To prepare you for such a reaction among your colleagues, let me suggest a possible response.

Anyone who has followed the computer or electronics industries can attest that the cost to acquire and to use a computer and most electronic devices for a given task has dropped by much more than 96 percent in the last few decades. Performing a series of calculations by using a spreadsheet program is a good example. If we measure costs in constant purchasing power, it's very clear that the reductions have been well beyond even 99 percent.

Some will counter that such opportunities don't apply in areas involving scarce natural resources (such as oil, gold, platinum, and rare minerals). Some producers have, in fact, changed the way that the resources are discovered, extracted, and processed to make huge savings. Did you know, for instance, that the price and costs for aluminum were once much higher than for gold or platinum and the available aluminum supply was tiny? Since then, technical innovations turned aluminum into a resource so inexpensive that we often throw aluminum foil away after a few seconds' use without giving the action a second thought.

Anyone who bought shares in the most efficient producers of scarce resources equal to the value of their personal or organizational annual purchases of such resources would have found that the gains in value of such securities would have much more than offset any increased prices paid for the natural resources, thus providing another way to reduce costs.

Others have found different ways to design an offering that uses fewer scarce resources and yet provides more benefits. Some have completely stopped using scarce natural resources, relying instead on "waste" sources as the key inputs.

Still other people will argue that needing highly skilled people (such as those who are involved in producing biotechnology breakthroughs) cannot be avoided in some industries, and such costs cannot be reduced. Many would have made a similar argument just twenty years ago that software programming costs could not be reduced very much, yet the cost to produce a line of software has declined quite a lot due to new software tools and the availability of more people in low-wage countries who are well trained to program and to test software.

Some people are forgetting in making such objections that cost reductions apply to more than just raw material and people costs. For instance, establishing the safety of new biotechnology products often incurs greater expenses than for their development. Software testing costs a vast multiple of what software writing does, and software testing doesn't require rare geniuses in order to be done well. In fact, some software (such as the Linux computer operating system) is developed and tested at no cost to users.

Why can such great cost reductions be made in almost any area? It's worth remembering Pareto's Principle, as defined by Dr. Joseph M. Juran: 80 percent of the results of any human endeavor come from 20 percent of the effort. In any substantial activity within an organization, this principle means that some people are probably sixteen times more effective than the least effective people. In an even more common activity across many organizations, scaling continues to increase differences in performance so that we can presume that some people are hundreds of times more effective than the least effective person who can add enough value to cover employment costs. By simply understanding and employing the lessons of the best performers in any activity, we can reduce costs by 96 percent.

If we go further and consider how business models might be improved and what the ideal practices are, we can make even larger cost reductions. One of my favorite examples comes from the Aravind Eye Care System in India. A cataract operation there costs less than 2 percent of what a similar operation does in England; and the clinical outcomes for patients are better at Aravind. If you can make such improvements with surgery, imagine what you can accomplish with something that's much simpler and potentially less dangerous to do incorrectly. If you would like to learn more about how such a cost reduction was achieved, read *Infinite Vision* (Berrett-Koehler, 2011) by Pavithra K. Mehta and Suchitra Shenoy.

The remaining challenge comes, of course, in that many doubters don't know how to even begin to make such substantial improvements. As with the other subjects in this part of *Your Breakthroughs*, the eight-step process for making 2,000 percent solutions described in Lesson Seven will get you there.

Often, the first step will make most of the difference: measuring as many things as possible to locate what benefits are actually being received and used, and at what cost. There may well be a pitifully small usage benefit compared to high costs for customers and end users in terms of time, effort, and resources. I say so because that's usually the case. Companies usually focus on providing what they want to provide without becoming sufficiently aware of what's actually used and how.

To see more examples to stimulate your thinking, I encourage you to read those sections of *The 2,000 Percent Squared Solution*, *Business Basics*, and *The Ultimate Competitive Advantage* that are dedicated to cost reductions.

Lesson Thirteen Assignments

1. What aspects of company and stakeholder costs related to your offerings are not being measured now?

2. How could such costs be measured?

3. Where are there few benefits compared to the costs involved?

4. How can you best use the 2,000 percent solution process to reduce costs of providing, acquiring, and using your offerings by 96 percent compared to the value that is gained?

Lesson Fourteen

Reduce Investments

The song of the terrible ones will be diminished.

— Isaiah 25:5 (NKJV)

We turn now to reducing by 96 percent your and your stakeholders' investments to provide and to use an offering. Before shifting into how to accomplish such a result, let's consider some of the financial effects.

Growing revenues by 20 times is obviously necessary to having a larger enterprise, one that can have a more substantial impact. Reducing costs by 96 percent makes expansion highly profitable and helps to finance growth. What does reducing stakeholder investments do for finances?

Let's start with a typical manufacturing company. Such a firm will have two dollars of sales for every dollar of net investment (gross investment minus the total of depreciation and amortization). Thus, a million-dollar revenue manufacturer needs approximately $500,000 of investment capital (provided by debt and equity). Acquiring this money can be a big hurdle for an entrepreneur. As a result, most of the larger manufacturing companies have many investors who combine to provide the needed debt and equity.

Next, let's shrink the amount of capital needed by 96 percent. When we do that, $500,000 of investment capital becomes $20,000.

That's still a lot of money, but for a low-cost enterprise that earns several hundred thousand dollars a year, it's a drop in the bucket.

In addition, your total cost of capital is a lot smaller ... no matter how much or how little you pay for the amount of capital you use. For instance, at 10 percent interest borrowing $500,000 would cost $50,000 a year (before considering any tax deductions to offset some of the cost). In comparison, if you only need to borrow $20,000 at 10 percent interest, your annual pretax borrowing cost is $2,000.

But an enterprise that is highly profitable and growing rapidly is going to need a lot more capital. Imagine now that you want to expand from being a $1 million a year manufacturer to becoming a $10 million a year manufacturer. Normally, that would mean adding $4,500,000 in investments. By reducing investment needs by 96 percent, you would only require $180,000 more investment capital. If you have a good track record and well-documented business plan, many banks will finance that much investment knowing that you will earn it back in just a short amount of time. As a result, your choice of capital sources is wider, and the difficulty of gaining the capital is much reduced.

Let's now consider the typical $10 million a year manufacturing company. Let's assume that it grows revenues by 10 percent in a year. That growth means $1 million more in revenues and $500,000 more in required investment in the next year. Most manufacturers of that size earn about 4 percent of sales after paying income taxes. That profit margin translates into earnings of $400,000, and all of that amount (plus an additional $100,000) would be needed to pay for the growth. As a result, no money could be paid to shareholders in dividends without borrowing for this purpose. The value to owners would rise, but that increased value would have no cash component until the owners sold their stock in the enterprise.

Compare that situation with having reduced reinvestment needs by 96 percent. When that's the case, the increase of $1 million in revenues requires only $20,000 more capital. As a result, $380,000 in earnings can be paid out to shareholders after financing growth.

If the organization also correctly employs the 96 percent lower-cost methods described in Lesson Thirteen, profits are twenty times larger ($8 million) and the dividends that can be paid to investors are much larger ($7.98 million). When that's the case, investors see the value of their shares rise by at least 2,000 percent and the value of their dividend payouts rise by almost as much as the earnings increase each year. It's like getting paid twice for making the same investment.

As you can see, there are huge owner benefits for reducing the cost of capital, improving cash flow, and increasing dividends.

But those aren't the most important benefits from reducing investments by 96 percent. Let's look at seven strategic advantages:

1. By requiring very little capital to grow, accessing money is never going to limit growth. Thus, during times of rapid industry expansion, you should be able to gain market share just by being more able to afford adding capacity.

2. By having very small investments in assets and having a huge profit margin due to cutting costs, you have enormous flexibility in making changes to your business model. For example, let's imagine that you decided to replace all of your assets in a $10 million a year manufacturing business. It would only cost you $200,000, what your company earns after tax in a little over three weeks. As a result, you could afford to totally upgrade your business model as fast as you could think of an improvement you wanted to make.

3. Because your investment is so small, the value of your enterprise is much higher. You deliver lots of profits *and* cash flow. As a result, you can use less stock to make acquisitions. Then, when applying your superior low-investment business model, you can quickly increase the value of any business you buy. You have plenty of cash to change its business model all the time, too. As a result, you can quickly take over your competitors, subject only to any legal restraints, and your competitive risk is very small.

4. Because your need to make new investments is so small, you free up lots of time to work on other areas of improving your operations and outperforming competitors in serving stakeholders. Consequently, process improvements should be installed at least three times more frequently.

5. Without a need to be concerned about capital constraints, you can adjust much faster to changes in the market. Thus, when the world changes (as it seemed to do in 2007 when many advanced nations hit the wall economically due to housing-price and borrowing-fueled bubbles collapsing), such a firm can adjust more rapidly to the new realities by switching to offerings that fit the changed needs of its stakeholders.

6. Reducing investment needs often leads to lower costs. For example, companies with limited investments don't have as large charges for depreciation, amortization, and interest expenses. When you visit a contract custom-manufacturing facility, for instance, the assembly station will typically receive its components just a few minutes before production begins, the assembly and testing processes will be completed in a few more minutes, and the item will be out of the facility on its way to customers in not too many more minutes. The infrastructure costs for such an activity are not much different from what a highly efficient, low-overhead garage shop could do with highly skilled, low-cost help.

7. Stakeholders gain parallel benefits from reducing their investment intensity, allowing them to improve their circumstances and to adapt to changed circumstances much more easily and rapidly.

With your greatly improved understanding of why reducing investment intensity is valuable, you are probably now eager to know what some of the most useful methods are for doing so. I've listed a few of them below:

- *Produce almost instantly.* Doing so allows you to eliminate receivables and inventories while permitting you to require prepayment or payment simultaneous with provision.
- *Eliminate receivables and slash inventories.* One way of accomplishing this result is by providing custom offerings to give customers an incentive to pay sooner and to allow you to exactly match provision and orders. Doing so may require developing new kinds of equipment or receiving more complete forms of supplies.
- *Reduce investments in land, buildings, and equipment.* Quite a few things help including redesigned offerings that require fewer physical elements, outsourcing to more effective suppliers, operating in countries where such investments are much less costly, finding ways for employees to work from home, and becoming more space-saving.
- *Teach and encourage stakeholders to reduce investments.* In doing so, you reduce the cash needed for them to participate in producing or using your offerings by as much or more than you do in providing the offerings. Doing so increases their ability to acquire, use, and gain benefits from your offerings.
- *Work with part-time and nonprofit suppliers.* Such suppliers will be able to operate with less investment than you either with lower cost land, building, and equipment, or with increased use of existing investments.
- *Have everyone in the organization work from home or public places.* Doing so may eliminate all need for land, building, and equipment.
- *Operate virtually.* This method means doing on line all activities for obtaining customers or providing offerings. Such an approach might mean providing electronic offerings or outsourcing everything that cannot be done electronically.
- *Be a marketing-only organization.* This approach means having others design, provide, and service the offerings. You just acquire the customers.
- *More efficiently operate activities for customers.* In this method, you gain efficiencies by doing more kinds of activities so that

the land, buildings, and equipment required by you and your customers are greatly reduced.

• *Add grants and subsidies.* Such financial resources reduce how much your organization has to spend in meeting its investment needs.

• *Use financial strategies to reduce the size of equity in your organization.* Such an approach might involve doing more leasing and borrowing on a non-recourse basis.

If you would like to learn more about any of these methods listed above, please see the lessons in Part Four of *Business Basics*. Those lessons will tell you more about what to do.

Lesson Fourteen Assignments

1. Identify the five most important strategic benefits that your enterprise would gain through reducing its need for investment capital by 96 percent.

2. Determine what it is about your current business model that requires so much investment capital compared to your revenues.

3. Investigate how competitors operate in ways that reduce their investment needs compared to what you do.

4. Research how companies in other industries operate with less investment capital than you do.

5. Identify five ways you could improve your business model to greatly reduce your investment needs while increasing your effectiveness in serving stakeholders.

6. Consider how similar or greater benefits could be provided through these five business-model improvements.

Lesson Fifteen

Increase Benefit Value

"Give, and it will be given to you:
good measure, pressed down, shaken together,
and running over will be put into your bosom.
For with the same measure that you use,
it will be measured back to you."

— Luke 6:38 (NKJV)

In this lesson, we focus on increasing the value of benefits for end users, customers, and customers' customers. We begin by considering end users such as individuals, families, small groups, nonprofit organizations, and governments, as well as for-profit companies.

How might end users gain enormous increases in the value of their benefits? While there are many potential value-improvement triggers for end users, including customers and other stakeholders teaching end users how to increase all forms of stakeholder value, benefit value increases more typically occur due to your company or the end user's supplier providing offerings that automatically deliver either all or most of the value improvement.

Let me describe an example related to 2,000 percent solutions (ways of accomplishing 20 times more with the same or less time, effort, and resources, as illustrated in *The 2,000 Percent Solution*, AMACOM, 1999). If I write a book that tells end users how to make 160,000 times more profits (as *The 2,000 Percent Squared Solu-*

tion does by directing that the lessons in the book be repeated for expanding revenues by 20 times and reducing costs by 20 times), end users who buy, read, successfully apply, and keep effectively reapplying the lessons of that book can eventually enjoy 160,000 times more profits. In the process, the economic values of their businesses would typically increase by about 160,000 times, as well. Now, let's consider working on expanding cash flow by 64,000,000 times, such as by repeatedly applying the lessons in *Business Basics*. When done correctly, cash flow will increase by that amount, as will the economic values of the businesses to which the lessons were applied.

The offering doesn't have to be a product to cause large value increases. The offering can be a service. Let's consider The Billionaire Entrepreneurs' Master Mind. After training in how to expand the market and revenues by 20 times and to reduce costs by 96 percent for each offering, end users of this service who apply the lessons can gain 400 times more profits. If end users then also learn and apply how to reduce investment intensity by 96 percent, their cash flow also increases by 8,000 times (a 20-fold increase over just developing the first two complementary 2,000 percent solutions). Putting in place a third such improvement will equate to adding another 20-times increase in economic value for end users over the two complementary solutions. If end users then successfully reapply each of the three lessons twice, their cash flow expands by an additional 511,999,992,000 times. And because the master mind doesn't charge 511,999,992,000 times more ... the value for members of The Billionaire Entrepreneurs' Master Mind compared to the cost in time, effort, and money just keeps getting better and better as they apply more of what they learn.

These product and service examples relate to knowledge transfer for end uses. Benefit transfers through offerings that add stakeholder value can be more direct than that.

Here's a product example. The Amazon.com Kindle reader and the company's support systems for producing and distributing written materials have revolutionized the potential for someone to learn.

On a Kindle reader, hundreds of books can be stored and easily accessed for comparing one source to another. The type size can be adjusted to make reading easier. Each book costs less because it is in a digital version. Because a whole library is now portable, study can be done in more environments, including while traveling or during breaks at work. If we include the value of the space-saving feature of substituting for physical books to reduce how much office or living space someone needs or uses, the economic benefits are undoubtedly much greater than 20 times the cost of a Kindle for anyone engaged in a learning project, such as writing a thesis or dissertation. And to gain the benefit, a learner just has to buy and use the product and related books in this form.

Let's look at a service example of direct increases in the value of benefits. Imagine that an end user's supplier has valuable rights that the end user is allowed to exercise. Such rights might involve being able to share valuable information with other people in a network, perhaps something like an individual using a Facebook-like page on an access-controlled network that provides large numbers of people with extremely easy ways to share highly useful information.

Another analogy might be a Web site on an Internet-like network accessible by specialized search engines capable of always taking you to exactly where you need to go. In such cases, the supplier's network is made more valuable by having more end users who share greater amounts of helpful information. The same value-multiplying effect on benefits also applies to the supplier's ownership value. A practical example of this service concept would be a highly efficient branded cooperative that made small companies more effective. The cooperative might do almost everything for the small companies except actually connect with their customers. As a result, each end-user company would gain the same low-cost benefits as everyone else in the cooperative, while also benefiting from owning part of the cooperative. The value of each end user's company could then expand even more if the cooperative could legally assign territories so that the number of end-user companies was held at the optimum level relative to the number of their customers and prospects. In a country that lacked enough qualified providers of a certain essential type (such as plumbers, for instance), such a cooperative might also be able to advocate more appropriate standards for government licensing and gain a virtual monopoly over training providers. If done properly, the cooperative might help a youth with no skills become the owner of a highly profitable and rapidly growing business.

You can see from these examples that providing a 20-times value enhancement for end users will not be automatic. There may be some learning, thinking, and working involved for the end users. In many cases, it may well be that the supplier's supplier (and so on) will have to play an important role in creating the step-up value for the end user before the large increase in economic value will occur.

Think of the potential. If an end user can gain 20 times more economic value from an offering, the value of the end user's activities related to the offering is often going to go up by more than 20 times the combination of the offering's value, plus the time, money, and effort involved in using it. When that's the case, what are end users going to do? Well, they are probably going to find a way to buy and use more offerings from the supplier. When that happens, the end user's economic value will continue to soar in exponential ways. It's like having the ability to turn lead into gold at little or no cost.

What can end users do with that potential? They can cut costs of what they do by 20 times. They can work 96 percent less. They can increase their incomes by 20 times. They can invest 20 times more. And so on. The choice is the end user's. Such flexibility should make a person feel more peaceful before going to sleep each night.

You may be wondering how all of this potential applies to those who have no enterprise to benefit from using any offering enhancements. In such cases, freed-up time can be used to engage in other personally or economically valuable activities. Or for someone who feels he or she has enough personal value in hand, the time can be solely applied to being more fruitful for the Lord. Naturally, the potential value increase will not always be realized unless end users are provided with information and encouragement to make constructive use of whatever value they obtain.

Let's turn our attention now to customers and their customers. Because businesses are often in closer contact with their customers than with their end users, opportunities to notice and serve customers' needs can often be more easily grasped than for adding value to end users. Improving value for customers and their customers can also be a powerful way to extend value to end users through making customers more effective.

How should we treat customers? In Luke 10:34 (NKJV), our Savior used the parable of the Good Samaritan to explain who our neighbor is (anyone we come into contact with) and what it means to love our neighbors as ourselves (to provide whatever assistance we would want if we were in someone else's circumstances): "So he went to *him* and bandaged his wounds, pouring on oil and wine; and he set him on his own animal, brought him to an inn, and took care of him." Surely, applying the stakeholder concept to customers should be based on Jesus' teachings about how to love our neighbors.

We should also see our customers' customers as stakeholders in the sense of their being just like slightly more distant neighbors. Here's a way to think about this similarity. Since you have direct contact (or easily could have in most cases) with your customers, you can see them as being like the neighbors who live next door to you. While you may never see or speak with your customers' customers, their impact on your customers can be just as great as yours is ... or possibly even greater. It's as if a customer's customer lives on the opposite side of your customer's house from where you live, as your customer's other next-door neighbor, but separated from you by some barrier that makes access quite difficult.

Let's shift now to considering what kinds of benefits can be supplied to customers and their customers. While there are many potential ways to improve value, including teaching customers how to increase value for their stakeholders, more typically the increased value is derived by the supplier company (your firm) providing offerings that deliver either all or most of the value improvement. In that sense, the opportunities are much like those I describe concerning the advantages delivered by the combination of the Amazon.com Kindle reader and the related digital offerings and services.

Let me provide another product example to show how value can be provided to customers. Let's imagine that your company makes a highly desirable electronic product, such as an outstanding smartphone that never needs recharging. If you only sell such a phone through one service provider, then anyone who wants this smartphone is also going to buy a service contract from that carrier. If the prices and profits on those plans are high and tens of millions of people buy, the exclusive carrier selling the phone can increase its shareholder value by 20 times while similarly increasing value for many of its stakeholders. To ensure that the equity-value expansion isn't hidden, the phone carrier could offer for sale public shares representing a small percentage of ownership in a subsidiary that only provides service for your outstanding smartphone. Those few shares would skyrocket in value, and everyone would know the worth of the subsidiary's shares that the carrier still owned. In most cases, the value of the carrier's shares would also expand by a high percentage of that subsidiary's premium public value.

You may quibble with this example as it applies to adding value for the customers' customers. What about the person who buys and uses the phone in her or his work? That customers' customer (if not an end user) can also enjoy a 20-times larger value by being able to accomplish more profitable activities, due to the phone making it possible to work a higher percentage of the time while mobile. For instance, just imagine the increased value to a salesperson needing to obtain and quickly communicate much information while traveling. There are also bound to be more applications written for use on this phone than on others, applications that will further enhance the value of its unlimited mobile usefulness.

You might respond with a question about where the 20-times increase in value is for the ordinary people who buy (customers'

customers) or receive and use (end users) the smartphone for personal applications. Of course, the value of benefits depends on how they employ the phone. If they want to find bargains so they spend less, such a phone could allow them to do more of that, say, while searching for a low-price foreclosed house to buy in a great neighborhood. Such a phone could help if they want to do homework more conveniently so that they can spend more time practicing the piano and thus sooner become a highly paid performer. Naturally, if the increased benefits relate to advancing God's Kingdom, the value of the benefits can be eternal and priceless.

I believe you can see from many of these examples that customers obtaining a 20-times value enhancement will not be automatic. There may be some learning, thinking, and working involved for the customer. But such a large advance in economic and other forms of value could be captured.

Once again, think of the potential. If a customer gains 20 times more economic value, that must mean at a minimum that the value of the customer's activities connected to using the offering is often going to go up by more than 20 times the cost of the offering, plus the time, effort, and money involved in using it. When that is the case, what are customers going to do? Well, they are probably going to act like end users and find a way to buy more offerings from the seller. When that happens, their economic value will continue to soar in exponential ways. It's like having the Midas touch so that whatever you come into contact with turns to gold, but with the advantage of the touch's effect being selectively up to you to apply so that no loved ones become golden statues by mistake. How nice!

What can customers do with this potential? As with the end users, customers can cut costs by 20 times, work 96 percent less, earn 20 times more, or invest 20 times as much. And so on. And, naturally, the same is true for customers' customers, providing even more value for the customer by expanding its business volume.

Lesson Fifteen Assignments

1. How can your organization's offerings be improved in ways that will increase the economic or personal value of your end users, customers, and customers' customers or their activities by 20 times?

2. How can your organization transfer knowledge to raise end users', customers', and customers' customers' economic or personal value by 20 times?

3. How can your organization provide exclusive arrangements to end users, customers, and customers' customers that will increase their economic or personal value by 20 times?

4. How can you teach end users, customers, and customers' customers to increase their value by 20 times, independent of any increased value of offerings, any operational knowledge transfers, or any exclusive arrangements?

5. How can these end-user, customer, and customers' customer benefits be transformed into improved relationships that will make it easier for your company to increase by 20 times its economic value and ability to provide for other stakeholders?

Lesson Sixteen

Accelerate Innovation

"You are the light of the world.
A city that is set on a hill cannot be hidden.

"Nor do they light a lamp and
put it under a basket,
but on a lampstand,
and it gives light
to all who are in the house."

— Matthew 5:14-15 (NKJV)

I believe that the words of Jesus in Matthew 5:14-15 (NKJV) capture this lesson's perspective very well. To paraphrase His wisdom in terms of this lesson's topic, I observe as follows: If you set a good example in innovating, that example will become the way those in your industry think and act.

Let me begin by sharing some of what I have published previously on this subject. The following material is drawn from Chapter 11 of *Adventures of an Optimist* (Mitchell and Company Press, 2007) in which I lay out the case for the exponential benefit expansions that can follow from organizations combining several complementary breakthroughs (ways of enhancing results by at least 20 times with the same or fewer resources, time, and effort that fully multiply the benefits of one another):

Isn't it great that people are such copy cats? This virtually universal instinct can be relied on to help us create another 20-times boost in benefits: an increase in the number of people who apply the same improvements as do the most successful creators of multiple 2,000 percent solutions.

Many people will be aghast at the suggestion. Why make it easier for others to copy you? Isn't it better to keep your best methods a secret? Well, while that approach often works best, there are important exceptions.

In many instances, an industry is being held back by the unprofessional way that some competitors operate. Improve the choices for customers, and more people will be willing to buy from an industry. California wines for many years had a deserved reputation as usually being inferior to imports. The typical target end user was a skid-row alcoholic. Wines were made as cheaply as possible to provide a lot of alcohol for the buck. When a few vintners began to emulate fine European wines, they knew they had to employ new practices because growing conditions are different in California. By sharing hard-won knowledge with other California wineries, these vintners began to develop fine wines that eventually won acclaim against European wines and established a huge demand for the best California products.

An unexpected benefit of giving away such valuable knowledge is lighting a permanently bigger fire under the company's own efforts to improve. Adding those improvements, in turn, will speed industry growth and provide for even more multiplied benefits. In most cases, there is not much to worry about concerning competitive advantage; organizations will be spreading management processes rather than revealing details of proprietary knowledge that's unique to their most valuable offerings.

People vary in how good they are at copying. So it may be necessary for thousands of other organizations to attempt copying successful 2,000 percent solution-based organizations before total benefits will expand by another 20 times. That's no problem: The world is full of organizations that would benefit from working on such solutions.

An organization seeking to eventually deliver a great many more benefits will normally want to open its doors wide enough to help others copy what it has done in adding revenue, operating cost reductions, capital turnover improvement, reducing capital costs, benefiting stakeholders who are neither customers nor shareholders, and letting copy cats learn from their success in those dimensions. In many cases, the scale for applying the improvements will be even larger in other industries.

A wise master of these dimensions will probably find opportunities to use this sharing to add still more great customers, suppliers, distributors, partners, employees, and sources of new ideas for the company's own activities. It may also be possible to create a joint venture with an educational organization to earn a respectable profit from providing this information.

A good way to begin is to seek publicity about the company's or nonprofit organization's successes. From there, be sure the information-sharing activity can afford appropriate marketing and educational activities to attract and help those who want to copy.

It's also a good idea to work on the learning process so that it can be delivered by using 2,000 percent solutions to speed and to lower the cost for both the company and those who want to copy. Learning these methods will also be helpful for reducing the costs of getting new employees up-to-speed in the company's best ways of making progress.

In sharing those perspectives, I built on some assumptions about human nature. Let me spell out five of the most important of these assumptions:

1. A highly successful organization will easily shift into complacency and begin devouring many of the benefits of what has

already been accomplished unless substantial threats focus attention on making further major improvements.

2. Innovation is accelerated by management becoming more familiar with what is the state of the art.

3. When more people know what the state of the management art is, the state of that art will advance more rapidly.

4. Copying an industry leader or leaders can be highly beneficial to such leaders, much in the same way that supporter and fan behavior can help social leaders improve effectiveness.

5. Choosing innovation paths that benefit from copying allows for multiplied improvements that no single firm could accomplish on its own. As an example, if there had only been one automobile company, today's road and bridge systems would probably be much more limited.

I spell out these assumptions to invite your questions and challenges. Feel free to contact me at donmitchell@fastforward400.com/. I also share the assumptions to help you understand that the purpose of stimulating innovation and copying is to expand stakeholder benefits by 20 more times ... not to provide lots of economic gain for your competitors at the expense of your organization's stakeholders.

Some might be tempted to dismiss such a broader focus on creating benefits from innovation as being some form of impractical idealism. While many of those who advocate such a broadening of the benefits from innovation base their thinking solely in what matches some personal concept or increases their emotional comfort, The 400 Year Project takes its guidance differently. First, direction comes from God's Word, the Bible. Second, insights into how to apply the Bible's wisdom have been gained from the Holy Spirit concerning the many practical ways that encouraging innovation can be good for everyone. Such increased benefits, in turn, can power virtuous cycles of greatly expanded company capabilities, resources, accomplishments, and benefits for sharing that multiply the results with each cycle.

Let me also explain what I mean by the "value" from innovation. When economists refer to this term, they usually have some utilitarian purpose or dimension in mind. In ordinary speech, of course, value also suggests acquiring something for less: a bargain. In contrast to the first two meanings, we often think of a value as describing what we esteem for guiding our lives, regardless of its current or potential financial worth. While this lesson often overtly focuses on value in material terms, either owning something that increases in economic worth or acquiring offerings at less cost, the lesson also advances Biblical values by basing the advice on the perspective of what God values. While we may not know exactly how to measure value in God's terms, we should certainly not pay any less attention to advancing it.

For instance, once again consider Jesus' words in Matthew 6:24 (NKJV): "No one can serve two masters; for either he will hate the one and love the other, or else he will be loyal to the one and despise the other. You cannot serve God and mammon." (If you aren't familiar with the word *mammon*, it refers in this context to worshiping *riches*, as though they were being personified as a god.) In relating ways to better operate businesses, we should always keep in mind that any such benefits should be directed towards advancing God's Kingdom, rather than some selfish purpose of our own. Otherwise, we will simply be worshiping money rather than God, a terrible sin. We should see using any money developed in this context as simply a means for accomplishing that most important purpose, God's will.

I mention this point now because I have seen variations of some methods described in this lesson misapplied to violate laws and morality, such as by conspiring with competitors to take advantage of customers and end users. What's the lesson from such applications? I cannot recall seeing any lasting good come from such misdirected uses. So I hope you will apply this information to demonstrate God's greatness to the world and to use the resources He supplies through these methods to glorify Him while serving His purposes.

You should also realize that the laws of each nation differ concerning what activities are permissible for stimulating, contacting, cooperating with, and working with competitors to take certain actions. While undoubtedly each idea presented in the lesson is perfectly legal somewhere, any given action may not be allowed where you do business. When you believe you know what actions you want to take that are encouraged by this lesson, I urge you to check with appropriate legal counsel to verify that your plans are wholly acceptable there before taking any actions.

Other 400 Year Project books contain useful guidance for ways to use resources for God's purposes. If you aren't yet familiar with these books, I suggest that you read some or all of them before or while you read and apply this lesson. A good starting point is *2,000 Percent Living* (Salvation Press, 2010), which describes how to be 20 times more fruitful for the Lord. If you want do delve deeper into the subject of being fruitful, I also suggest *Help Wanted* (2,000 Percent Living Press, 2011). For those who want to focus on witnessing, I recommend *Witnessing Made Easy* (Jubilee Worship Center Step by Step Press, 2010) and *Ways You Can Witness* (Salvation Press, 2010). For anyone who wants to help make a whole nation more fruitful for the Lord, be sure to read and apply *The 2,000 Percent Nation* (400 Year Project Press, 2012).

As you read about the many ways to increase innovation, you may find it helpful to think about how the knowledge could help with expanding and improving a community of believers. Such a reference should increase your focus on making fruitful use of what God provides through these amazing methods, serving to reduce the temptation to use the resources in un-Godly ways.

By implementing all the appropriate lessons from the 50 in *Advanced Business for Social Benefits: Stimulate Competitor Innovation and Copying* in conjunction with the 50 lessons in *Advanced Business: Exponentially Increase Stakeholder Value* and the 50 lessons for expanding market growth, slashing costs, and eliminating unnecessary investments in *Business Basics* (400 Year Project Press, 2012), a company can increase benefits for its stakeholders by 3.2 million or more times.

To make this present lesson easier to understand and use, I discuss ways to accelerate innovation from four perspectives:

1. Take the initiative to innovate.
2. Improve customer effectiveness.
3. Encourage employees.
4. Stimulate competitors to do more innovating and copying.

While working with preeminent organizations that prided themselves on their innovation effectiveness, I was more often struck that these firms were doing more to manage what was happening in the laboratory than to do all of whatever else could be accomplished for increasing innovation. I never detected that these leaders were opposed to doing more activities to enhance innovation, but, rather, that they failed to appreciate most of the opportunities for doing so. In the first perspective, we help such leaders expand their horizons to appreciate what might be done by one organization to increase innovation by everyone in an industry.

To begin, you should survey and evaluate your company's and the industry's innovation and copying methods. After that, accelerate the frequency of introducing new offerings. Apply lean innovation methods as you do. Seek first to gain new customers who demand multiple sources. Then, create breakthrough business models that competitors can copy. With your next generation of offering improvements, emphasize what can be compellingly demonstrated in advertising. Also, develop superior offerings helped by trends that competitors are sure to notice. In doing so, set a new standard of user satisfaction. From there, fill out your offering line with easy to copy items. When appropriate, endorse competitors' offerings to enhance their revenues and desire to copy to keep your endorsement.

If competitors resist copying, innovate to gain highly admired bragging rights and make improvements that will attract their highest profile and least profitable customers in profitable ways. Then, upgrade all your new offerings in ways that will make competitors' offerings seem dated. If necessary, publicize flaws in competitors' plans that do not involve copying your offerings. If all else fails, innovate to outperform a competitors' best features. They will then be forced to respond with copying and innovations.

Once competitors become active in copying, make it easier for them to reverse engineer your new offerings, leave gaps in offering features to encourage competitors to innovate in those ways, while also leaving gaps in your offering line for the same purpose. Publish your innovation methods and plans. Finally, acquire dominant industry suppliers and make improvements in their offerings competitors can access.

From the second perspective, we look beyond the organization and its offerings to consider ways to help customers be more effective as a mechanism for increasing the value they receive. Doing so is often the most valuable type of company innovation.

Begin by educating customers in appealing ways how to gain more value from the existing and future offerings. From there, help customers shift their focus onto more value-enhancing opportunities. After that, share more development information with customers to gain their reactions and to "leak" news earlier to competitors. Solidify your reputation and image with customers by using authenticity advertising that emphasizes the key role your organization plays in adding benefits to the industry. Finally, focus as much innovation as possible on making offerings more valuable due to more people being able to communicate and share valuable information.

The third perspective involves moving beyond the idea of employees as valuable human resources and stakeholders who should be rewarded by the organization to also seeing the substantial role they can play in developing and conditioning an industry to be more innovative and effective. While these ideas may seem wrong, let me assure you that it can be very helpful to create an environment in which you can so easily adjust to employees leaving that you can encourage more of them to join competitors, where they will undoubtedly improve the ability of their new employers to copy what your organization does. You should also encourage employees to develop internal units that copy your organization. When such units become effective enough, sell them to the employees or the public so that they can operate independently as new competitors.

In the final perspective, there are activities that your company can encourage that will probably stimulate responses by competitors, viewed solely from their self-interests, to enhance their effectiveness in adding benefits for all stakeholders as innovators and copiers of what you and others do. Begin by developing an improved industry standard that provides more benefits to stakeholders. From there, develop and license standard equipment to competitors that enhances stakeholder benefits. After that, license your intellectual property to competitors while requiring that certain features be included in their offerings that will expand stakeholder benefits. In doing so, permit "clones" of your offerings. Go further and become a private-label supplier to your competitors, allowing them to put their brands on what you produce. Because some competitors will be ineffective in developing brands, you should create complementary ones and sell them to competitors.

Where legally permissible, many more direct ways of enhancing competitors' innovation and copying can be done. You can probably form joint ventures with them to develop technology or benefits. You can sell their offerings for them to your customers, which will put pressure on competitors to copy whenever your offerings become too much more advantaged compared to theirs. Providing services for competitors can upgrade their effectiveness in innovation and copying. Training their employees can also be helpful for these purposes. Making it known how profitable the opportunities to copy are can help attract new competitors. By acquiring, upgrading, and selling competitors, you can enhance their abilities to innovate and copy, as well.

Across the industry, you can improve innovation and copying by sponsoring syndicated research that any competitor can subscribe to, founding public research institutes anyone can access, and sponsoring university research that competitors can use. In addition, you can launch public contests that competitors can join to reduce costs while improving designs, adding convenience, customizing offerings, and enhancing benefits.

By the time you finish applying these methods, your understanding of what it means to "do business" will have permanently become more fruitful. You will appreciate many new ways your company can use innovation and innovative practices to improve itself, as well as to increase the benefits that stakeholders receive. In the process, you'll come to see stimulating competitors to take more beneficial actions as one of your most abundant and inexpensive resources. Shifting to this approach will make you feel as if a large number of people have suddenly begun lifting their fair share of a heavy burden you have been carrying alone: Your difficulties in increasing innovation will be much less, and you'll be highly encouraged to have so many helpers assisting with bearing any new loads.

If you would like to know more about these methods, individual lessons on each point are available in *Advanced Business for Innovation: Stimulate Competitor Innovation and Copying*.

Lesson Sixteen Assignments

1. How can your organization's activities be improved in ways that will increase the economic or personal value of your end users, customers, and customers' customers or their activities by 20 times and encourage or stimulate competitors to copy and innovate on what you do?

2. How can your organization transfer knowledge to raise competitors' effectiveness in innovation and copying by 20 times?

3. How can your organization use increasing competitors' effectiveness in innovation and copying to improve its own innovation effectiveness by 20 times?

4. How can increasing competitors' and your own effectiveness in innovation by 20 times be used to increase stakeholder benefits by a greater amount?

Lesson Seventeen

Serve Social Needs

"A new commandment I give to you,
that you love one another;
as I have loved you, that you also love one another.
By this all will know that you are My disciples,
if you have love for one another."

— John 13:34-35 (NKJV)

Why should a company serve social needs? Let me begin by sharing some of what I have published previously on this subject. The following material is drawn from Chapter 11 of *Adventures of an Optimist* in which I lay out the case for the exponential-benefit expansions that can follow from organizations combining six complementary breakthroughs (ways of enhancing results by at least 20 times with the same or fewer resources, time, and effort that fully multiply the benefits of one another) to increase stakeholder benefits by over 64 million times:

Let's poke around among some of those areas that economists like to complain no one pays any attention to.

What do I mean? Here is an example: The tragedy of the commons is a problem familiar to economists. Provide something for free to everyone, and the privilege will be abused until the common resource all but disappears. In early New England towns, a central area was left open for general use. These town commons would be grazed down to the dirt by farmers' cows and sheep until no one could graze livestock there anymore.

Those who study social problems point to air and water pollution, traffic congestion, and overcrowding at free events as current examples of the same issue. In studying these problems, scholars are usually quick to point out that while solving these problems has great value for everyone, there's not enough profit potential to encourage any individual or organization to simply be responsible to the general good.

I have a little secret for you: Those scholars don't seem to know about 2,000 percent solutions. Centuries of pollution and waste have left the world filled with valuable opportunities to fix what is already a mess. A simple example is that many new mining operations don't dig up any ore at all; they simply reprocess the piles of tailings left over from earlier ores that were processed for a different mineral.

One of my students in Asia found that his company could make much more money by going to zero emissions than it could by being a polluter. Why? Waste can be turned into something valuable if you focus on the opportunity. What's more, the same company increases its profits from waste elimination that returns cleaner river water after processing than the water it originally pumped into the plant.

Forecasters are predicting great problems because of steadily declining supplies of clean water, increasing air pollution from developing countries, and great additions of toxic materials into the soils and buildings of poorer countries (such as carcinogenic chemicals, asbestos, and heavy metals). Clearly the social costs of continuing these trends will be enormous in terms of reduced life spans, disease, and medical care.

Despite the gloomy forecasts, 2,000 percent solutions are undoubtedly available. However, such solutions are highly unlikely to be developed by the least effective organizations, minimally educated people, and weakest governments. Chances are quite good, though, that these problems can be profitably solved by those with know-how for creating 2,000 percent solutions.

Let's go back to the mine example. Even more profit could have been gained initially if a more effective miner had been processing ore from the beginning to extract more types of minerals and leave less waste in piles. What if the world's leading companies in ore processing technology added a business activity to provide outsourcing services to mines for processing ore? Such a company could bid for the right to process the ore from mines, install the latest equipment, and operate in ways that would leave the least amount of waste. Soon, the technology company's size would be more than 20-times larger by having added another line of business that also created enormous social benefits.

Let's update that idea for containing air pollution in China. Major sources of the pollution in that burgeoning country are power plants burning coal and electrical generators using petroleum. All the soot that goes into the air now could instead be turned into something profitable either by generating more power from the same fuel or turning the waste into something valuable. Pollution control equipment makers could provide an outsourcing business similar to the one I proposed for ore processing equipment makers to profitably reduce waste. By applying their capital and know-how, large improvements could follow.

My suggestion is that each organization that wants to create more benefits find and operate in ways to profitably reduce the economic costs created by the world's environmental pollutants by 20 times the value of the organization's own profits. Figuring out the numbers might require having access to a few specialists to identify costs. As an example, if air pollution was bad enough in a given location, the pollution might be reducing life expectancy by 10 years. Let's say that the people affected could have earned an extra $100,000 over those 10 years. If 10,000 people live 10 years longer, that improvement would have an economic value of one billion dollars before looking at other benefits such as less need for health care from lung-related ailments. If those same people who live longer are the company's customers for other offerings, another chance is provided to improve an organization's profitable growth.

Why is providing this kind of benefit a good idea when you aren't helping your own customers? Let me explain by beginning with an economist's argument. If you reduce global economic costs by 20 times your current profits, you've just expanded the ability of the world's customers to buy. There's a general increase in purchasing power that benefits everyone. Many people remember that Henry Ford decided to pay his worker's five dollars a day as wages, well above what he needed to pay to attract good workers. Mr. Ford did this because he realized that he was better off with employees who could afford to buy the cars they made; if other employers followed through on this example, car consumption would be greatly helped. Likewise, if others follow your example, general purchasing power rises further for you and everyone else.

There's also a substantial preference for doing business with companies that reduce harmful pollution and solve other expensive social problems. More customers will seek you out as a result. For companies that directly serve consumers, that preference can be enough to turn you into an industry leader.

In addition, such companies have a much greater ability to attract top talent. Many people would like to work as employees for, be partners with, invest in, or be suppliers to those who are making important improvements. Many idealistic young people will be drawn to larger companies only for this reason, knowing that smaller organizations have potentially less impact in dealing with similar kinds of issues.

Naturally, there's individual self-interest in providing such benefits as well. Do you want to suffer some disease because others have done a poor job of containing harmful materials? I'm sure the answer to that question is no, so it benefits you personally to create more of such benefits.

In sharing those perspectives, I built on some assumptions about human nature and the current situation for providing social benefits. Let me spell out five of the most important assumptions:

1. A highly successful organization will tend to do more of the same when expanding its activities. In doing so, leaders can easily begin to focus on smaller opportunities relative to the organization's size, due to such opportunities being more easily captured and profited from.
2. Working on huge expansions in benefits from solving social problems can be morally inspiring, enormously energizing, and mentally liberating for those who share a strong desire to provide such benefits.
3. Because business philosophies have so long favored looking for opportunities almost every place except where social benefits will be the greatest, there should be many missed opportunities here, especially on a large scale.
4. Governments often operate activities that provide social benefits. Due to the nature of politics, such engagements can end up being compromised in many ways.
5. The economic value of many social benefits that are too infrequently provided is often a large multiple of the cost to provide the benefits. Financing that covers the cost of producing the benefits until such time as the economic value is realized will enable many more social benefits to be efficiently supplied.

I spell out these assumptions, in part, to invite your questions and challenges. You can contact me at donmitchell@fastforward.com/. I also share the assumptions to help you understand that the purpose of serving social benefits is to create more for society, as well as to increase an organization's profits. You may have been surprised to learn that I argue for increasing social benefits by 20 times more than corporate profits. While that relationship might appear to be based on some sort of "do-good" impulse without a firm foundation, the argument is, instead, based on the idea that with so many more benefits being provided compared to the profit earned, it will be easier and more attractive to produce and profit from providing such benefits. I draw that conclusion, in part, based on the realization that many traditionalists will oppose your organization's attempts to provide social benefits while seeking a profit, seeing the two goals as inherently in conflict. I've observed such opposition time and again when public benefits were provided for the first time by profit-seeking organizations. Obviously, then, the more you do to provide social benefits compared to the profits, the fewer people who are going to see there being some sort of harm from mixing social benefits and private profits. Accordingly, you won't experience as many roadblocks and delays in launching and expanding your activities.

Some might be tempted to dismiss such a broad focus on creating social benefits to earn a profit as being based on some form of impractical idealism. While many of those who advocate such a broadening of the benefits from any activity base their thinking solely in what matches some personal concept or increases their emotional comfort, as I also describe in Lesson Sixteen this lesson draws on different guidance. First, direction comes from God's Word, the Bible. Second, insights into how to apply the Bible's wisdom have been gained from the Holy Spirit concerning the many practical ways that profiting from more effectively serving social needs can be good for everyone. Such increased benefits, in turn, can power virtuous cycles of expanded company capabilities, resources, and benefits for sharing that will multiply the results with each cycle.

This lesson also describes ways that the interests and efforts of companies, their stakeholders, and those who receive benefits can be so complementary, even without an intention to do so, that any improvements will automatically translate into much more effectiveness and benefits for all. Let me also explain what I mean by "serving social needs well." When experts refer to this term, they usually have some practical dimension or purpose in mind. In ordinary speech, of course, "serving social needs well" also suggests doing something for the public in a high-quality way: desirable effectiveness for many people. In contrast to the first two meanings, we often think of "serving social needs well" as describing what we desire for others to have, regardless of its practical value to them. While this book often overtly focuses on serving material needs, either providing something that increases economic worth or acquiring something that is needed at less cost, the book also advances Biblical values by basing the advice on the perspective of what God sees as "serving social needs well." While we may not know exactly how to measure doing so in God's terms, we should certainly not pay any less attention to advancing it. God's measure, for instance, surely means adding lots of love while providing.

As I also mention in Lesson Sixteen, once again consider Jesus' words in Matthew 6:24 (NKJV): "No one can serve two masters; for either he will hate the one and love the other, or else he will be loyal to the one and despise the other. You cannot serve God and mammon." (If you aren't familiar with the word *mammon*, it refers in this context to worshiping *riches*, as though they were being personified as a god.) In relating ways to better operate businesses, always keep in mind that any such benefits should be directed towards advancing God's Kingdom, rather than some selfish purpose of our own. Otherwise, we will simply be worshiping money rather than God, a great sin. We should see using any money developed in this context as simply a means for accomplishing that most important purpose, God's will. I hope you will apply this information to demonstrate God's greatness to the world and to use the resources He supplies through these methods to glorify Him while serving His purposes. As Lesson Sixteen mentions, other 400 Year Project books contain useful guidance for ways to use resources for God's purposes. You can review that list there.

As you read about the many ways to increase providing social benefits, you may find it helpful to think about how the knowledge could help with expanding and improving a unified community of believers. Such a reference should increase your focus on making fruitful use of what God provides through these amazing methods, thereby reducing your temptation to use the resources in un-Godly ways.

By implementing well appropriate lessons from *Advanced Business for Social Benefits: Profit from Serving Social Needs* in conjunction with the 50 lessons in *Advanced Business for Innovation: Stimulate Competitor Innovation and Copying*, the 50 lessons in *Advanced Business: Exponentially Increase Stakeholder Value,* and the 50 lessons for expanding market growth, slashing costs, and eliminating unnecessary investments in *Business Basics* (400 Year Project Press, 2012), a company can increase benefits for its stakeholders by 64 million or more times.

This present lesson primarily concerns the following topics:

1. Selecting benefits to provide
2. Developing and adjusting stakeholder relationships
3. Launching such a program

To select the right benefits to provide, you need to pick social benefits that can be greatly expanded and that will also substantially enhance company profits. Here are nine related opportunities to do so that are drawn from case histories in *Advanced Business for Social Benefits*:

1. Attract more customers and purchases because of customers wanting to support the social purpose.
2. Obtain premium pricing due to the strength of customer desire to support the social purpose or to the marketing benefits received.

3. Reduce costs due to attracting much volunteer help or receiving smaller charges from some suppliers who favor the purpose behind the increased social benefits.
4. Experience fewer costs due to a higher drive among employees, partners, and suppliers for productivity, willingness to work harder in less favorable conditions, and demanding less in payments and benefits.
5. Avoid investments due to stakeholders doing more of such investing.
6. Increase sensitivity to improving cash flow by all stakeholders because of its effect on providing more for those who receive social benefits.
7. Encourage innovative business models that build on the trust and preference for providing and receiving the social benefits.
8. Potentially receive subsidies from stakeholders to launch, expand, or sustain the benefit provision.
9. Directly create more demand for the firm's offerings due to the resulting social benefits.

To succeed, you need to look closely at current and potential customers to identify ways that your business model should be revised to solve social problems and serve social needs well in ways that will increase your attractiveness to purchasers from your firm. We see that customers hold the key to most of the potential advantages for an organization from serving social needs well.

For many organizations, end users of offerings are seen much more dimly and imperfectly than are customers. However, you should gain insights from how end users react to changes in your business model that provide more social benefits.

Consider, too, how suppliers can enhance providing social benefits well while also helping you attract more customers, end users, and other supporters of your activities. If current suppliers aren't able to do what's needed, finding and developing new suppliers can be necessary.

Similarly, employees are of great importance in finding solutions for pressing social problems and effectively increasing the provision of scarce benefits. Much of your credibility in achieving your purpose will be determined by how well employees go about doing such important work.

Employees' families can be an important source of encouragement for employees, stakeholders, and those who might decide to become stakeholders. Such families' comments are often taken more seriously than what a respected "objective" source might say about your organization's activities to supply more social benefits. You should also consider the importance of limiting negative comments by employees' families that can create skepticism concerning the company and its efforts.

Owners have more influence over what an organization will do than many other stakeholders. It's important to establish the credibility of a solution before asking owners to support it, as well as the significance of succeeding for expanding owners' value in the company. You also need to focus on the kinds of non-economic advantages provided to owners when the company seeks to greatly increase social benefits as a means of expanding company profits. Such advantages will often be more appealing to some owners than simply having more money.

You also need the right partners to accomplish results that none of the organizations could achieve on their own. Identify the ideal partners and determine what relationship to seek with each one.

Adding different types of distributors can increase the efficiency and effectiveness of providing social benefits and earning profits by doing so. Case studies to consider include the Grameen-Danone joint venture and the Aravind Eye Care System. Be sure to look into gaining even more advantages by adding different types of distributors than other organizations have.

Carefully investigate the potential for attracting volunteers to perform tasks that might otherwise be done by employees and suppliers for pay. While nonprofit organizations have often relied on this approach, too few for-profit organizations with appealing social practices have done so.

Strangers are too often ignored as a potential resource for accomplishing more in providing social benefits. Due to the appeal of your purpose, those who have had no more contact with your activities than hearing about what you are doing can become valuable contributors by sharing their reactions to your benefit provisions with others, performing short-term tasks, and providing valuable information about ways to improve.

Consider also how being a good example by providing more social benefits can lead competitors to take complementary actions to expand such benefits. Doing so well can be helped by drawing extensively on concepts contained in the prior lesson and in *Advanced Business for Innovation*.

Every organization affects the communities in which it operates. Positively engaging with such communities can increase the social benefits that are received, reduce harm, and improve profits.

Also, look into how your company interacts with governments to seek ways to provide benefits for and to gain support from governments that multiply the results from your company's own efforts.

Experts can become very valuable contributors to a company's social-benefit expansion by adding experience, knowledge, and credibility. However, such experts must first become interested in what you intend and then become willing to contribute. It's a new kind of marketing task that can be very rewarding for your organization.

You should also engage authorities to support your solution. Authorities differ from experts in being able to influence large numbers of stakeholders, regardless of their skill and knowledge in the subject area. For instance, a popular president of the United States might influence many people to engage in a beneficial activity while knowing little about how to accomplish the goal. Franklin Delano Roosevelt's support for the March of Dimes is an example of what can be achieved in this way.

Experts and authorities aren't the only useful sources of public support. Foundations can also make an important difference in similar ways, while also funding experiments, sustaining support during lean times, and multiplying the social benefits that are supplied.

The largest potential group of contributors is the general public. From among those who don't yet know what you are doing and have no connection to current stakeholders can come most of your new contributing stakeholders. With enough of such people, you will be able to greatly increase the social benefits you can provide and enhance your company's profits.

You should look next into establishing a firm foundation for an irresistible cause tied to your social-benefit expansion. I recommend you develop ideas by studying the March of Dimes as an example.

After doing so, attract more attention for and support of your irresistible cause. As a result, the social benefits you plan to increase will be expanded as much as possible due to the support of stakeholders and the general public. In doing so, stay focused on what the Bible and the Holy Spirit direct. As part of this work, develop compelling true stories to attract interest, support, and actions for the irresistible cause. To the extent that the stories relate to advancing God's Kingdom, the stories will be more persuasive. When you are ready, hold an unmistakable launch event to attract attention to and support for your irresistible cause.

Once launched, add cheerful givers by building commitment to support the irresistible cause. After that, effectively increase commitment through experiences that many people can participate in and feel touched by. In so doing, the original ways that commitment was built should be expanded and streamlined.

When much of such commitment is in place, it's time to train committed people to perform the key tasks required by the irresistible cause.

In addition to the process I've just been describing, there's a second way to advance social benefits by 400 times: replacing a government activity. While the opportunity is large, the potential opposition can be even greater. One way to get started is by developing public opinion that favors installing such a replacement.

Another way to replace a government activity is to demonstrate the value of governments financing beneficiaries. With access to such funds, beneficiaries can then choose to purchase social benefits that you provide more efficiently and effectively than the government does.

You should also consider using private financing to fund greatly expanding the provision of social benefits. As one option, you could provide such financing directly. In this way, beneficiaries can be better protected from harm.

Another option for replacing a government activity is by teaching beneficiaries how to finance themselves.

As you can well imagine, there's an obvious third strategy for expanding social benefits by more than 400 times and profits by at least 20 times while doing so: replacing private enterprise activities, whether by nonprofit or for-profit organizations. Look first to replace activities that have high social costs. Next, attempt to replace private-enterprise activities that provide few social benefits, such as cigarette manufacturing, marketing, and distribution. Finally, evaluate the opportunity to improve any business whose social benefits can be directly increased by more than a hundred times. With the effects of the expanded direct benefits, the combination of direct and indirect benefits will usually expand by at least 400 times.

All of these points are developed in separate lessons found in *Advanced Business for Social Benefits*. As you work on this lesson, your understanding of what it means to "do business" will become much more fruitful. You will appreciate many new ways your company can effectively address long-standing, harmful public problems, as well as increase the benefits that your stakeholders receive. In the process, you'll come to see solving social problems and supplying large quantities of social benefits as a spiritually rewarding calling. Shifting to this approach will add a spiritual dimension to managing a business.

You will also delight in receiving the support of many new people and be highly encouraged to have so many added helpers.

Lesson Seventeen Assignments

1. How can your organization's activities expand the amount of social benefits by at least 400 times in ways that will increase company income by at least 20 times?

2. How can your organization replace government activities that are ineffective to increase social benefits by at least 400 times in ways that will increase company income by at least 20 times?

3. How can your organization replace private activities that are ineffective or harmful to increase social benefits by at least 400 times in ways that will increase company income by at least 20 times?

4. In answering the first three assignments in this lesson, how can the increased social benefits be generated in ways that will broaden how many types of beneficiaries are helped?

Lesson Eighteen

Engage the Underemployed

My brethren, do not hold the faith of our Lord Jesus Christ,
the Lord *of glory, with partiality.*
For if there should come into your assembly
a man with gold rings, in fine apparel, and
there should also come in a poor man in filthy clothes,
and you pay attention to the one
wearing the fine clothes and say to him, "You sit here in a good place,"
and say to the poor man, "You stand there," or,
"Sit here at my footstool,"
have you not shown partiality among yourselves,
and become judges with evil thoughts?

Listen, my beloved brethren:
Has God not chosen the poor of this world to be *rich in faith*
and heirs of the kingdom which He promised to those who love Him?
But you have dishonored the poor man.

Do not the rich oppress you and drag you into the courts?
Do they not blaspheme that noble name by which you are called?

If you really fulfill the *royal law according to the Scripture,*
"You shall love your neighbor as yourself," *you do well;*
but if you show partiality, you commit sin, and
are convicted by the law as transgressors.

— James 2:1-9 (NKJV)

Why should a company engage the underemployed? Let me begin answering that question by sharing some of what I wrote previously about this topic, in Lesson 11 of *Adventures of an Optimist*:

> Most of the world's people are desperately poor. Their lack of resources leads to permanent problems. Some babies don't properly develop their brains for lack of a few hundred dollars in nutrients. Lives are ravaged by diseases that are preventable with clean water, inexpensive vaccines, and easy-to-make medicines. Hundreds of millions of people with above-average intellect never receive enough education to develop their minds to anywhere near their full potential. Entrepreneurs capable of leading thousands to economically useful lives lack the investment capital to train and employ those thousands.
>
> What's the root of the problem? It takes a long time and a lot of investment in people before individuals can earn their keep and support others. Short-change the most valuable parts of that time and investment, and the value of the lost potential will be an enormous multiple of the resources that aren't expended in the near term.
>
> Large organizations won't, in most cases, be able to think of ways to earn a near-term profit from solving these problems of helping people achieve their potential. Does that mean we are at the end of opportunities to create billions of times more benefits? I don't think so. Other approaches offer potential.
>
> Research conducted by my students in Africa has shown that there are millions of partially able entrepreneurs who can become leaders who create enormous economic and social progress. How could this potential be turned into a happy result? Establish a new type of entrepreneurship — enterprises that will profitably employ hundreds of millions of people who now have few prospects for earning much of a living.
>
> How might organizations based in developed countries profitably improve the effectiveness of such entrepreneurs? I can see sever-

al possibilities; here are a few choices for helping these entrepreneurs:

- Develop new business models that benefit from employing lots of energetic, but undereducated, entrepreneurs. An example is providing such entrepreneurs with opportunities to directly sell your organization's offerings. Firms like Avon are already having success in this regard. Such business models will be more successful, of course, if inexpensive entrepreneurial education is included.
- Partner with underdeveloped entrepreneurs by providing information, training, capital, and support to the partnership while the entrepreneurs supply their efforts, time, and determination. The most successful of such entrepreneurs could later be hired by companies to develop relationships and partnerships with still other underdeveloped entrepreneurs. This business model could be especially attractive in delivering technical services in places where a local language and awareness of local customs are needed in order to be effective. ServiceMaster, for instance, could partner in this way with underdeveloped entrepreneurs to provide excellent cleaning services for stores, restaurants, hotels, and hospitals.
- Establish business models that turn high performing employees in poor countries into business owners. Chains of mom 'n pop retailers could be operated to serve as tryouts for couples to purchase and operate the stores. The resulting chain would be stronger through combining its knowledge, marketing, systems, and purchasing clout.
- Manufacturers could develop modular ways to expand into a country, beginning with making or assembling simple, labor-intensive components that are expensive to ship. These production modules could be set up and operated by the manufacturer at first until running smoothly. Later, the production

units could be sold to people who work in the enterprise and have done a good job of learning how to lead and operate the production. Those units could then become supplier partners. Customer awareness of the company's efforts to provide local content and ownership would probably assist in selling more of the resulting items in that country.

- Manufacturers could also provide training and licenses to distribute their products in a given country. This approach would be most attractive in sparsely populated locales in which distribution is difficult. In the beginning, such networks could be focused on selling the simplest items and providing the least valuable replacement parts. Those who did well could eventually be upgraded into establishing authorized repair centers.

- Transportation companies could establish common carriage warehouses where fledgling entrepreneurs who cannot afford facilities could rent secure spaces for valuable items. These warehouses would then prosper from more shipping being done to and from the facility by these entrepreneurs.

- Organizations of all kinds could utilize a policy of emphasizing outsourcing to local entrepreneurs. If nothing else, such a policy would help those who are educated but don't know much about running businesses to get their feet wet in entrepreneurial ventures. Here's an example: Instead of having their own training departments for basic literacy and numeracy skills, companies might hire local teachers to provide such knowledge and experience during evening and weekend classes. Training in various basic technical skills might be hired out to vocational school teachers for other night and weekend classes. Hospitals might provide opportunities for their best nurses to train nurse's aides in exchange for additional compensation.

There is an enormous multiplier effect of such activities in uplifting lives. First, the number of gainfully employed grows very rapidly. Of course, most of these people will have low-wage jobs, but that's how economic development usually starts. The holders of those jobs will certainly be better off than before. Second, local purchasing of simple consumer goods will expand very rapidly, creating the opportunity for more entrepreneurs to produce and sell those products. Third, you will rapidly create a generation of entrepreneurial role models who will inspire others to take this career route. In some underdeveloped countries, it's very unusual now to have such role models. Instead, teens try to learn to be entrepreneurs from other teens who don't know any more than they do. Fourth, the expansion in goods will create a need for much more transportation and storage, which will expand the easier entrepreneurial opportunities still further. Fifth, by involving educated people as entrepreneurs, you are bound at some point to stimulate the development of low-cost, part-time schools that specialize in preparing entrepreneurs for areas where demand is greatest. For instance, such schools can help reduce enormous shortages of trained leadership and personnel in fields such as plumbing, electrical work, automotive and equipment repairs, and advanced construction. When many more people can then earn adequate livelihoods through trade or manufacturing rather than subsistence farming, larger-scale agriculture can also expand, making it possible to substitute equipment for human work and animal energy. You can expect that the number of people receiving sufficient nutrition and education will rapidly increase. Establish one successful entrepreneur in a family, and chances are that entrepreneur will find ways to help the rest of the extended family. Make these shifts in ways of doing things across a whole nation, and you reduce the likelihood that during times of drought the country will lack foreign reserves to buy food and medicines. As a result, overall health, knowledge, productivity, and wealth will improve on a sustainable basis.

There is another path to progress for underemployed people: Help some of these people to advance far beyond the usual best practice by becoming skilled in developing 2,000 percent solutions, series of complementary 2,000 percent solutions, and excellent solutions. Having even one such person in a community should make it possible to find many ways to engage with underemployed people and, in turn, for those people to supply breakthrough after breakthrough to advance the profitable activities of a firm in their local communities.

One of the criticisms aimed at programs for helping the poor is that such programs "do for" the poor, rather than empowering the poor to create and implement their own solutions. A company wishing to upgrade the skills of underdeveloped people could have its pick of all but a few of the best minds in many nations to learn about making breakthroughs. Then, such individuals could find activities that would profitably engage quite a few more underemployed people on the company's behalf. The cost in time, money, and effort for training and paying such an individual until she or he is productive would be modest. Almost any medium-size or larger enterprise would have trouble finding the cost at the end of the year. Yet the potential returns could be enormous. Naturally, funding of any breakthroughs would be evaluated in the same ways as any other profit-seeking program. Pilot projects would precede any sort of major investment.

Another possibility would be for groups of companies to combine as sponsors of the kinds of global online contests that are described in *The Ultimate Competitive Advantage*, *Advanced Business for Innovation*, and *Excellent Solutions*. By combining the incentive of aiding poor people with financial rewards for such achievement, such a contest should produce some remarkable new business models, approaches for making underemployed people quickly productive, and methods for avoiding harm while making such changes.

If companies are not interested in making such investments, I remind you also of *Help Wanted* (2,000 Percent Living Press, 2011) in which I describe the need for a million tutors globally who are able to train others in developing and implementing breakthrough solutions. A community, a foundation, a local donor, or a person trained in making such breakthroughs could decide to provide such training for others. The costs could be recovered by obtaining royalty rights on the revenues that develop from the efforts of those who are trained, up to the investor receiving a reasonable return on the initial investment.

I'm sure you'll have better ideas than I have presented here. I look forward to hearing from you. Please contact me at my e-mail address: donmitchell@fastforward400.com/.

Lesson Eighteen Assignments

1. How can your organization's activities expand the engagement of underemployed people by at least 400 times in ways that will increase company income by at least 20 times?

2. How can your organization cooperate with other organizations to expand the engagement of underemployed people by at least 400 times in ways that will increase company income by at least 20 times?

3. How can your organization encourage individuals to begin private activities that will expand the engagement of underemployed people by at least 400 times in ways that will increase company income by at least 20 times?

4. In answering the first three assignments in this lesson, how can the increased engagement of underemployed people be generated in ways that will broaden how many types of underemployed are helped?

Lesson Nineteen

Increase Stakeholder Effectiveness

But the wisdom that is from above is first pure,
then peaceable, gentle, willing to yield,
full of mercy and good fruits,
without partiality and without hypocrisy.
Now the fruit of righteousness is sown in peace
by those who make peace.

— James 3:17-18 (NKJV)

In *Your Breakthroughs*, we have occasionally discussed sharing with others what has been learned by an individual or an organization. That approach is an important element of gaining the fruits of *2,000 Percent Living*, as a significant way that complementary 2,000 percent solutions can be developed and enhanced. In this lesson, I present what to some will seem like a radical idea: Enhance the effectiveness of *all* stakeholders in ways that will yield enormous benefits for them, as well as for your company. In the earlier lessons, the focus on helping stakeholders is mostly limited to assisting customers and end users to make better use of offerings, to suppliers providing inputs that could enable better offerings, and to partners making more valuable contributions to joint ventures.

Here, I extend the concept much further: *Upgrade the biggest opportunity area in each stakeholder's life, regardless of its apparent connection to enhancing sales or profits of your offerings.* Once again, I must beg your indulgence as I explain the logic behind this point. Otherwise, you will think what I am describing has no possible application for being part of a complementary 2,000 percent solution that will exponentially raise the level of benefits of all the other solutions we've been covering in this part's lessons. To the contrary, I think that this approach may have greater potential to increase complementary benefits than any of the others I've already discussed with you.

But of course, for-profit-company owners are going to wonder if I'm advocating taking their money and using it for a charitable operation. Let me address such a concern by first providing a thought experiment.

Imagine that a poor, but well-intentioned, person wins a lottery worth five hundred million dollars. Will that person spend more? Will that person use money to solve personal problems, such as ill health and lack of decent living conditions? Will that person be willing to help others in his or her family, as well as friends?

I'm sure you agree that many of such actions will be taken in such an instance. I use that example because we've all read about what individuals do after winning a big lottery prize. Yes, they often waste much of the money, but they often do some good with it, as well. I like the example because it's easy to see that money can solve some problems, while creating new ones such as attracting scam artists.

Most people and organizations are in a somewhat analogous situation. There's a blockage related to some lack that keeps them from fulfilling much of their most positive potential. For an undereducated person who is bright, the lack is not learning enough. For an organization that is deficient in technical know-how, the lack can be overcome by gaining or accessing such know-how. For an individual or an organization that doesn't know what is lacking, good advice is needed for what to add. I'm sure you will agree that being released from a limitation makes it possible for an individual or an organization to do much more. Not all individuals and organizations will take full advantage of the new opportunities, but at least some improvement is likely.

Next, imagine that your firm's stakeholders have all gained such a release from lack. What might the effects of that result look like? Well, they would all be more productive. Many of them might be more innovative. All of them would be thankful that they no longer had such a limitation.

Now, consider what it would be like to have received help to remove such a limitation from your profit-seeking firm. How might such an experience have influenced your relationship with whoever provided the help? Unless an individual or organization is hopelessly sociopathic, there would probably be a strong sense of gratitude and obligation that those benefited would seek to express in words and deeds. If your firm shared its needs for help in ways that such individuals and organizations could contribute, don't you think that there would be a desire take such actions to help you? And, naturally, some of the desire would turn into helpful actions. If the actions had been well selected so that your organization gains large benefits, surely profits would greatly expand. In addition, a bond between your organization and the stakeholder or stakeholder organization would have been forged or strengthened that would translate into loyalty that would influence attitudes and actions for some time to come.

Naturally, you shouldn't rush into implementing such a solution without experimentation. I suspect that while it would be ideal to have a totally individualized approach for each person or organization, doing so may not be possible. However, ways of measuring what stakeholders need might be standardized. From the findings, knowledge could be developed for contributing the most important elements of what is lacking. You could take on supplying one type of need at a time, becoming effective at fulfilling a first one before developing a second way to help.

I suspect that the best approach would be to focus on those needs that people feel most strongly. Such a list might include helping the next generation in a family to have a better life, dealing with any debilitating circumstances that make people feel demeaned, opening up exciting opportunities, overcoming anything that seems like too much to bear, and so on.

Since owners are likely to look at such activities very suspiciously, I suggest that developing ways to help customers is probably least likely to be seen as a waste of time. Typically, companies have done surveys of customers to help them understand how to make better use of company offerings. That's still a good thing to do, but such investigations could be expanded to include helping with other "hot" issues, such as why a customer firm is having trouble selling its offerings, difficulties with handling expansion, technical problems that seem insoluble, and so forth where solving the problems would enable many more purchases of your firm's offerings. Once such issues were resolved, it would probably become clear that such organizations are also missing opportunities, either because of their not being perceived or because no one knows how to address them. While it would probably be taking on too much to actually solve all such problems, your organization could probably benefit by helping such customers to learn how they can help themselves or to acquire reliable assistance elsewhere.

In thinking about taking such actions, I'm reminded of the part of Lesson Sixteen about acquiring competitors, fixing them, and reselling the entities. If your firm has developed such skills and has had good experience while applying them, some of those competencies could apply to helping customers in similar ways. In fact, for customers whose owners are planning to cash out, you might find it profitable and helpful to engage in similar purchasing, fixing, and reselling. In thinking about doing so, keep in mind that many other customers may see such actions as threats because you are now their competitors, which would hurt sales to them. A better approach in some industries could be to help effective customers acquire and improve other customers.

Where might you go next after helping customers? Well, owners and stakeholders would probably be comfortable with doing more to assist end users, especially if studying customer needs has shown obvious issues where end users need help that is unrelated to your offerings ... but which could expand usage of your offerings.

I don't want to become too specific here in terms of prescribing what your organization should do. My experience as a management consultant has taught me that the kind of help people feel they need most is often quite simple to provide and takes little more than caring enough to find out the details and to talk about possible solutions with them. While doing so personally, I have lost count of the number of times that a simple comment by me led to a life-changing redirection that someone later described as a major event in achieving some success. When we start to see ourselves as connected to and dependent on the capabilities and effectiveness of *all* stakeholders, it begins to make sense to look for ways to enhance those capabilities and such effectiveness.

While you may be starting to wonder how so much can be accomplished, I have some advice for you: Relax!

I doubt if your organization will be able to do much more than play a role in diagnosing what's needed for many of your stakeholders. After knowing what kind of help they need to become more productive, the chances are almost perfect that some other individual or organization can better serve that need than you and your organization can. Of course, in matters related to your offerings, your organization will usually be the best source.

Start with helping to make improvements your stakeholders and you think would be most productive and useful. In the process of being so engaged, you'll learn of many other, potentially more valuable, opportunities, as well as gain insights into how to best increase stakeholder effectiveness.

Lesson Nineteen Assignments

1. What concerns do your shareholders or owners have about the value of increasing the effectiveness of *all* stakeholders?

2. How can those concerns be respected while seeking to increase stakeholder effectiveness?

3. What does each stakeholder think are the most useful ways to increase effectiveness?

4. How can your organization identify the best ways to make such improvements?

5. How can your organization help stakeholders gain access to resources that would make such improvements easier to accomplish?

6. How can you turn such assistance into a more cooperative relationship in which stakeholders will assist with many needs that you cannot easily supply for yourself, but that they can be highly effective in providing?

Part Four

Excellent Solutions

Have I not written to you excellent things
Of counsels and knowledge,
That I may make you know
the certainty of the words of truth,
That you may answer words of truth
To those who send to you?

— Proverbs 22:20-21 (NKJV)

Some people are discouraged by what they know about the state of the world. For instance, personal knowledge, observation, an online search, or listening to the news reveals that many people lack some of the basics for sustaining a healthy and productive life: clean water, food, medicine, shelter, education, and a job. Some people who are well supplied with the basics recall times when their own circumstances were more favorable than now and are discouraged about the future. Others are concerned that some people seem determined to harm as many other people as possible and personally live in fear.

If you share any of these concerns, developing excellent solutions (ways of increasing benefits by 10 trillion times through one set of changes while using the same or less time, money, and effort) can provide silver linings for dark clouds. Realize that there is more than sufficient time, effort, physical resources, and funding available to greatly improve the spiritual, moral, health, emotional, and physical circumstances of almost everyone on Earth. While some make that argument based on redistributing some of what those with more have to those who have less, excellent solutions upgrade what we all do and how we conduct our lives to provide such benefits.

Why then do so many people lack what they obviously need? Part of the answer is that too few excellent solutions have been developed and applied for making better use of existing resources.

After learning how to devise and to apply such solutions, you will greatly improve your own life, as well as the lives of others.

Before explaining more about becoming an excellent-solution innovator, let me suggest an analytical process that could speed your application of excellent solutions: Travel mentally forward in time to learn the future's lessons that can be applied today. As a lad, I was fascinated by science fiction, especially stories involving time machines and time travel that provided knowledge from the future about opportunities to avert problems today. At the end of such stories, I was often struck by how applying common sense would have delivered similar insights.

Since then, I've learned valuable ways of mentally traveling into the future to bring back such insights. While creating and applying breakthrough solutions, I have not tried to perceive what the future will be in the way that a Biblical prophet might do through seeking a message from God. I don't deny the value of such an approach, but God usually doesn't provide that kind of guidance to me. Instead, I usually do something simple, such as combining current conditions and past trends to project into the future what could happen if the trends continue.

Why is such a mental exercise useful for finding excellent solutions? I choose to take these mental trips forward in time, in part, because I want to escape being blinded by what I see around me. No moment in time captures all the possibilities open to us, and the vividness of being in the present can blind us to most of the other possibilities for today and tomorrow.

I also make such mental excursions because they help to shine a brighter light on the best future possibilities. While some helpful aspects of today are becoming more difficult or expensive, other helpful influences are becoming less expensive, easier to do, and more valuable. When a helpful trend is changing faster than a negative one, possibilities begin to open for how to use the positive trend to overcome any potential harm from the negative one.

Here is an example of what I mean. The percentage of people learning and regularly applying advanced quantitative analysis skills has been decreasing. That trend reduces the capacity to use such analysis to improve benefits for everyone. However, that negative trend is more than countered by a positive one of increasing calculating power and the software to use it so that each analyst is far more productive. If we extend both current trends into the future, it's clear that effects of the positive trend vastly overwhelm the effects of the negative one.

We then need to return to the present to see what can be done now to make the best use of the improving capability. For creating excellent solutions in the context of this example, the question becomes how to use the enormous increases in calculating power and effectiveness of software to accomplish more. Investigation would reveal that existing analytical power is more than adequate for the purpose, but that too little data exist on which to do many analyses. In a number of cases, the answer for establishing more excellent solutions is simply to develop more kinds of data that are relevant to accomplishing increased results with the existing time, resources, and effort.

Finally, I mentally muse in terms of these time dimensions, knowing that most breakthroughs have been based on insights first written down and communicated at least 400 years before they went into use by most people. As a consequence, I can look for excellent solutions by appreciating that the necessary elements for the solutions already exist and are known to at least some people, but that these same elements are not yet fully appreciated, properly combined, and effectively applied. My mental voyages often yield insights into what knowledge to look for in the past and present. Once such knowledge is found, the challenge of creating most excellent solutions is simply to reduce the time required to understand, apply, and expand the use of any breakthroughs made possible by the solutions.

You'll learn more about how to do this kind of thinking as you study the next four lessons. As you do, feel free to extend any trend changes that interest you far into the future to see what conclusions you reach. I think you'll be fascinated by what you learn from doing so. I look forward to hearing about your thoughts and learning as you apply such thinking. Feel free to e-mail me at donmitchell@fastforward400.com anytime you have an observation to share or a question to ask.

When you work on adding to the storehouse of excellent solutions, it doesn't matter what country you live in, who just gained political office, where you were educated, what you know, the nature of your work, what your parents did for a living, what you look like, how old you are, or what kind of a home you live in. You are already equipped with the resources to create and to apply such solutions ... except for the information in these lessons. After reading about *what to do* and *how*, your excellent solutions can be established in any place and from any background to transform your life in far more powerful ways than you are now imagining.

In Lesson Twenty, we embark by determining what your role should be while creating or applying excellent solutions. For most people, that role will include being part of a team. If God has called you to help with an excellent solution, He has specially prepared you to be interested in and to fruitfully apply talents and skills that He has given you. Improving your knowledge of excellent solutions and thinking about how to create and implement such solutions by considering this part's lessons will increase your fruitfulness, as well as enhance the effectiveness of those who copy your solutions.

In Lesson Twenty-One, we examine how to develop an excellent solution through the two master processes for doing so. *My purpose here is to show how the Godly benefits of your actions can be increased by trillions of times while employing the same or less time, resources, and efforts than you and others are already applying.*

Without going into the processes to be used, let me first put excellent solutions into perspective. In *Your Breakthroughs*, you have already learned about two kinds of breakthrough solutions in parts two and three. These are:

1. **Accomplish at least twenty times more with the same or less time, money, and effort: a** *2,000 percent solution.* As Lesson Seven demonstrates, the first seven steps of the eight-step process can enable productivity to rise by 20 or more times. By following step eight of the process to repeat the first seven steps, you can then make another 20-times improvement to your first 2,000 percent solution. That repetition can increase benefits by 400 times the initial level. After that, each repetition of the process can multiply the most recent level of benefits by another 20 times. With seven or more repetitions, increased benefits exceed 20 billion times while applying no more time, resources, or effort.

2. *Link complementary 2,000 percent solutions* **whose benefits perfectly multiply one another's fruitfulness.** Complementary solutions provide at least a 20-times benefit increase in terms of each solution's dimensions while also multiplying the benefits of other 2,000 percent solutions by the same amount to create some other benefit. Two complementary solutions (such as increasing revenues or those served by 20 times, as well as decreasing costs by 96 percent) expand benefits by 400 times (benefits and profits, in this example) with the same or less time, resources, and effort. By adding enough complementary solutions, benefits can be expanded by billions (with at least seven such solutions) or trillions (with at least ten such solutions) of times. Think of these opportunities as providing a 2,000 percent solution for making 2,000 percent solutions by increasing the sources of benefit expansion.

Let me now relate excellent solutions to these earlier types of solutions: **Create and implement an *excellent solution*, one breakthrough solution that provides at least the same combined benefit expansion as ten complementary 2,000 percent solutions (or nine rounds of improvements for a 2,000 percent solution) under any set of external conditions, aided by unstoppable human reactions that speed the rate of implementation.** Think of such a solution as being like a 2,000 percent solution for making many complementary or repeated 2,000 percent solutions. That observation is true because you only need to make one set of changes through one solution.

Is there a fourth, and even more valuable, category of solutions? Why not? God created the world, knows all things (including what comes next), loves us, and wants the best for us. By looking at the progression of these solutions, it's pretty easy to take a guess as to what the fourth solution could be: a 2,000 percent solution for making excellent solutions. I look forward to receiving whatever Godly knowledge will be revealed in this regard, and to being immensely blessed by sharing it to bring honor and glory to our Almighty Father; the Lord, Jesus Christ; and the Holy Spirit.

In Lesson Twenty-Two, we turn to exploring the benefit dimensions of excellent solutions.

In Lesson Twenty-Three, we consider how to start unstoppable chain reactions that will help an excellent solution to provide more benefits sooner.

Keep in mind as you read these lessons that I am condensing a great deal of information into a small space here. For a full appreciation of these topics, you'll need to read *Excellent Leadership* (400 Year Project Press, 2015), as well as either the nonprofit or for-profit edition of *Excellent Solutions* (400 Year Project Press, 2014). As you read these lessons or work with these other resources, feel free to send your questions to donmitchell@fastforward400.com/.

Lesson Twenty

Determine Your Role

I, therefore, the prisoner of the Lord,
beseech you to walk worthy of the calling
with which you were called,
with all lowliness and gentleness,
with longsuffering,
bearing with one another in love,
endeavoring to keep the unity of the Spirit
in the bond of peace.
There is *one body and one Spirit,*
just as you were called
in one hope of your calling;
one Lord, one faith, one baptism;
one God and Father of all,
who is *above all, and through all,*
and in you all.

— Ephesians 4:1-6 (NKJV)

What a great adventure you are beginning! The knowledge you gain and apply about excellent solutions will enable you to surpass your wildest imaginings of what you can accomplish with and for God. I will be praying for the success of all your endeavors to glorify Him while serving His purposes. I look forward to learning about your plans and tracking your progress. I would also like to help. Please send your questions about your role with an excellent solution to donmitchell@fastforward400.com so that I can do so.

Thank you for being interested in praying for and working to create and implement an excellent solution. I'm sure that your believer's faithfulness in doing so will be noted and rewarded by the Lord when you are in heaven, as well as by having God more abundantly bless your life on Earth, especially in its spiritual dimensions. How wonderful are such prospects!

Unfortunately, the Bible indicates that some believers won't answer the calls that God makes, causing those who don't respond to delay or to miss the chance to participate in God's plan.

I'm sure you want the best God has planned for you! With the help of this lesson, you'll be clearer about what God intends for you to do with regard to an excellent solution. Be sure to act on what you learn.

Tell others also about any excellent solutions that attract you. Involvement with one of these solutions could also be part of God's calling on their lives, and you may be the only messenger who God has selected for communicating this purpose.

Many people are needed to develop, implement, and subsequently improve an excellent solution. Knowing that some people might not immediately respond, the Lord may have called more people to play these various roles than are needed. Don't let that observation slow down your response to His call! Keep in mind that many fewer may be called to become leaders of excellent solutions than are called to perform other essential roles. The sooner you start, the more likely it is that He will direct you into one of the most beneficial roles. In considering this comment, please be aware that there are many types of leadership roles, as well as many other important tasks to be done for developing, implementing, and improving an excellent solution. Performance of all roles is essential, so be happy about whatever your calling turns out to be. As the Apostle Paul noted, where would the head be without the body?

This lesson will help you determine what the Lord is calling you to do for a particular excellent solution. In following His directions for attaining the purpose, remember that God will provide whatever information you need at the perfect time, which may or may not be while you read this lesson, or even while you first study this book. However, feel confident that whatever you implement by following this lesson will be valuable for God's Kingdom, His plan for an excellent solution, and His plans for you.

This lesson addresses these questions concerning your callings from God:

- Are you called to work on an excellent solution?
- What contributions are you called to make?
- What preparations should you make to become a more fruitful contributor?
- Are you called to be a leader of an excellent solution?
- What leadership role(s) are you called to perform?

We begin by determining whether you are called to work on an excellent solution. Here are some Bible verses to start your thinking:

Now they came to Jericho. As He went out of Jericho with His disciples and a great multitude, blind Bartimaeus, the son of Timaeus, sat by the road begging. And when he heard that it was Jesus of Nazareth, he began to cry out and say, "Jesus, Son of David, have mercy on me!"

Then many warned him to be quiet; but he cried out all the more, "Son of David, have mercy on me!"

So Jesus stood still and commanded him to be called.

Then they called the blind man, saying to him, "Be of good cheer. Rise, He is calling you."

And throwing aside his garment, he rose and came to Jesus.

So Jesus answered and said to him, "What do you want Me to do for you?"

The blind man said to Him, "Rabboni, that I may receive my sight."

Then Jesus said to him, "Go your way; your faith has made you well."

And immediately he received his sight and followed Jesus on the road.

— Mark 10:46-52 (NKJV)

The miraculous restoration of Bartimaeus' sight demonstrates several key elements of how callings can be perceived and appropriately acted on to serve God's purposes. As we see in other parts of the Bible, Jesus taught that human physical deficiencies (blindness in this case) don't necessarily reflect someone's sin, but such lacks can, instead, serve as opportunities to bring more glory to God. For instance, in granting Bartimaeus' request to receive sight, Jesus showed that He had supernatural power of the sort that the Old Testament indicates would be demonstrated by the Messiah.

Let's consider what led up to this miracle. If Jesus had not traveled through Jericho, He would not have encountered Bartimaeus. The Bible indicates that Jesus sometimes selected routes that allowed Him to come into contact with specific people whom He was seeking, such as the Samaritan woman at the well. While the Bible is silent about whether such an intention preceded this encounter, it's certainly possible that this meeting was not an accidental one on Jesus' part.

Also notice that once in the vicinity of Bartimaeus, Jesus did not step up to him and start a conversation. Without the entourage and the commotion that accompanied Jesus, Bartimaeus might not have even known that Jesus was present.

Instead, Bartimaeus had to become aware of Jesus and persistently seek Him before the miracle could occur. Without sufficient faith in Jesus, Bartimaeus might not have been determined enough to gain Jesus' attention and ultimately to receive his sight. Jesus' words also suggest that Bartimaeus' faith may have contributed to his healing in ways beyond being merely persistent in attracting Jesus' attention.

Our actions are often necessary elements of God accomplishing something important. In this instance, Jesus always had the power to help Bartimaeus, but it took Bartimaeus first doing what he could before the miracle occurred.

After the miracle, Bartimaeus was immediately transformed into a follower of Jesus who traveled behind Him down the road, serving as a living testimony of Jesus being the Messiah. Certainly, that's one way to bring God glory.

Let's translate these elements into possible methods for learning your calling with regard to an excellent solution. Note that your calling doesn't depend on your personal view of your potential. Jesus often chooses those who might seem to others to be least able to fulfill His purposes. As Bartimaeus did, begin by drawing closer to God. It's easy to do. Keep in mind that Jesus is always present when two or more believers are together. In this manner, Jesus is always seeking to be with us when we are in the right company. We just need to speak to Him and listen to what He says. At the same time, the Holy Spirit is fully present inside each believer, guiding us and answering our questions. Jesus also taught us how to pray in His name to gain direct access to our Heavenly Father.

Since the Triune God can be brought completely into contact with us by praying in the name of Jesus with other believers, we should do so and ask our Heavenly Father; our Lord, Jesus Christ; and the Holy Spirit to reveal whether we should work on an excellent solution. In such prayers, keep in mind that we may have to be persistent, just as Bartimaeus was. Realize that any delays in response could reflect, among other things, imperfect timing on our part in asking the question, a desire on God's part to test our faith by seeing how steadfast we will be in seeking, and a need for us to develop in some way before we can become usefully involved with the excellent solution.

Why do I mention such delays? Let me describe some of the delays I've experienced with regard to excellent solutions, even though I appear to be someone who has been called to work on developing such solutions. I've been praying quite consistently since 1995 for God to increase my effectiveness so He could receive more glory. While He has certainly enabled me to increase such effectiveness, He didn't even hint at the possibility of anything approaching an excellent solution being possible until 2007. The reality of how to accomplish such a solution wasn't revealed to me until 2012. So if my experience is any indication of verifying a calling concerning an excellent solution, your timing may not be immediate or even very fast. Be patient. Keep praying in faith to learn whether He has such an intention, while being fully submitted to doing His will rather than yours.

While asking if you are so called, be sure to do so with as much faith as you can that God has reserved and can prepare you for an amazing role in developing and supplying an excellent solution. As Jesus indicated, it was Bartimaeus' faith that made him well. If your faith isn't sufficient, the calling may not be confirmed until you develop more faith.

How can you build enough faith? One way is to cleanse your heart of unrighteousness by repenting your sins as soon as they occur and asking God to help you to do better. In addition, I think it's essential to focus in your prayers on ways that the excellent solution will bring God glory and advance His Kingdom. The clearer such results are in your heart, mind, soul, and spirit as you pray, the easier it will be to have sufficient faith that He wants the result.

Having created me, God well knows that I lack imagination, and He accordingly helps me to appreciate His plans more fully by being quite direct in His communications. As one method of making His plans explicit, God has directed His Holy Spirit to dictate the words, phrases, and sentences for me to include in The 400 Year Project's books. Knowing that such information can also come from the enemy who is in the world, I always carefully check to see whether what I have heard is consistent with the Bible. My verifications so far have always been successful!

Other direct communications to me from God have included visions, dreams, and words spoken by strangers. The Bible also mentions instances of some people receiving messages spoken by angels. Perhaps you will receive such a message. Wouldn't that be awesome?

However, God may have granted you more imagination than He did me. Should such be the case, His confirmation of your calling to work on an excellent solution may be less direct than the words, visions, and dreams I have received. You may simply feel peaceful when you think about a specific excellent solution and role. Or, a Bible verse may verify to your heart and spirit that you should proceed.

Don't forget that God also uses His natural world to send messages. In my case, He knows that I love to watch cardinals. When He wants me to know that good things are coming, He sends a cardinal a day or two before. When He wants me to know that He's about to do something wonderful, I am overrun with cardinals. These timely messengers are always appearing, despite the rarity of seeing cardinals where I live during the coldest months and my not having provided any seed to attract them.

After you receive a confirmation of your calling, then determine what contributions you are called to make, our next subject. Once again, let me start with some Bible verses to set the stage:

For the gifts and the calling of God are irrevocable.

For as you were once disobedient to God, yet have now obtained mercy through their disobedience, even so these also have now been disobedient, that through the mercy shown you they also may obtain mercy. For God has committed them all to disobedience, that He might have mercy on all.

Oh, the depth of the riches both of the wisdom and knowledge of God! How unsearchable *are* His judgments and His ways past finding out!

"For who has known the mind of the LORD?
Or who has become His counselor?"
"Or who has first given to Him
And it shall be repaid to him?"

For of Him and through Him and to Him *are* all things, whom *be* glory forever.

— Romans 11:29-36 (NKJV)

If you have already received confirmation that you are called to work on an excellent solution, congratulations! If you have gained neither confirmation nor denial, keep asking. If God has said "no," ask what you should be doing to bring Him glory and to advance His Kingdom.

Let me describe another way to seek your calling: Consider the contributions you might make. Part One of *Excellent Solutions* describes how to set goals for an excellent solution. You could read and apply this information. If you do, keep plenty of notes about what happens that could be indications of God's purposes for you. You should include any feelings you experience while doing the tasks, Bible verses that make a special impression, people you meet who say things that impact you, and any noteworthy encounters with animals, plants, or any other objects that have a special meaning for you. Feel free to add to this list any other encounters and experiences that grab and hold your attention.

Lesson One in *Excellent Solutions* advocates choosing problems to solve that ignite your Godly passion, fire your curiosity, and warm your heart. Should God have chosen you to play a key role in developing an excellent solution, you may find at least one of such problems bursting into and remaining fixedly in the center of your consciousness.

If you don't have such an experience, perhaps you are called, instead, to be part of delivering an existing solution. Search around for opportunities to provide such solutions, including some role with The 400 Year Project. As you do, pray to be led to what you should be doing. As you consider what role to play, see if one of the activities compellingly attracts your attention. If you cannot find any solution-oriented activities that greatly inspire you, please send me an e-mail to donmitchell@fastforward400.com/. I'll be glad to suggest other solution-development or -provision activities for you to consider. Once you become aware of several such existing activities, you'll probably develop a sense of what God wants you to do for one or more of them.

Lesson Two in *Excellent Solutions* directs you to explore all dimensions of an excellent-solution's goals. If you are to lead a solution, the Holy Spirit will tell or show you what you need in regard to such goals. If you don't receive any directions or aren't making much progress on developing goals, test whether your calling is to explore excellent-solution opportunities with others. To do so, look for similarly called people and then work together. While exploring for and with others, your experiences will probably spotlight the role or roles that God has called you to play.

Lesson Three counsels you to consider the possibilities for providing multiple benefits. Similar to Lesson Two, you'll either make great headway on your own or you'll need to work with others. In the latter case, what happens after you connect with the others can indicate your role or roles.

Lesson Four in *Excellent Solutions* explains ways to start an unstoppable chain reaction. Since such an insight can only come from

God, receiving one is a clear indication that God wants you to lead an excellent solution. If you don't obtain such guidance, look for others to work with who have received all or some of such inspiration. In the course of working with these inspired individuals, you'll get a sense of your role or roles.

Lesson Five guides you to define benefits and who receives them. If you have emerged as either the leader or as one of the leaders through applying the first four lessons in *Excellent Solutions*, I am sure you'll find this task to be relatively straightforward by drawing on the Holy Spirit's guidance.

Lesson Six in *Excellent Solutions* focuses on sharing and explaining the solution's goals. To accomplish this work, even the anointed leader for developing an excellent solution will usually need to draw on the skills of those who are good at expressing and spreading ideas. Such collaborations should be naturally occurring at this stage, while assembling a team for further development of the solution.

While engaged in any of these collaborative roles, realize that you may also be called to be the excellent solution's leader in the sense of coordinating all the development and provision activities. God may have intended others to become involved as blessings for them, as well as you, through such collaborations.

Let's look next at preparing to make your contributions from the perspective of a proverb about how preparation is more important than strength:

The ants *are* a people not strong,
Yet they prepare their food in the summer;

— Proverbs 30:25 (NKJV)

In whatever role you play for an excellent solution, it's highly valuable to begin by identifying and eliminating any harmful beliefs and ways of thinking about what to do. Part Two of *Excellent Solutions* describes bad thinking habits that can affect the development or provision of an excellent solution, as well as ways to overcome such thinking. These lessons also reference other 400 Year Project books, such as *The 2,000 Percent Solution*, *The Irresistible Growth Enterprise*, and *2,000 Percent Living*, that contain helpful information for replacing harmful habits with highly fruitful ones. I'm sure you remember, as well, Lesson Six's information about stalls and stallbusting.

You will also need specific kinds of knowledge to increase effectiveness. For instance, your activities on behalf of an excellent solution that are intended to improve education will benefit from knowing ways to speed and enhance learning. Once involved in such a subject, you may also find it useful to add background knowledge, such as insights from psychology, to appreciate why certain results may have occurred during trials of various methods.

In other cases, you may find that *new* knowledge must be developed for the excellent solution to fulfill its potential. If no one else does so, you may have to be the one who fills the knowledge gap. I mention this possibility because I have had to do much learning about undocumented methods during The 400 Year Project. As you proceed, relax and smile. God will supply whatever you need.

In addition, stay in prayer to learn how God wants you to develop in spirituality, knowledge, specific skills, or otherwise. He will show you what to do and how to do so.

We consider next whether you are called to make a leadership contribution to an excellent solution from a perspective found in Nehemiah:

Then it was, when the wall was built and I had hung the doors, when the gatekeepers, the singers, and the Levites had been appointed, that I gave the charge of Jerusalem to my brother Hanani, and Hananiah the leader of the citadel, for he *was* a faithful man and feared God more than many.

— Nehemiah 7:1-2 (NKJV)

These two verses from Nehemiah are instructive for leading an excellent solution. While God called Nehemiah alone to lead repairing the wall around Jerusalem, as soon as the task was complete Nehemiah gave authority over Jerusalem to Hanani, his brother, and Hananiah, the leader of the citadel. Although you cannot know what plans God has for an excellent solution's leadership until He reveals His intentions to you, keep in mind the Bible's examples of the initiating leader being replaced or supplemented by sustaining leaders. For instance, even before Moses' disobedience angered God, Moses found himself overwhelmed by the number of disputes to be judged. After his father-in-law pointed out that he needed help, Moses appointed other judges to handle minor matters. Similarly, the apostles appointed some men of good reputation who were filled with the Holy Spirit and wisdom to serve tables at the common meals to free the apostles to spend more time on the pastoral work that God had called them to do.

Let me expand on these Biblical examples to describe what may occur with regard to the leadership of many excellent solutions. Notice that God didn't appoint any multiple leaders to share the overall authority during the development stages of important activities described in the Bible. One possible reason is that God didn't want His leaders to be distracted from Him by needing to pay a great deal of attention to one another. From these examples, I suspect that most excellent solutions will initially have one overall leader who identifies what needs to be done, finds people to perform the tasks, and coordinates all the activities during the solution's development.

In many cases, there will also be a need for leaders of specific developments that affect part of the solution, implementation activities, and ongoing improvements of an excellent solution. The need for such leaders will be especially evident where extensive experience and skill are required to obtain the best results.

In addition to such continuing leadership roles, I foresee that leaders will also be needed for less frequently occurring tasks. Think of such leadership roles as being similar to leading projects.

Where a task is quite large, further specialized leadership may be needed to apply specific skills or experiences in various locales. Such leaders will often need to operate with a high degree of autonomy.

In addition, every activity benefits from informal leaders who set good examples, encourage others, and provide comfort to those who need it. While informal leaders may not have titles and assignments indicating their roles, benefiting from their help may be more essential to success than what is gained from the activities of those with formal authority.

How will all of these roles be filled? At first, many people will play multiple roles. Any overburdened leaders should be quick to follow the examples of Moses and the apostles in granting authority to others who are willing and well equipped to lead. In addition, some people will just start doing whatever needs to be done, acting as leaders where no one has been designated. From such experiences, the full complement of leaders for an excellent solution will emerge through a combination of either demonstrating the anointing that God has placed on each life or the inspiration that God has sent to direct each person.

As you read about and considered all such roles, I suspect that some roles touched your heart, mind, soul, and spirit more than others. You probably thought, "That sounds like me," or "I'd love to do that." Let these reactions help you appreciate whether you have been called to be a leader of an excellent solution, as well as in what ways. Keep praying, and you will receive confirmation at some point for what you should begin doing. As you patiently pray in faith, keep in mind that your first assignment may be quite different from what you will eventually do for an excellent solution. Like the faithful servants described in the parables of the minas and talents, God may intend for the excellent solution to first develop you to play a bigger role in His plans.

In the last section of this lesson, we consider what leadership roles you are called to perform from the perspective of Jesus:

"So the last will be first, and the first last.
For many are called, but few chosen."

— Matthew 20:16 (NKJV)

In the parable of the vineyard workers, Jesus carefully explained that the rewards for serving God would be exactly whatever God had promised, no more and no less. The amount of work done or the duration of that work wouldn't affect the rewards. As in many of His teachings, Jesus made it clear that those who seek precedence for some personal reason aren't doing what's wanted or needed. Christians should, instead, focus on serving others in selfless ways. Jesus set the example in this regard by sacrificing His life so we might have access to Salvation, as well as by washing His disciples' feet, including the feet of Judas Iscariot who betrayed Him, at the Last Supper. Although many are called by God to act in such a way, few will pass the tests that involve putting others first.

Keep these lessons in mind as you consider what you have been called to do for an excellent solution. You may well have been called to a leadership position. However, you may still have to be chosen to fulfill such a position based on how faithfully you discharge the trust God has placed in you. You may also have lessons to learn before He will find you ready to lead.

Although God has often placed me in leadership positions of great responsibility, my first jobs working outside of my family's gardening business involved lots of heavy lifting and toilet cleaning. Such work isn't what some Harvard undergraduates (which I was at the time) would have expected to be doing during their summer vacations. However, I learned important lessons: Physical labor is extremely demanding and doing dirty jobs with a smile requires having spiritual peace. Similarly, when I was in my early sixties, my first volunteer job at a church I attended involved moving the furniture to set up the service ... and cleaning the toilets. I found both tasks to be just as physically demanding and spiritually educational as I did when I was 18. While leading during the intervening years, I was often reminded that doing whatever it takes to get the right result often falls on the leader's action agenda. I cannot count the number of times while serving as a leader that I've chosen to do tasks that were extremely menial or unpleasant solely because it wouldn't have been right to ask anyone else to undertake the work. I'm glad God prepared me well in advance for what was going to be required.

Similarly, your preparations for excellent-solution leadership in any one of the possible roles may not involve anything that looks like leadership. For instance, in the decades before The 400 Year Project began, I often gathered and analyzed data while unsuccessfully seeking answers to questions that God had placed in my heart. In every case, I couldn't figure out the answer and had to admit to God that the task was beyond what I could do. God seems to like it when I admit such failures. He always comes along later and shows me the answer from His perspective. I am always astonished by how far away I have been from ever reaching the solution. You may well be tested in the same ways. Be prepared to act in faith, knowing that God will keep His promises and help you.

So even if no immediate leadership opportunity appears, but you feel called to lead, contribute in whatever ways anyone will let you. Chances are that you will have just put a foot on the first step of a ladder that could take you to one of several leadership roles that God wants you to play.

Your Lesson Twenty Assignments

1. Is God calling you to play a role in preparing or providing an excellent solution?

2. If you are so called, what contributions has He planned for you to make?

3. What preparations should you make to become a more fruitful contributor?

4. Are you called to be a leader of an excellent solution?

5. What leadership role(s) are you called to perform?

Lesson Twenty-One

Master Processes

Listen, for I will speak of excellent things,
And from the opening of my lips
will come *right things;*
For my mouth will speak truth; ....

Proverbs 8:6-7 (NKJV)

If you have been chosen to develop an excellent solution, you should first set and communicate your goals and also eliminate or overcome any bad thinking habits (what I call "stalls") for you and your organization before you start creating such a solution. I appreciate that you may not yet feel ready, and I humbly ask that you trust me on this point for just a bit.

To understand your readiness, let me begin by describing some things about excellent solutions that you may not know. Many challenging activities such as composing operas, developing new sports techniques, writing novels, and finding subatomic particles can take quite a few years to accomplish and require special talents. By contrast, although the results of the very first excellent solution you complete will greatly exceed the current world's record for that particular kind of performance, the time involved to do so will be reasonable, and you probably won't need any special talent.

Do you feel a little better prepared? You may still have a question or two. Why will you do so well by applying less time, resources, and effort than are required to make many less significant accomplishments? Your performance will benefit from following a path that's vastly shorter, faster, and easier to use than the ones usually taken for providing more of the benefits you seek.

A race where advantages and disadvantages are applied unequally among competitors (such as by the handicap system applied in horse racing) is one way that I think about understanding the differences between what you will be doing and how others usually seek to increase such benefits. Imagine that you will be racing against millions of people who will have substantial disadvantages, and the first person to cross the finish line will win an astonishingly desirable prize. Because you care about the results, you are determined to have the victory.

The source of competitors' disadvantages is that each person chooses his or her own route. In this race most people will select a difficult route that is 12,000 miles long while looking for and obtaining assistance from few other people.

The race rules prohibit using mechanically or electronically enhanced means. Most people will use some combination of walking, running, swimming, paddling canoes, and riding horses. Even if someone is quite athletic and tireless, it's going to take a long time to reach the finish line.

Next, imagine that the rules also permit setting your own starting point. Due to understanding more than all others do about what needs to be done during the race, the course you choose requires traveling only a fraction of an inch to reach the finish line and you will draw on the assistance of many more people than the number of people competing against you.

Who do you think will cross the finish line first?

I make this comparison because I want you to appreciate that excellent-solution breakthroughs come from using the method ... rather than from having greater talent and more extensive training, practice, and experience. Even an incredibly inefficient person who uses such a vastly superior method will accomplish much more than the top performer who applies an obsolete, much less effective method over a vastly longer course.

To make the same contrast between methods in another way, it's as if those using the excellent-solution method are passengers on a supersonic jet while the most able competitors are crawling on their hands and knees over rocky ground.

By now, you are probably quite interested in learning about how such a superior method might work. Let me introduce you to the *steps in the first of two excellent-solution processes.*

In *Step One*, you will explore what is darkest, most hidden, and most misunderstood about supplying and making good use of the benefits you want to greatly increase. You will begin by talking to and learning from those who are feeling the most hopeless about providing or receiving more benefits. You'll then explore the murky places they point to, find opportunities there for hope, and gain understanding concerning the rampant discouragement. Since few have looked deeply into these disturbing circumstances to learn how to either change or to turn the circumstances into advantages, you are certain to find lots of opportunities within the usually avoided areas.

A useful Biblical example of Step One is found in Joseph's faithfulness to living a righteous life. Despite having done the right thing by fleeing from temptation to commit sexual sin while a slave in Egypt, Joseph was imprisoned after being falsely accused by his master's wife. While he was incarcerated, it looked to many people as if Joseph's prospects were unavoidably poor: After many years, he might be eventually restored to serving someone else outside the prison as a slave.

However, during these dark days Joseph strengthened his character and increased his connection to God. Because of these changes, God blessed Joseph in ways that led Pharaoh to release him from prison and make Joseph his second in command over Egypt, then the most powerful nation on Earth. As this example shows, with God's help prospects are never poor, no matter how dark and desperate they might seem from a human perspective!

In *Step Two*, you'll enlist free and low-cost help from as many idea developers as possible to find and take advantage of the best ways to combine useful practices to change and make better use of the disturbing circumstances. Conducting a series of sequential global online contests will rapidly develop and connect many complementary solutions to form part of the process you'll apply to make a productivity breakthrough in providing benefits. To date, no one has fully harnessed the potential of such contests to make excellent solutions.

A Biblical example for this step is found in Exodus. Just before leaving Egypt, God directed the children of Israel to ask their neighbors for gifts of gold, silver, and clothing. Entirely due to God's favor, the Egyptians generously and gladly gave this precious booty. Thus, one nation freely emptied itself of its most valuable resources to enrich God's people. Because God owns everything on Earth, there's no limit to what His bounty can provide or from where it might come.

Step Three shows you how to plant highly fruitful seeds in the form of inspirational stories that contain the potential to yield huge harvests of benefits. Planting the seeds will lead many other people to also plant these seeds. Such an expansion will occur as a result of looking for, improving upon, and sharing powerful stories that teach and inspire people to do what needs to be done for producing and delivering many more highly fruitful benefits.

Jesus told many parables about seeds and their potential to improve lives that influenced His disciples to take richly fruitful actions. In a parable about the importance of sharing the Gospel and their own testimonies, Jesus indicated that some people would help create spiritual harvests of saved souls that were 30, 60, or 100 times greater than what they sowed. Jesus appears to have been talking about how one person's witnessing can help lead many other people to repent their sins and gain Salvation. The newly saved people, in turn, can share the Word and their testimonies in similar fashion, multiplying the initial witness's fruitfulness. This lesson about the value of sharing personal testimonies and describing the life of Jesus continues to teach and encourage witnessing today that contributes to such expanded fruitfulness. For instance, imagine if the first person saved turns out to become a great and active witness who helps lead millions to Salvation. Just think of that!

While applying *Step Four*, you will help increase the individual goals, confidence, and effectiveness of those who provide and use the excellent-solution benefits so that the productivity of whatever inputs they employ is greatly multiplied.

On two occasions, Jesus spoke to thousands of hungry people where there was little food readily available. He graciously multiplied the little food there was until all were abundantly fed. Even the leftovers greatly exceeded the original amount He multiplied. These examples helped the apostles realize that they could successfully take the Gospel message to the whole world, even if they started with a handful of people and few or no physical resources. The apostles gained faith that God would meet their needs while they were engaged in serving Him to help increase the number of believers. Based on such confidence, witnessing helped expand Christianity from being practiced by only about 100 people to becoming the dominant religious belief in Western civilization.

Step Five explains how to reach out to people at risk during the times when they feel the most vulnerable. Doing so will transform those who are helped in awe-inspiring ways, establishing or restoring their faith and confidence, as well as filling those who serve them with great joy and increasing their desires to help.

In a number of cases, Jesus and the apostles met people with such severe infirmities and sicknesses that the afflicted had given up hope of ever experiencing a desirable life. When the afflicted were healed, the effects on those who observed or heard about the miracles were almost as great as they were on the healed people. Thus, faith and taking appropriate actions were encouraged for one and all.

Step Six calls for establishing and increasing always-available resources that can be used wherever they are needed by anyone. You can think of such capabilities as being like a combination of the dispatch centers that take emergency calls and the first responders who are dispatched to assist with medical care, dangerous conditions, firefighting, and protection from criminals.

Jesus was wonderfully capable of identifying such extreme needs and arriving just in time to meet them. I particularly remember the two times when He appeared and provided great catches of fish. On another occasion, He sent Peter to catch a fish, promising that he would find a coin in the fish that would pay Peter's and His Temple taxes. Jesus' timing and provision were sometimes perfect for reasons other than speed, such as when everyone had given up hope for Lazarus because he had been dead in his tomb for four days, yet Jesus resurrected him.

Step Seven directs you to prepare more seed sowers of the fruitful methods you've identified. Much as Christianity originally expanded due, in part, to more people learning how to be missionaries and going where no one knew about the Gospel, your excellent solution needs people who well understand its ins and outs to explain and prepare others to use more advanced versions of the solution's most fruitful activities. Think of these people you will prepare as being like those who train the trainers who teach their own organizations a new practice. For the most substantial and widespread excellent solutions, a core of thousands of such trainers of trainers will be needed.

In the book of Acts and the New Testament's Pauline letters, there are many examples of the important roles played by witnesses, evangelists, missionaries, church planters, and pastors of newly established congregations to ensure that sound doctrine and practices were in place so that unified, spiritual progress ensued. This attentiveness was important for avoiding and overcoming any divisions among fellow believers.

When applying *Step Eight*, you will amplify the most helpful information about what you have discovered so that its use will spread to many more people. Think of this step as being like putting a loudspeaker next to each person on Earth and sending useful messages through the loudspeakers that describe exactly what that person needs to do next to apply the most beneficial aspects of the excellent solution.

From the Bible, I'm reminded of Jesus promising the baptism and indwelling of the Holy Spirit as the preferred way to provide timely information and encouragement for directing the lives of all believers. At the time of His promise, Jesus noted that the effect of this provision would be greater than what Jesus Himself could provide if He remained in person with the apostles.

If you would like to learn about these steps in more detail, they are spelled out in Part Three of *Excellent Solutions*.

Instead of being satisfied with what you now know and are doing, I strongly urge you to learn *a second method for developing and establishing excellent solutions.* I believe this added knowledge will be immensely valuable to you ... even if you never apply the second method.

Why? Understanding of any method is much improved by being able to compare it to a different one designed to be used for the same purpose. While working one day with a student who was developing a method for identification, I saw an example of how valuable comparisons can be for improving understanding. The student was quite puzzled about how to begin identifying differences until I suggested that he assemble a number of the objects. As he inspected and interacted with the objects, he began to note many distinctions among them. Through drawing on these observations, he began to list many methods for identifying something through comparing it to something else that had already been identified. He commented at the end of the process about how much comparisons had helped him.

Hopefully, one benefit for you from studying the second method will be to highlight differences in the two methods that will make each one clearer to you. Consequently, you will be more likely to choose and better apply the more appropriate method for the excellent solution that you intend to establish.

I also believe that some people will find the second method easier to understand and apply than the first one. For example, the second process places fewer burdens on the excellent-solution developer. Additionally, the second method is more similar to the 2,000 percent solution process that many readers have already studied and employed. Because of this similarity, I had originally planned to include only this method in *Excellent Solutions*. Then, of course, the Holy Spirit intervened on May 1, 2013, by revealing to me the first astonishingly effective method. Furthermore, the second method contains elements that will remind you of some parts of the first method. Much in the way that the Prophet Elisha was blessed to receive a double portion of the Prophet Elijah's spirit when Elijah was taken to heaven by a fiery chariot (2 Kings 2, NKJV), you have been doubly blessed by having the potential to accomplish more than twice as much with excellent solutions by using both of these methods to supply different benefits for which each method is especially well suited.

In *Step One of the second method*, you will define more measurements of the solution's benefits. You may be wondering how this step is different from defining benefits and who would receive them. Think of Step One for this second method as more closely examining benefits to see more clearly what aspects of supplying and using the benefits should be expanded.

As further explanation, consider Matthew 6:19-21 (NKJV) where Jesus advised His believers to focus on laying up eternal treasures in heaven rather than physical treasures on Earth where decay, rust, and thieves can take away what has been earned. He pointed out that a key benefit from focusing on creating eternal treasures is keeping a person's heart concentrated on heaven, where such treasure is found. Similarly, more and better benefit measurements will focus greater attention on the most important aspects of developing and implementing an excellent solution.

Step Two calls for considering ideal-practice characteristics. Ideal practices are the most productive ways that anyone could expect to accomplish important tasks in the next five years by using whatever technology and knowledge will be available. In previous 400 Year Project books about the 2,000 percent solution process, Carol Coles and I outline many examples of such practices for individuals, as well as organizations. We also analyze the examples to define practices that routinely provide near-perfect performance, while requiring few resources. Some of that information can be found in Lesson Seven.

Because most people are quite aware of their own imperfections and faults, they tend to have low opinions of themselves and to believe that they and others can accomplish relatively little. Jesus, explained, however, in Matthew 5:48 (NKJV) that He sees us differently, as having perfect potential: "Therefore you shall be perfect, just as your Father in heaven is perfect."

Step Three shows how to imagine solutions that provide the required level of benefits through applying unlimited resources. You may be wondering why finding such solutions can be helpful for an excellent solution. Let me explain. This step enables some people to overcome their initial disbelief that such a benefit expansion could be accomplished in any way, even before they consider the potential challenges of doing so with no more time, resources, and effort. Successfully tackling the opportunity without resource constraints has repeatedly been shown to be a good way of removing mental barriers that can limit useful thinking.

Let me remind you of what God said in Isaiah 55:9 (NKJV) about gaining greater wisdom:

"For *as* the heavens are higher than the earth,
So are My ways higher than your ways,
And My thoughts than your thoughts."

Taking a bigger perspective of what might be accomplished allows us to draw a bit closer to God's perfect perspective concerning what can be done with His help.

During *Step Four*, you will improve on what was learned in Step Three by finding more effective ways to provide and use vastly increased benefits. You will ask as many people as possible to participate in making improvements to the "best" solution that utilizes unlimited resources for supplying and using the intended benefits. Naturally, many of such Step-Four improvements will reduce the required resources. In other cases, however, better benefits may be identified. While the work involved in the second method's Step Four might remind you of the first method's Step Two, this Step Four differs by just working to enhance one way of creating abundant benefits, making it easier to identify improvements.

For conducting such an activity I'm reminded of the prayer to God in Isaiah 25:6 (NKJV) for the Lord to provide abundantly for His people. In the case of Step Four, God will direct His people to identify astounding ways to provide virtually unlimited benefits at little cost and with minimal effort. Locating such improvements will be aided by Internet sharing of the "best" solutions so far and encouraging incremental improvements to these solutions. Seeking and using the improvements have a number of similarities to the online contests used for the first method.

Step Five of the second method describes testing the most promising aspects of the unlimited-resource solutions that employ the fewest resources. While many ideas look good on paper, most of them don't work nearly as well in practice. Testing is by far the best way to differentiate what will be sufficient from what only appears to be able to get the job done.

In this regard I'm reminded of the exhortations by the Apostle Paul in 1 Thessalonians 5:16-21 (NKJV):

> Rejoice always, pray without ceasing, in everything give thanks; for this is the will of God in Christ Jesus for you. Do not quench the Spirit. Do not despise prophecies. Test all things; hold fast what is good.

Note that only after also testing does Paul say to hold fast to what is good, that which survives the testing. We should do likewise.

Step Six seeks further advances in effectiveness. Improvements are again widely sought, this time for just the solutions with the most successful tests. People who could wrangle over theories for years without necessarily finding any better answers can easily pick apart a tested theory to point out improvements in applying it and what other theories should also be applied. The second method makes unprecedented use of crowdsourcing's potential. I can hardly wait to see the results!

You can think of this step as being like reapplying Paul's exhortation to test in 1 Thessalonians 5:16-21 (NKJV). We will hold fast to what worked well in the initial tests and then seek even better approaches to test. The result will enable us to hold fast to even more of what is revealed to be good by the testing.

During *Step Seven*, the best of the improvement ideas from Step Six's round of enhancements will be tested. In this regard, Step Seven is similar to Step Five. However, Step Seven differs from Step Five by publicizing and encouraging others to duplicate the best results from the second-round tests. By also encouraging others to conduct such advanced tests, it's highly likely that even better solutions will emerge. Because the methods that are being tested at this point have already been shown to be highly effective, it's important to begin using such solutions. In particular, some environments or applications may enable higher effectiveness from a method, so it makes sense for any full-fledged excellent solutions to be immediately put in place by those who first sense such high-potential opportunities.

This step reminds me of the description in Joshua 6:27 (NKJV) of Joshua's success as a result of God's support. At this point in an excellent solution's development, it will be clear to most people that the Lord's hand is with the solution, and intense interest will develop in what's going on, encouraging people to make further fruitful innovations and provide more benefits to those who need them.

In *Step Eight*, a solution is fully implemented as soon as it has been proven capable of providing at least the equivalent of ten complementary 2,000 percent solutions for increasing the productivity of delivering benefits relative to the present amount of time, resources, and effort. When you reach that point, tell the world what you are doing, enlist whatever help you require, and engage in what tests show will work best. Some of the implementation steps for the first excellent-solution method may be applicable here. Feel free to draw on them.

Taking this step reminds me of the Apostle Paul's letter to Philemon (Philemon 1:21, NKJV), in which Paul begged his friend to forgive Onesimus and to charge that erring man's faults to Paul. When the time is right from God's perspective and the proper appeal is made based on a firm and Godly foundation, we should expect that more will be accomplished through an excellent solution than the minimum that we seek.

Step Nine might feel a bit like attending a reunion to those who have been learning and applying the many solution methods developed since 1998 by The 400 Year Project. This step calls for repeating the method's first eight steps. You might think that such a direction is overkill. Let me beg your pardon and politely disagree. Remember that locating even minor improvements during a repetition of the process will release trillions of times more benefits. Surely that's worth a little more time and effort!

This step reminds me of some of my favorite Bible verses, where we are directed to rejoice in all circumstances:

Rejoice in the Lord always. Again I will say, rejoice! Let your gentleness be known to all men. The Lord *is* at hand. Be anxious for nothing, but in everything by prayer and supplication, with thanksgiving, let your requests be made known to God; and the peace of God, which surpasses all understanding, will guard your hearts and minds through Christ Jesus. (Philippians 4:4-7, NKJV)

God promised to provide for the needs of His children, even before developing any excellent solutions. What an extra reason to rejoice that He is willing to stoop to allow us to play such active roles through excellent solutions to make the kind of provision He wants for His Kingdom. Praise God always!

While no one outside of heaven can know why God has chosen to involve us in His spectacular provisions through excellent solutions, I can think of one possibility for you to consider: We live in an age when people are interested in gaining new knowledge and skills through working cooperatively with many others. For those who are drawn away from Him by such pursuits, what would be more natural than that He would open a door that would prove irresistible to them that would reveal more of His glory than they could perceive in any other way? Who knows if that's the right reason? I don't. We'll find out in God's own good time, I'm sure.

If you would like to learn about these second-method steps in more detail, they are spelled out in Part Four of *Excellent Solutions*.

Lesson Twenty-One Assignments

1. Which aspects of each excellent-solution method do you like best?

2. How does each excellent-solution method help you to better understand the other one?

3. How would your role differ in one method compared to the other?

4. Do you feel called to use one method more than the other?

5. What will you do first to implement that method?

Lesson Twenty-Two

Benefit Dimensions

"My grace is sufficient for you,
for My strength is made perfect in weakness."
Therefore most gladly I will rather boast in my infirmities,
that the power of Christ may rest upon me.
Therefore I take pleasure in infirmities, in reproaches,
in needs, in persecutions, in distresses, for Christ's sake.
For when I am weak, then I am strong.

— 2 Corinthians 12:9-10 (NKJV)

As these verses describe, God can make up for any weakness we have. However, He often requires that we first do our part, limited as it usually is. Our weaknesses show up in their potentially most harmful form when we refuse to seek providing enough kinds and quantities of benefits. Enshrine any shortcomings in these regards in goals, and the potential fruitfulness can be decimated. In this lesson, we consider how to be sure that enough benefit dimensions are considered during the goal-setting process. Be sure to stay in prayer to seek Heavenly guidance as you do.

Much like the way a young child exploring a toy chest picks a favorite toy and plays with it, ignoring all else that is around, we can be equally quick to think about and to work on only one of many potentially valuable dimensions for solving a problem. Let me give you an example.

Let's assume that you want to help youngsters read better. In thinking about possible goals for an excellent solution in this regard, you might choose to improve reading speed and how well youngsters remember what they read. Since there are standard tests available to measure both kinds of performance, you might set goals related to such tests that call for all youngsters being able to read at least X words per minute and to be able to recall Y percent of what was just read. Does that kind of goal setting make sense? Sure it does. In fact, many school systems and governments have established similar goals.

Are you ready now to start thinking about how to accomplish these goals? Not so fast.

Do you care how long a youngster can recall what is read? Sure you do. If you don't properly define the right length of recall in your goal, you may create a less helpful solution than would best serve your intention to increase reading benefits.

Okay, let's assume you want youngsters to be able to recall C percent of what was read six months later. Is that long enough when it comes to really important information, such as what is read in the Bible about the Ten Commandments? Well, maybe you decide that youngsters should have different recollection goals for various types of information. So you make such adjustments.

Are you feeling happier now? Probably not. But you could be feeling that you have done a better job of goal setting, which is certainly true.

Wait just a minute. There's more to consider. If youngsters don't like to read, it may not matter how well they can do so and recall what was read for a test. Perhaps it would be a good idea to have a goal for how much reading youngsters do. Hmm. That does sound like a good idea, doesn't it?

Does it matter what they read? Sure it does! Going through 700 juvenile novels about forming friendships or winning athletic contests may not bring sufficient knowledge to prepare someone to be an effective adult. Defining helpful reading material during goal setting will keep you busy for some time, I'm sure.

In thinking about useful knowledge, have you thought about the availability of helpful reading material that furnishes such knowledge? Perhaps not. In well-educated households where the adults are interested in assisting children to acquire knowledge, there are usually many fine resources and more can be either purchased or borrowed from a local library. In other homes, such materials may be absent and access to alternative sources may also be limited. Do you need goals in terms of reading material availability? Sure you do.

Well, do you also want young readers to be able to find whatever helpful information they need? If so, you need to add some goals for learning how to find the best reading material.

Does it matter to you whether young readers will ever use what they learn? Umm. That hasn't come up yet, has it? Perhaps you need some goals for usage, as well.

If you make goals for what is read and using it that apply to all youngsters, how well will those goals work for people with different interests? Do budding violinists need to do a certain amount of reading about vehicle mechanics? Some learning might not hurt, but how much is right? What do those who like to tinker with cars need to know about playing violins? Perhaps not much. All the preceding goals may need to be adjusted to reflect a given youngster's interests.

How far into the future should these goals reach? I've seen surveys indicating that the average American adult reads just a single nonfiction book a year. That book had better be a pretty terrific one, or little learning will occur. Maybe the goals should be connected to producing the right amount of lifelong reading and learning. Otherwise, upgrading reading skills may not yield sufficient benefits.

Some people find it tough to learn in classroom settings, and many more can little afford more education beyond what's free or low cost. Should there be different reading goals for these people so that they can compensate, in part, by learning on their own for what they won't gain from formal education? Perhaps that adjustment would be worthwhile.

Now, let's think about how rapidly knowledge is advancing. If I perfectly remembered everything I learned in elementary and junior high school but added no knowledge after that, I would be in sad shape. Why? Much of that "knowledge" turned out to be wrong. In addition, recently developed knowledge is more complete and actionable. So there's a need, as well, to know when and how to update what was learned. What should these goals be?

So far, we've focused on upgrading the bottom tier of young readers. Shouldn't there also be goals for upgrading readers from whatever level of skill they already have? After all, enhancing skill and usage for average and outstanding readers may bring different benefits for society than from only helping weak readers become more adequate.

Realize, too, that between a quarter and a third of American adults don't have adequate reading skills but are good at pretending that they do. Most of these adults need encouragement to get help, careful diagnosis of why they read poorly, and individualized instruction to improve. Almost none of these people are studying now in any school. What goals are needed for these adults?

So far, we've emphasized skills, access, interest, relevance, and helpfulness. But that's not all of what's involved with gaining benefits from reading. Many people have emotional difficulties made worse by reading problems, such as low self-esteem and insufficient confidence to engage in activities that would benefit many people. What goals are needed for such improvements?

To this point, we've focused on the individual reader. An individual's reading skills also affect those who come into contact with him or her. What should goals be for effects on these other people? Goals should probably consider at least family members, coworkers, friends, neighbors, those who are affected by a person's work and personal activities, and casual contacts.

Do you realize that parents' and guardians' reading practices can have a large influence on children? What should goals be for the reading examples, activities, and support that parents, guardians, grandparents, aunts, and uncles provide for children? What needs to be improved for the most benefit to be gained by today's children as well as by future generations?

Having focused on readers, those who affect them, and people they affect, we may have missed setting goals for technology. For instance, one way to make reading easier and more effective is by providing materials in formats that more people can quickly understand, use, and remember. We live in an age when new types of formatting are starting to occur that improve reading and comprehension, and we may not be far from the potential to accomplish more. In addition, how can technology be helpful for improving long-term recollection of or access to key information?

Readers are also only one group involved in reading, remembering, and applying information. What about writers? Rarely does improving reader benefits significantly enhance the evaluation or compensation of authors. Most writers are only held to the standard of writing correctly in terms of grammar and punctuation. Commercially, they are affected by how many people spend money to access their writing ... whether or not anyone ever actually reads or applies it. Clearly, if writers produced texts that were much more appealing, easier to understand, and more helpful, the benefits gained from applying existing reading and recollection skills would be greatly increased. What goals should be applied for upgrading writers' skills and encouragement to be more helpful to readers?

Surely, you also remember the old saying: "A picture is worth a thousand words." Well-illustrated writing can convey much more information and reduce the time and effort required to learn. In other cases, drawings, illustrations, plans, and photographs can be vastly superior as stand-alone resources for appreciating and using information. And videos can often provide even more benefit. So, do we need goals also for creating and using purely visual information?

Sure we do, if we are interested in enhancing what youngsters can learn and accomplish, rather than just how well they can read and remember.

In these goal discussions, we've mostly emphasized going from one level of accomplishment to a higher one. While it's certainly good to encourage improvement, how do we know how much improvement is enough? Perhaps we should also be measuring performance goals compared to the potential for what can be accomplished, rather than by just improving performance from today's level. What role should the individual's desire to accomplish more play in setting these goals?

While I could certainly continue exploring how to set goals for improving reading, I'm sure you get the point: It's difficult to set the right kind of goals, even for an activity for which you have much knowledge and personal experience.

I'm sure you also noticed from this discussion of reading goals that a more careful investigation of what goals to set can greatly expand the potential benefits a solution provides. Such investigation

- opens your mind to the possibility that your initial focus is incomplete or mistaken.
- expands your perceptions of what the most important issues are.
- encourages you to be more thorough in determining what goals to set.
- helps lead your thinking toward more valuable gains.
- adds other potential beneficiaries for consideration.
- increases your openness to looking for possible breakthrough solutions.
- directs your thinking towards other resources that could help.

As a substitute for trying to identify all such goal-setting issues solely through your own efforts, let me offer a template for more systematically exploring and considering possible goal dimensions. If you are familiar with *The Ultimate Competitive Advantage*, you'll recognize these perspectives as part of what defines a business model. If you would like to learn more about how to use these perspectives for goal setting, you may find that book to be a helpful resource. The goal-setting template dimensions are:

- *Who* is and can be affected, and in what ways?
- *What* is done differently by each participant?
- *When* is something done and when do the results from these actions occur?
- *Why* are certain benefits sought and given approaches applied?
- *Where* are the actions taken, do their effects occur, and are their results felt?
- *How* are beneficial, neutral, and harmful results provided and received?
- *How much* help is provided and with what kinds and quantities of resources?

Let's look at each of these dimensions, beginning with *who is and can be affected, and in what ways*. It is easy to underestimate how many people are substantially affected by a problem you want to address with an excellent solution. Typically, someone's mind is drawn first to those who are most vulnerable and visible, such as youngsters who struggle with reading. Beginning with these people is a perfectly fine place to start. Just don't stop there.

I find it easiest to move next to thinking about others who may also gain direct benefits from making improvements. After noticing young readers who struggle with reading, it's natural to also think of those adults who have the same problem.

Given that your mind may have been first drawn to those who are vulnerable, be sure to also consider those who are in average and superior circumstances, or who are already performing at higher levels. It may be worthwhile to enhance their circumstances, skills, or opportunities. In many cases, considering such a wider body of potential beneficiaries is essential to finding an excellent solution with virtually universal effects, such as the 2,000 percent solution process does for shaping breakthroughs that use the same or less time, resources, and effort. I find it easiest to think next about those who are personally connected to the people most directly affected by the problems that have been identified so far. These personally connected individuals may include family, friends, neighbors, those who worship together, and acquaintances.

Considering these people always leads me to think about future generations, especially those who won't be born for some time. In considering the future perspective, the size of potential benefits can often be enormous. After thinking about creating the most benefits for future beneficiaries, my mind always shifts about what's most important to emphasize in goal setting.

Many people have jobs, and it's usually easy to think about those who are affected by their work such as customers, end users, beneficiaries, colleagues, suppliers, partners, distributors, investors, lenders, and the communities in which the organization operates.

It's also good to think about whomever else might play an important role in accomplishing more. In our discussion of young readers, book authors appeared to be important. Although we didn't discuss them, teachers are another influential group. More reading improvements would occur if teachers knew more about identifying ways a reader could improve and received more training and resources for how to help. Those who provide visual resources in articles, books, or online, such as photographs, diagrams, and videos, are also important for accomplishing more, both for readers and for teachers.

From there, it's important to let your mind drift a little bit wider to think about any other possible large categories of people who are helped or hurt by what you've been considering as a problem. For instance, poor reading, limited understanding, and incomplete recall can contribute to expensive errors that harm patients, create difficulties in finding and holding jobs, lead some people to commit crimes that affect their victims, and contribute to driving accidents from misunderstanding what should be done (such as an illiterate driver hitting a well-marked, low overpass with a truck). Seeing the costs and potential benefits of reducing these effects can also be helpful for identifying more broadly aimed excellent solutions.

I also encourage people to circle back several times to review the list of who is affected before moving forward into actual goal setting. You'll be amazed by how many other types of affected individuals will eventually occur to you.

Let's now describe how to consider *what is done by all partici-pants*. Expanding what you know about what all participants do is all to the good. Unless you are exceptionally well informed, you will discover lots of important information. Take whatever time you need to check the accuracy of what you believe you know, identify what you don't know, consider what can be easily learned, and gain valuable knowledge in cost- and time-effective ways.

Let's continue with the reading example. Chances are that you don't know much more about how youngsters learn to read than how you, the friends of your youth, your siblings, and your children (and possibly a few of your nieces and nephews) learned. Unless you are quite young, such information is probably dated and may not be very relevant except for people your own age and the ages of young people you had a chance to observe while they learned to read.

In any case, many different learning methods have been used in recent decades, and you need to know at least a little about the most important aspects of the major, as well as the most and least effec-tive, ones. You should also learn about research in how young and older readers have acquired and are acquiring skill in applying what they have read.

You should also study the methods used to help those who have difficulty benefiting from the most often used teaching methods. In some aspects of reading, remembering, and applying information, there may be no formal process to observe, such as if you were look-ing at reducing time spent preparing tax returns. In such instances, you'll need to access studies done with statistically adequate samples of appropriate populations or to conduct your own surveys to learn how individuals describe what they do.

As you can imagine from the prior two paragraphs, learning what is done by all participants can be a much bigger effort than merely defining who is and can be affected and in what ways. Rejoice in this greater data-gathering task. While acquiring this information, you are likely to find bits of data that will help lead you to an excellent solution.

Let me lay out the process for learning what is being done by all participants. Start with your list of "who is and can be affected" and make notes for each category of persons concerning what you believe is being done or has been done by the people in the category, as well as those who affect people in each category. Concerning young people who are learning to read, your list of those who affect such youngsters would include parents and guardians, other family members, teachers, the youngsters' friends, those who read aloud with children, people who advise about and provide learning resources (such as audio recordings of phonetic sounds, *Sesame Street* episodes about letters, and flash cards), authors, and illustrators.

Each category of those who affect the learning readers should be described for what they do or have done. Look for research that spells out what those practices have been and are today, and especially seek sources that include good measurements. If you have trouble locating comprehensive, quantitative sources, find often-quoted authorities. Then, look at their articles and books. If what you locate still doesn't provide what you need, contact those authorities for help. If you aren't able to reach them or don't receive the assistance you need for any reason, seek, instead, guidance from editors of the most authoritative journals and periodicals. Be sure to consider also any government studies of these issues. Officials responsible for such work are usually happy to help, and they can often provide unpublished details that shed more light than what has been published.

If searches for comprehensive sources are fruitless, begin looking for more narrowly focused resources that describe just certain aspects of what some people do with some of the affected. If you find major gaps not filled by such narrower resources, you'll need to conduct surveys.

Chances are that designing and fielding surveys aren't among your skills. Rather than master the task on your own, look for help. If you can afford it, naturally you can hire an appropriately experienced professional to assist you. In many cases, a professor will be less expensive than the commercial equivalent and will often provide a superior result. If you have a tight budget, see if a local university has a graduate student who needs financing for similar work and offer to pay for some of the survey expenses.

If conducting a survey turns out to be a dead end, instead conduct individual interviews with authorities who should have lots of observational experience to share. The sum of such responses won't be entirely accurate, but you will succeed in going well beyond what you could learn on your own.

I also suggest that you take time to observe some of the more common and most effective current practices and to ask those involved about what they are experiencing. Such observations and discussions will flesh out the more abstract information provided by written materials, studies, surveys, and interviews. You may also gain insights that direct you to sources that you otherwise would have missed.

As you look for such information about what is done and experienced, be sure to cast your net widely enough to find valuable sources that you might not have previously encountered. For example, much has been learned in recent years about how people read through various kinds of brain scans. So realize that it is not just reading specialists and teachers who will have useful information about this subject.

I think that's enough information for you to understand a general approach for significant learning about what is done by all participants. Let's shift now to considering *when something is done and when the results from these actions occur*. It's easy to pass over too quickly or incompletely in identifying the ideal timing for actions and their results. Why? The positive and negative effects for most of what is done are usually limited to certain circumstances and times, many of which are hard to observe and measure.

Pareto's Principle teaches that in most circumstances, 80 percent of the positive and negative results are associated with just about 20 percent of what's done. While any given set of observations will not exactly follow Pareto's Principle, you should assume until proven otherwise that small numbers of people, actions, situations, and resources will account for almost all of the positive and negative variations from what has gone before and from the results experienced by the remaining people through their actions, in their situations, and with their resources.

By pinning down the factors that are highly associated with positive or negative consequences, you come one step closer to understanding what can be done to avoid harm and to increase benefits beyond what normally occurs. Before drawing any conclusions, be sure to check (and test, if necessary) for the ultimate sources of causality. Otherwise, you could emphasize something that coincidentally occurs at or near the same time, but that by being changed won't make much of a difference.

Here's a helpful example from www.ideachampions.com of how a cause of negative consequences was tracked down. Birds were making a mess at the Jefferson Memorial in Washington, D.C. Using harsh chemicals to clean up the mess was harming the memorial. Many possible solutions were considered, focused mostly on removing the birds or keeping them away from the memorial.

Someone in the Park Service investigated further and discovered that the birds were coming to feed on an unusually large number of spiders. The spiders, in turn, were multiplying because there were lots of midges for them to eat. The midges were so abundant because they procreate in the amount of light perfectly provided by turning on the memorial's lights one hour before dark.

The Park Service concluded that changing the lighting would greatly reduce the birds' mess. As a low-cost test, the Park Service delayed when the lights were turned on until an hour after dark, and the midge population greatly declined. The bird mess was ultimately reduced. Through this test result, the cause and how to reduce it were identified, and the memorial didn't have to be cleaned as often, with as harsh chemicals, or as thoroughly.

Notice that without a careful search for the ultimate cause of the increased bird mess, the Park Service might have chosen much less effective or more expensive solutions (certainly not excellent ones) such as hiring more cleaners, using different chemicals, making loud noises to scare the birds away, trapping birds, poisoning the spiders (and possibly some of the birds, as well), enclosing the memorial so birds and people couldn't go inside, moving the memorial, or totally closing it.

In considering what's being done, be sure to note *everything*, regardless of whether the intent of an action is to create a desirable result. If you see a sudden increase or decrease in some result that you want to encourage, look first for what changes were made at about the same time. In the case of the Jefferson Memorial, any indication that the lights had previously been turned on at a later time could have triggered a faster identification that lighting was causing the increased bird mess.

In looking for causality, be sure to also consider if there's a reason why something might be influencing the result that you want to achieve. Otherwise, it's easy to draw the wrong conclusion from whatever relationship you find. Let me explain with an example. For instance, most people respond positively at first to any change that they don't dislike. Because of this tendency, it's important to test whether it's a certain type of change that produced results ... or merely the novelty of a positively perceived change. Such cause-and-effect relationships can often be pinned down by running dual experiments involving different types of changes until you note that some of the benefits begin to fade for a certain type of change.

This problem of identifying the cause is similar to what pharmaceutical developers face in determining whether a new molecule can improve certain health results: If you give people sugar pills and describe them as a powerful new medicine, some of these people will improve as much or more than if they were ingesting an effective new medicine designed for that purpose, a response that's referred to as the placebo effect.

Learning experiments have revealed something similar associated with strong beliefs. For instance, students do better when their teachers are told that either they (the teachers) or the students are especially gifted in teaching or learning. The teacher's belief in a more favorable outcome obviously plays a role in this phenomenon, an influence called the Pygmalion (or Rosenthal) effect.

In your searches for cause-and-effect relationships, be sure to inquire about any other kinds of psychological influences that create tangible results so that you can identify what, in fact, needs to be changed. It may well be that an excellent solution will require creating novelty, positive beliefs about future results, and actual efficacy concerning some circumstances inherent to the change you make.

After you identify what actions have large positive and negative effects and when those effects occur, also take some time to think about when useful actions could be taken, but aren't, and when results are not occurring, but would be especially valuable. From those thoughts will come insights into useful goals, as well as clues for creating an excellent solution.

While identifying causes and their effects is so important that many books have been written solely about it, we must leave it now. If you are having trouble in this regard or just want to have your conclusions checked, I suggest you spend some time with a person trained to draw such conclusions either to help you structure your investigation or evaluate what has been learned. Most universities have professors with the requisite skills. Those who teach statistics are almost always able to be helpful.

Let's now consider a different subject: *Why are certain benefits sought and given approaches applied?* This subject requires identifying what current beliefs are and which of the beliefs cause people to act or accept the actions of others. While you might think that understanding such perspectives concerning less than excellent solutions would be all but irrelevant, such information is absolutely essential to finding ways to encourage people to change from what they do now that's less productive to what is, in fact, vastly more effective.

Here's an example of what I mean. Imagine that you want to encourage youngsters to eat more green vegetables. You might start by finding out which green vegetables would be most helpful for improving health and effectiveness for youngsters.

If we were considering young people who were at risk for cancer, such an investigation might lead to finding some unusual vegetables topping the list, such as Brussels sprouts. If you just started cooking and serving this vegetable, you might find that some youngsters didn't like its appearance or taste and wouldn't eat very much.

If it is essential for these youngsters to eat this vegetable, you might find valuable clues for encouraging them by considering why some other youngsters initially didn't like the appearance or taste of Brussels sprouts ... but eventually came to like them. From such an investigation, you might find recipes, modes of preparing and serving the vegetables, and related food items that improved the appearance, palatability, and aroma of Brussels sprouts for youngsters. It would also be important to ask those who prepared the vegetables as well as those who ate them why they did what they did and what they experienced.

For instance, you would eventually learn that overcooked Brussels sprouts can taste unpleasantly bitter. Overcooking also destroys many of the cancer-fighting benefits from eating this vegetable.

Such a search would undoubtedly turn up that no matter how well prepared, some youngsters never develop much of a taste for Brussels sprouts. In such cases, it might be important to see if the helpful vegetable could be diced or pureed and included as an ingredient in tasty soups and vegetable drinks.

Keep in mind that all such searches for beliefs and motivations should include everyone who may have an influence on the decisions. In this example, scientists identified that certain ingredients in food have cancer-prevention benefits. Were the scientists primarily concerned for those who have not yet had cancer, for those who have cancer now, or for those who formerly had cancer and are at risk for a recurrence? Their perspectives may affect how scientists think about what alternatives to propose. An excellent solution that could attract more support from these scientists might provide benefits to more classes of people in more ways.

For most youngsters, parents or guardians will actually be purchasing and preparing the food. How do parents and guardians think about what foods to provide? Their decisions may be also influenced by personal attitudes that favor, in part, using food as a reward for children, rather than primarily as a source of health benefits. Other parents and guardians may lack knowledge of and skill in food preparation that will affect what they will try and how well they will perform in providing the food. Still others may have limited time to prepare special meals and will need time-saving suggestions.

Appearance, taste, and aroma aren't the only issues for youngsters. Concerns about health vary from child to child. Individual youngsters are also more or less inclined to do or to rebel against what adults want them to do. The sound of a food's name or its mouth feel can also be big factors. How can these attitudes become assets or be overcome in cases where they now are liabilities?

I was recently reminded of the importance of such issues while reading a biography of Louisa May Alcott, the author of the juvenile classic *Little Women*. During the American Civil War, she faithfully served as a nurse before becoming quite ill. Since she was serving far from home and was too ill to be consulted about her treatment, her physicians decided on their own what medicines to use.

One of their preferred treatments involved a concoction that was loaded with deadly mercury. Her health was undermined by that treatment for the rest of her abbreviated life. No doubt her physicians chose that treatment, in part, because fighting off the harmful effects of mercury poisoning temporarily increased the immune response in some seriously ill patients in those days before antibiotics were available. The doctors also may have incorrectly believed that her body would remove the mercury over time.

In her day, proposing an alternative treatment would have required addressing some of these kinds of reasons as to why the physicians were deliberately poisoning their patients in ways that would cause them much agony and weakness before prematurely dying. Since what I'm describing is so closely related to identifying stalls (bad thinking habits) and stallbusters (ways to eliminate stalls), I'm sure you appreciate what I'm proposing: Find the belief behind the mental habit that determines behavior and find ways to encourage (if correct) or to overturn (if incorrect) the belief, as needed.

Let's now consider *where the actions are taken, their effects occur, and their results are felt.* After you know what actions are taken, you will probably have a pretty easy time determining where they occur. I hope you are pleased to discover that this goal-development task isn't very challenging.

Before you relax too much, let me mention an opportunity to learn more: Thinking about where actions are taken may also lead you to identify some actions that you hadn't previously identified.

Such thinking is also good for exploring where the effects of the actions occur and the results are felt, which are much more difficult to learn. Most people greatly underestimate the impact of their own actions on others. They are even less likely to notice the impacts that their organizations have, especially where those affected are silent about the effects. In cases where an effect is simply on the physical world in ways that are hard to detect, the likelihood of noticing and observing where effects occur is quite small. Naturally, if the location of the effect is missed, the consequences that are felt by others are also likely to go unidentified.

At such times, I'm often reminded of the methods used by the fictional detective Sherlock Holmes. The pipe-smoking Englishman spent a great deal of time in Sir Arthur Conan Doyle's stories and books studying obscure subjects, such as how to identify the source of tobacco from sniffing a slight whiff on some clothing or by examining a cigar's ash. By carefully observing what was present and missing at crime scenes and places where the victims and people connected to a crime had been present, Holmes would then think carefully about what the most probable answers were about who did what, when, and why.

One kind of investigatory process can be helpful for locating where effects occur and the results are felt. Begin by imagining as many potential effects as possible, while not being concerned if some of these possible effects might not occur. For identifying possible effects, also ask others for their ideas. Their differing views may help you to appreciate what you would otherwise miss.

Then, reverse the process that Sherlock Holmes used and seek clues that indicate such effects have occurred, are occurring, or will occur in the future. If you can visit the locations where such effects may be observed, do so. Consider if there are simple tests you can use to identify effects. For instance, manufacturers may be able to use chemical reactions to identify if materials used in their processes or products have leaked into the environment or into other places where they should not be. In doing so, don't neglect opportunities to ask those present what they have observed, especially about how earlier conditions may have been different from the current ones.

Also investigate locations where there's no reason to expect that there might be effects. You are likely to be surprised to find effects where there's no apparent reason for them. When that happens, you are in a situation much like Sherlock Holmes in many of the stories, needing to figure out how the effect (or clue to the effect) came to be where it shouldn't be.

In the process of following Holmes's example, you'll probably learn about cause-and-effect mechanisms that are not widely known and appreciated. For example, did you realize that under certain circumstances it can be relatively likely for a good swimmer to drown in the desert?

That's because the scarce rains in such dry areas can cause minerals to partially dissolve, forming all-but-impossible-to-penetrate sedimentary stone just below the desert's sandy surface. When a cloudburst occurs, the water can't soak very deeply into the soil. As a result, a little concentrated rain can become a roaring torrent in a narrow canyon, covering the ground to well above a person's head and moving so swiftly that swimmers cannot stay afloat without being powerfully pounded into rock walls that can easily knock them out. Under these circumstances, someone caught in such a "flash flood" may die of drowning in the desert, despite being a good swimmer.

The only clues to what happened will be lungs filled with fresh water and severe injuries all over the drowned person's body. Without care, someone might incorrectly conclude that the drowned person had been beaten into unconsciousness by an assailant before being murdered in a pool of water.

Because of the potential for such "seemingly impossible" results to occur, I always recommend that those seeking to set good goals randomly check for effects that might not yet be understood and learn how others react to those effects. Although some people might find it frustrating to spend such time and effort and yet learn nothing, validating that no other effects and reactions are occurring is, in fact, learning something valuable. While looking, you are likely to find unexpected effects and reactions, some of which may create valuable insights into how to produce an excellent solution.

Let's now turn our minds to *studying how any beneficial, neutral, and harmful results are provided and received.* Many people want to begin goal setting by considering this dimension of how any beneficial, neutral, and harmful results are provided and received, appreciating its importance for pointing toward better solutions. When that urge overtakes you, realize that the prior steps in this lesson are essential for identifying more of the actions, conditions, and circumstances that can lead to beneficial, neutral, and harmful results. Without taking the earlier steps seriously, you would just focus on whatever little you knew that was correct and be misled by whatever incorrect and incomplete impressions and suppositions you had. Yes, you would move much faster toward setting goals, but mostly in a way similar to when someone only sweeps up the broken glass from an automobile accident that can be seen under a street light at night, leaving alone all the glass in dark places. In the process, you may well miss most of what you seek. When important effects are ignored, your search for an excellent solution will be stalled by your impatience and ignorance. In addition, your solution will have far fewer benefits than are readily available.

In some situations, harmful and beneficial effects can flow from a single action. Consequently, what looks like a neutral result may simply be a combination of positive and negative effects with equal impacts.

As a result, it's important to identify all the positive, seemingly neutral, and harmful effects of the various actions, conditions, and circumstances. In doing so, you must attempt to identify the cause-and-effect relationships so that harmful effects can be eliminated or reduced and positive effects are magnified or increased in frequency.

Here's a medical example of what I mean. You might find that a small percentage of youngsters who receive a certain vaccine also experience severe infections. Naturally, you would like to eliminate the infections while vaccinating all children. You should identify if the infections have anything to do with the production, transportation, storage, or age of the vaccine. If those activities and circumstances seem unrelated to the infections, you should also investigate how the vaccinations are administered by medical personnel. In doing so, you might find that the children are being exposed to antibiotic-resistant bacteria due to insufficient cleansing precautions by those who vaccinate them. As a result, you might change the way the vaccines are packaged and applied so that any flawed hygiene by the medical personnel would cause many fewer infections.

Similarly, for any seemingly positive effect it is important to isolate what aspects of the circumstances and what is done provide the bulk of the benefits. If a hundred things are done in a given set of circumstances, and only three of the actions are effective, greater benefits may be created by redirecting the time, resources, and effort spent for performing the ninety-seven actions that make no difference.

In considering the sources of effects, it's also essential to consider the actions, conditions, and circumstances that occur in addition to what those taking the primary actions do. In many cases, for instance, the person who receives the benefit or harm has a large impact on the results. In making this observation I'm reminded of how many adults fail to finish taking a full course of antibiotics after starting to feel well. When less than a full dosage is applied, small numbers of harmful bacteria can survive and multiply, causing a recurrence of the infection and increasing the likelihood of antibiotic-resistant bacteria strains developing.

I'm sure you will find these kinds of investigations to be interesting and satisfying. I wish you well in your efforts.

Finally, then, let's look at *how much help is provided and what kinds and quantities of resources are used.* Improved resource allocation is essential for defining and implementing excellent solutions. My experience has been that there are always more than enough resources to accomplish anything, but most of the resources are either being applied in ineffective (or, worse yet, harmful) activities or are idle. By redirecting existing resources under such circumstances, astonishing improvements can follow.

In the prior discussion, you learned to identify how beneficial, neutral, and harmful results are provided and received. Matching the resources to the actions and circumstances that caused those results provides an inventory of resources that can be reallocated in more useful ways. Thus, the measurements required here become quite important for determining what goals to set. Without realizing that plenty of resources exist, but need to be redirected, your excellent-solution goals may be far too modest in terms of what you attempt. In addition, your solution should address all dimensions for redirecting resources into more productive activities.

Some people can feel a little overwhelmed by the task of quantifying the help that is provided now and what resources are used. If that's you, relax. In most cases, an approximate answer is more than adequate for goal setting. For instance, you will probably find that the most useful kinds of help are seldom provided and that few resources are applied now for these activities. In making that determination, it doesn't matter for goal-setting purposes whether the frequency of help is 0.00001 percent or 0.1 percent. Both are tiny compared to the potential to accomplish more.

What's more important in such a circumstance is to be reasonably accurate in determining how many resources would be needed to help 100 percent of the time. Once you know that number, you will probably be able to compare it to the uses for which existing resources are being applied and see if there are enough resources today … or if more resources need to be developed.

Here's an example of what I mean about resource availability that relates to improving reading. If you determine that people with dyslexia would benefit from having reading materials formatted so that only one word appeared at a time on an electronic screen, you would quickly learn that almost no articles, books, and other resources are already available in this format. While the gap between what's available and all reading material is huge, you would eventually learn that people with dyslexia only need to use such formatting for a brief while. In that case, you could determine how many books and articles of what sort would be necessary to help dyslexics acquire better neural connections for reading.

If the work involved is pretty routine, you could then estimate how many hours of such formatting are needed from people who have average skills. You could compare these requirements to how many volunteer hours are now devoted to helping dyslexic readers, and you would probably find that there are more than enough hours to get the formatting done in a reasonable amount of time.

Should you decide to investigate if making the improvements could be further accelerated, you could also check how much money is donated by organizations and individuals as well as what governments supply for helping dyslexic readers, and you would probably find that only a small portion of these funds would need to be redirected in order to purchase sufficient formatting so that it could be completed sooner.

Be sure to inventory not only resources that can be easily redirected into new purposes, but also resources that with some work can be developed through adding capabilities. For instance, in helping dyslexic youngsters who need reading assistance, many reading specialists could be given additional training so that they, in turn, could train classroom teachers to earlier identify dyslexic readers. By providing that training to teachers, more youngsters would receive specialized help they need at a younger age. Consequently, the harmful effects of their dyslexia could be greatly reduced.

In some cases, you may not yet know how you might want to apply a given resource. Don't let that lack of clarity keep you from noting that the resources exist or could be created.

Further, realize that sometimes resources are being provided for dealing with the effects of what you want to avoid or improve. Be sure to consider that these resources might also be made available for dealing with the underlying causes of such effects. For instance, many unemployed people have reading problems. Some of the funds available for training them for new jobs might be made available to assist some with improving reading so they could qualify for a wider variety of jobs.

Single mindedness can be beneficial for implementing an excellent solution. However, *for the purpose of setting excellent-solution goals,* single-benefit *mindedness should be avoided.*

Let me explain why I say that. When you felt called to solve a problem with an excellent solution, your heart, mind, and soul were strongly attracted by just being aware of some potential beneficiaries and certain aspects (maybe even only one) of their needs. If you had only focused on these beneficiaries and such need or needs, you would have missed setting many other worthy goals for your excellent solution.

Similarly, many people can initially conceive of only one or a few benefits being created from taking action or making changes. That sort of thinking is as if you only considered whether eating a certain food would cause an allergic reaction for some youngsters.

The other benefits and drawbacks of foods also need to be considered so that optimal benefits are provided to youngsters, such as supplying essential vitamins and minerals, having enough protein and healthy fats, furnishing the right amount of calories, adding fiber, delivering essential cancer-fighting molecules, balancing blood sugar, improving metabolism, and appropriately dispensing energy. Planning a meal to provide more kinds of such benefits leads to certain kinds of ingredients, recipes, and preparation methods so that the resulting meal will be more beneficial than if someone simply seeks to avoid allergic reactions.

Wisely putting together a monthly meal plan could also accomplish much more than just planning a single meal that considers such nutritional and health needs. In planning dozens of monthly meals, other benefit goals might be added such as spending less money, reducing time spent for purchasing food and preparing meals, improving access to higher quality ingredients, and encouraging healthier snacking.

An expanded view of avoiding allergic food reactions might also include checking home, school, and recreational environments for possible sources of allergens that could make a youngster more likely to have food reactions. With less stress on an immune system from all allergens, foods might trigger reduced reactions. If that broader focus didn't solve the food allergy problem and limiting consumption of a food remained important, different sources of the food could also be tested (such as trying organic produce from various local farms) to see if any food sources induce fewer and less severe allergic reactions.

In thinking about such factors, let me remind you that we are still just considering the goals, rather than focusing on best ways to achieve an excellent solution. I provide this reminder about considering multiple-benefit opportunities now because those who cannot initially conceive of possible solutions are often quick to set goals that are too modest, ones that fall well short of being sufficient to qualify as an excellent solution. To expand your horizons a bit concerning what benefits to seek, view the potential for excellent solutions from the following perspectives:

- Single actions and changes that create multiple benefits
- Combinations of actions and changes that create multiple benefits
- Sequences of actions and changes that multiply benefits
- Timing of actions and changes to multiply benefits
- A mental framework for identifying ways to obtain more types of benefits from actions and changes as well as multiplying the resulting benefits by one another

You'll be glad you applied these perspectives.

Here's a thought process that can help you expand your horizons about benefits to add. Start identifying benefit opportunities by reexamining what you learned about how any beneficial, neutral, and harmful results have been and are being provided and received. In doing so, be sure to consider if any beneficial actions and changes provide or could provide other types of benefits beyond what you are focused on.

If so, find out what those other possibilities are. In doing so, you may begin to see ways to extend benefits that greatly exceed what your imagination originally revealed. In the process, don't be afraid to look for related actions and changes that might provide more of these previously unidentified benefits that are consistent with your purposes. Be open to discovering that some of these actions and changes might also multiply the benefits you have been seeking.

Then, compare the benefits that have been gained in taking those actions and making such changes to your ideas about who should be served; what benefits should be sought for them; why certain benefits should be sought and given approaches applied; what should be done by all participants to provide such benefits; when such actions should be taken and the benefits occur; where the actions should be taken, the effects occur, and the results be felt; how much help should be provided; and what kinds and quantities of resources to use.

As you would expect, there will be at least some gaps between what you know or your organization knows about how to provide and what you desire to make available. For example, no methods may be identified, as yet, for providing certain other kinds of benefits to some beneficiaries. Also, resources may be insufficient to deliver all of the benefits that you know how to provide.

If the differences are substantial between your knowledge of applying the available resources and what you want to accomplish, your confidence in setting excellent-solution goals may be undermined. It's a good idea to do enough investigation now into what's possible to increase confidence in the kinds of goals that you will probably be setting.

Another potential benefit from doing more investigation now can be learning about actions and changes that can provide other benefits that would be good to add to your goals. When that happens, you may be able to produce a much more excellent solution.

Begin by examining the list to find gaps in either identifying or accessing resources, actions, and changes needed to supply the desired benefits. Then think of reasonably similar benefits that are routinely provided in some other aspect of life. (For those of you who are familiar with creating 2,000 percent solutions, this thinking is analogous to beginning a search for future best practices by looking at other industries to find helpful practices and methods. See Chapter 7 of *The 2,000 Percent Solution Workbook* for more details.)

In doing such thinking, confidently assume that similar benefits to those you seek can be gained in highly effective ways by using methods you don't yet know. I urge you to assume so because this kind of faith has always been rewarded in my own searches for better methods.

Let me give you an example of what I have in mind involving reading improvement for youngsters. Let's assume that some young people experience debilitating headaches while reading that curtail how much reading they can do and how well they can do it. While there are many possible reasons for and contributing factors to such headaches (such as poor lighting, bad posture, needing glasses, using glasses with an out-of-date prescription, inadequate blood flow, low blood sugar, hunger, dehydration, caffeine withdrawal, adverse drug interactions, neurological problems, illness, tumors, and so forth), it's clear in all cases that few children are going to do a lot of reading while enduring great pain.

While headaches have many negative effects, a high percentage of people suffering from such pain can find ways either to lessen or to eliminate it. For those who can gain such relief and then be able to read effectively, you do not need to be concerned except in cases where more resources are needed for this purpose.

You would focus most of your attention on those with severe headaches. Although you or your organization either may not be expert concerning or involved with treatments, you can certainly avail yourselves of whatever knowledge exists about why, how often, and with what degree of pain youngsters experience headaches.

Let's assume that you want to first address how to gain the most immediate pain relief for the most afflicted of such youngsters. You might investigate what is known by first-aid instructors, emergency medical technicians, nurses, and physicians about what treatments are most likely to be effective in extreme cases and have the least risk of harm.

Let's assume that you also want to eliminate as many extreme headaches as possible in the long run. To do so, you might first examine what neurological specialists have learned about what can be done for those with chronic, extreme, and long-lasting headaches. It would be helpful to find out if any of such approaches would also be good for dealing with short-term, infrequent headaches that are very painful. Such knowledge of universal benefits would be desirable because youngsters and their families could be sooner focused on doing things that provide permanent benefits.

Check those treatments with public-health professionals to determine which ones are most likely to be practical to implement universally and for their suggestions about how that might best be done. After you acquire this knowledge, you should meet with those who are good at estimating the required cost and effort to implement various approaches. Ask them to help you design some effective, low-cost treatment programs for testing.

In parallel to such investigations, hypothesis-building, and experimentation, you might also speak with people in other fields where fast decisions have to be made for how to deal with poorly understood emergency situations, such as firemen and policemen. Although they may not have relevant knowledge about this particular problem, their experience in quickly diagnosing what's needed and applying the right resources at the optimal time might suggest methods for simplifying and improving your potential treatment programs.

For example, first responders have learned through much experience to extract major conclusions from small bits of sensory information upon which they immediately act. If the floor of a wooden structure is hot during a fire, that may well mean that the area below is also aflame and that the floor might soon collapse. In such a circumstance, you must get off that floor to safety as soon as possible. Similarly, if you note that a fire burns hotter after pouring water on it, there may be chemicals present that react with water to create harmful effects. You need to stop pouring on water and use the right chemical-fire retardants.

Such insights might then suggest that you identify signs of what is most likely to be causing a severe headache that could be used by youngsters and nonmedical personnel to narrow down to the more likely methods to immediately alleviate or to eliminate a headache, beyond just taking over-the-counter and prescription pain relievers. In this way, fewer actions and resources would be needed, and benefits would be obtained sooner.

Prepared with both the medical and first-responder information, you are ready to define tests. From the test results, you can then determine whether you have identified any usable solutions that will better match available resources to the benefits that you intend to supply.

In such tests, you may find that there are other outcomes that need to be considered. For instance, some treatments may be great for reducing pain, but they also cause youngsters to feel weak and disoriented (such as from certain migraine medications) so that learning isn't enhanced as much as with other treatments.

You may be feeling uncomfortable with the idea of doing so much investigation before you have even set goals for an excellent solution. Relax. Remember that you are building a sturdier foundation for the right goals, an important aspect of providing an excellent solution.

In this example involving headaches that interfere with reading, I want you to realize that some youngsters have many stress and health issues that make it hard for them to do well in school, as well as to read. Surely, some high school dropouts experience such issues. Headaches may be just an occasional symptom of these other problems. In the course of looking into headaches, you may realize that there are highly effective and affordable methods that can be used for all youngsters to identify what can help them to lead more productive and joyful lives, both mentally and physically, whether or not they experience extreme headaches.

Since part of the benefit from improving reading is to upgrade life quality for youngsters, surely dealing with more fundamental health and stress issues is consistent with what would be good to accomplish. As a result of such an investigation, your range of goals may well expand in a way that will provide both more kinds of benefits outside of reading, as well as more benefits in the aspects of reading that initially attracted your attention.

Consequently, you may look for ways to improve health and stress screening at a younger age to enhance learning capacity in ways that can be combined with education to help youngsters and their families find useful solutions sooner and with less expense and effort. In the process, you may reduce the effects of other factors that limit reading and learning.

In my own case, I was born very nearsighted. Somehow no one noticed that until I was nine. That's when a teacher sent me to be tested by the school nurse after observing how I used every recess and lunch period to go up to the blackboard to read what had been written there during the last lesson.

As you can see from this learning example, you want to stay open to lateral shifts in information and thinking that bring new issues to light that are fundamentally connected to your purposes, but that you haven't yet identified. In staying open to finding such helpful shifts, realize that you don't have to pin down answers at this point. You need, instead, simply to become more aware of possibilities.

Although such shifts may at first seem to complicate matters for you, in many cases the shifts may also open doors to simpler solutions. In this example, universal learning-related health screenings at young ages might be just such an opportunity.

For more examples of how to serve more kinds of benefits, see Lesson Three in *Excellent Solutions*.

Good hunting!

Lesson Twenty-Two Assignments

1. For the problem you feel called to address through an excellent solution, summarize what you have learned in this lesson concerning the following goal-setting dimensions:

- Who is and can be affected in what ways?
- What is done by all participants?
- When is something done and the results occur?
- Why are certain benefits sought and given approaches applied?
- Where are the actions taken and do their effects occur, as well as the locations where results are felt?
- How are any beneficial, neutral, and harmful results provided and received?
- How much help is provided and what kinds and quantities of resources are used?

2. Take what you learned from this lesson about the goal-setting dimensions and describe your initial thoughts about setting goals for an excellent solution in terms of:

- Who should be served?
- What benefits should be sought for them?
- Why should certain benefits be sought and given approaches applied?
- What should be done by all participants to provide these benefits?
- When should actions be taken and the results from those actions occur?
- Where should the actions be taken, their effects occur, and the results be felt?
- How much help should be provided and what kinds and quantities of resources should be used?

3. After reexamining what you just learned in answering questions 1 and 2, what other beneficial actions could provide other types of benefits beyond what you are focused on?

4. How do the benefits from your answers to question 3 compare to your answer to question 2?

5. How could any beneficial results be increased by adjusting the sequences, combinations, and timing of when desired actions and changes occur?

6. What seem to be the optimal sequences, combinations, and timing of desired actions and changes?

7. Do any remaining gaps in benefits relate to special circumstances or issues that can be addressed outside of the scope of your initial inquiry and focus?

8. How might any such special circumstances or issues be best addressed?

Lesson Twenty-Three

Unstoppable Chain Reactions

And so it was,
when Moses held up his hand,
that Israel prevailed;
and when he let down his hand,
Amalek prevailed.

But Moses' hands became heavy;
so they took a stone and
put it under him,
and he sat on it.
And Aaron and Hur
supported his hands,
one on one side,
and the other on the other side;
and his hands were steady
until the going down of the sun.

So Joshua defeated Amalek and
his people with the edge of the sword.

— Exodus 17:11-13 (NKJV)

When I was a youngster, controlled atomic chain reactions began to be applied for generating electricity. To help children understand the difference between an atomic blast (an uncontrolled atomic chain reaction) and an atomic power plant (a controlled atomic chain reaction), scientists designed some impressive demonstrations.

One of my favorite demonstrations of an uncontrolled atomic chain reaction was conducted in a large room filled with spring-loaded mouse traps that were each topped by two table-tennis balls. The narrator started the demonstration by throwing a single table-tennis ball into the room, and within a second the air was so filled with flying table-tennis balls that you couldn't see more than a few feet ahead. Within just a few more seconds, the energy stored in the traps was expended and quiet soon returned.

To me that demonstration was very powerful because it showed that you could move from no motion to universal motion almost instantly. Although I had no interest in setting off uncontrolled atomic chain reactions, I was impressed by the potential to stir actions that would create immediate, multiplied effects.

Since then, I have always wondered how such effects might be encouraged for people to influence one another. Early in life, I began to see examples. If someone stood at the top level of a stadium, perhaps one or two people in the vicinity would also stand up, but no other action would usually follow. If by standing up the person at top could strike a ventilation duct with a hand to make a loud noise, this person could induce a much larger reaction by rhythmically drumming on the duct while shouting a familiar chant. After such a beginning, the whole stadium would soon be clapping and chanting to the beat.

Occasionally, I played this role by starting the drumming and chanting just to help understand the cause and effect. I observed a similar phenomenon a few years later: If a person stood up in the first row of a stadium or auditorium in a way that blocked the views of the people behind the standing person, most of the people who couldn't easily see would immediately stand up rather than ask the first person to sit down. Each time one person stood up in front, four to ten people behind that person would also stand. Each of those standers, in turn, led another four to ten people to stand.

Within a minute or two, most people behind the original stander would be on their feet. Some people would stay standing, even if those in front sat down. Seeing that others were standing, some people in other sections would also stand, either in excitement or to stretch. Whenever such reactions followed among many of those on the bottom tier, almost the entire crowd would be standing during much of the event.

I began to think about the conditions that cause such reactions. The second example was due in part to obvious *self-interest*: People had come to the event to see what was going on. Interfere with their views, and they would stand up to gain a better look ... even if more effort was required. The first example was helped by a more subtle kind of self-interest: People enjoy feeling that they are part of an energetic crowd. To gain that feeling, many people will quickly take up chanting, dancing, and shouting slogans that connect them to the crowd. Even some normally reserved people will sheepishly do so.

Experiences and *habits* play roles, too. Many people have been in similar situations, and they have learned to enjoy the event more by acting in such ways.

I began to think about how self-interest combined with experience and habits could be used as substitutes for the two table-tennis balls sitting on each spring-loaded mousetrap to create a chain reaction by human beings.

Let me pull out some themes from what I learned and pose seven questions for you to consider:

1. Communications costs are rapidly approaching zero. What opportunities does that circumstance open for you?
2. Computing costs are near zero. What can you calculate and do now that you couldn't afford in the past?
3. Work can now be redesigned to produce higher-quality results at vastly lower costs. What activities can you now redesign to be more effective for the first time?

4. People are becoming used to do-it-yourself solutions that require their doing more to access and use information. What can you now provide for the first time that depends on such increased ability to perform and interest in do-it-yourself solutions?
5. Technology is advancing rapidly in ways that decrease costs and enhance effectiveness. What technology benefits should you be applying that you aren't?
6. Cost-reduction and effectiveness-enhancing opportunities are opening up more frequently than before. Are you studying enough about how to develop and apply new cost reductions and effectiveness enhancements?
7. Noticing new low-cost and effectiveness-enhancing methods is a critical first step for providing new types of excellent solutions. How are you monitoring what can be accomplished through excellent solutions?

Let's shift now from creating unstoppable human chain reactions to the practical problem of *how to accomplish such human chain reactions quickly and inexpensively*. Imagine that your greatest desire has just been fulfilled in a supernatural way and an angel told you to go quickly and tell others. I'm sure you'd head off as fast as you could.

When it comes to putting excellent solutions in place, realize that such supernatural interventions might not occur. Let's consider how we can accomplish such solutions as rapidly as possible while only being guided by the Holy Spirit.

Here's a key question for you: *What one change can you make to solve your problem that will set off a similar set of chain reactions that draw on* self-interest, experience, *and* habits *to increase effectiveness by much more than 20 times while also cutting costs for your organization (as well as for all your stakeholders) by 96 percent or more?*

Here's the answer I was directed to for accomplishing these goals for all of my activities: Help all my stakeholders efficiently learn how to create and teach others ways of combining at least ten complementary 2,000 percent solutions, as well as methods for developing excellent solutions.

As I'm sure you can appreciate, helping so many people learn these critical practices involves a lot of work over an extended period of time unless any stakeholders who learn from me also teach others, a practice I have encouraged throughout The 400 Year Project. I've been delighted that some exceptionally talented people have done well in sharing these methods with others. Praise God for them!

Naturally, we need to be concerned about how long it takes for an excellent solution to be developed and put into place. Think back to the table-tennis-ball demonstration. As you can imagine, a major challenge for such a demonstration is setting all of the mouse traps and putting table-tennis balls on them without starting an inadvertent explosion of balls. Such mistakes occur from time to time, and the difficulty of preparing the demonstration is great. Much time and effort are also required to gain just a brief view. The setup time is tens of thousands of times longer than the actual demonstration.

If you were to take the same approach to your problem, you might spend billions of dollars over decades to get to the point where a chain-reaction excellent solution would occur. Such a result hardly seems worth the effort.

As wonderful as a chain-reaction excellent solution is, I'm sure you agree that it would be enormously more valuable if such an excellent solution could be developed quickly and inexpensively. Although this point should be obvious, I have noticed that some people have been slow to focus on accelerating the development and implementation of breakthrough gains. Part of the problem seems to be that solution seekers tend to be overly optimistic. Another challenge is that many solution developers have no idea what's involved in making the improvements they envision. Without much knowledge about what to do, it's also easy to seek the right help from the wrong people, and the wrong help from the right people.

Goals are a good starting point for overcoming such problems. Be sure you have a goal requiring that your chain-reaction solution be identified and implemented in a short time period by applying modest amounts of resources compared to what you have available and can afford to commit.

Here are some strategies that can help you accomplish your goals for gaining breakthroughs faster and less expensively:

- See how a highly publicized global contest conducted on the Internet might provide you with access to better ideas at little cost.
- Examine benefit gains and cost reductions that can be easily and quickly tested on a small scale.
- Consider the difficulty and expense of various methods to provide benefit gains and cost reductions.
- Think about how challenging it would be to attract the talented people needed for implementation of the solution.
- Evaluate the natural interest that your breakthroughs will probably attract and how such interest can be used to speed progress.

Here's an example of what I mean. Let's return to the idea of helping all my stakeholders learn how to create and teach others how to define and implement ten complementary 2,000 percent solutions, as well as methods for developing excellent solutions.

I could easily sponsor a global contest for finding better ways to accomplish such purposes by publicizing the details on my blogs, Web sites, book reviewer profiles, press releases, and e-mails to people on the project's list. I could offer a prize of receiving tutoring from me for accomplishing the winner's choice of a 2,000 percent solution goal. The out-of-pocket cost for such a contest would be less than $500. The contest could be completed within 60 days of its beginning.

While the contest was being conducted, I could also review my experiences with helping others learn how to create 2,000 percent solutions and conduct small-scale experiments with teaching ways to identify far more effective, lower-cost methods. Promising experimental results could go immediately into broader-scale tests.

When the online-contest results were available, I could screen the possible solutions to see which ones might be easily and quickly tested on a small scale and focus next on trying such potential solutions.

After all the small-scale tests were completed, I should next consider the difficulty of applying the methods that worked well. Obviously, I would place a lower priority on methods that require lots of my time and attention while emphasizing approaches involving efforts that others could do better than I could at little cost in small amounts of time (such as creating interactive software-based versions of the materials I've prepared in the past through applying existing software templates). The difficulty of attracting the right people varies with the learning method. Ways of learning that do not need much review or supervision would be emphasized.

To check for natural interest, I could use a survey, test various ads through Google's AdWords, or tie my tests to creating solutions for topics with high Google search rankings. None of such methods would be expensive or slow. I could then test actual demand by making offers that would draw inquiries and measure the responses to identify the most appealing offers.

To reduce the risk of not making fast progress, I should simultaneously implement at least three different initiatives that would not compete with one another for resources or attention.

Naturally, if you are thinking of doing something that's for a manufacturing, retail, or capital-intensive business, you may not be able to move as quickly, cheaply, or smoothly ... unless, perhaps, you consider how outsourcing might give you more of the speed and flexibility you desire. Many outsourcing organizations now specialize in providing all aspects of designing and implementing breakthrough solutions. You just have to define what you want to accomplish. It can be expensive to work this way, but the costs might be lower than for your own efforts. If sufficient additional benefits are gained rapidly enough, the increased cost will be irrelevant.

Even if you are engaged in manufacturing, retail, or capital-intensive businesses, you can still do lots of cheap, quick testing by simulating benefits and observing stakeholder reactions. Then, you can rely on out-sourcers to speed implementation of the most appealing choices.

Lesson Twenty-Three Assignments

1. How could self-interest and habits provide more of the benefits you defined through the Lesson Twenty-Two assignments?

2. How could stakeholder experiences be a resource for providing more benefits?

3. How might stakeholders be encouraged to provide more benefits?

4. How can you apply the following themes to deliver more benefits?

- Communications costs are rapidly approaching zero. What opportunities does that circumstance open for you?
- Computing costs are near zero. What can you calculate and do now that you couldn't afford in the past?
- Work can now be redesigned to produce higher-quality results at vastly lower costs. What activities can you redesign to be more effective for the first time?
- People are becoming used to do-it-yourself solutions that require their doing more to access and use information. What can you now provide for the first time that depends on such increased ability to perform and interest in do-it-yourself solutions?
- Technology is advancing rapidly in ways that decrease costs and enhance effectiveness. What technology benefits should you be applying that you aren't?
- Cost-reducing and effectiveness-enhancing opportunities are opening up more frequently than before. Are you studying enough about how to develop and apply new cost reductions and effectiveness enhancements?

• Noticing new low-cost and effectiveness-enhancing methods is a critical first step for providing new types of excellent solutions. How are you monitoring what can be accomplished through excellent solutions?

5. How could you apply any of the follow strategies to provide more benefits?

• A highly-publicized global contest conducted on the Internet to access better ideas at little cost
• Easily and quickly testing benefit gains and cost reductions on a small scale
• Considering the difficulties and expenses of applying the methods that provide the benefit gains and cost reductions
• Thinking about how challenging it will be to attract talented people to help you implement
• Evaluating how much natural interest your breakthroughs will attract and how such interest can speed progress

6. How can your excellent solution become more irresistibly attractive to all stakeholders so that they will provide more support for providing the benefits?

• What characteristics are most irresistibly appealing to the stakeholders who are most important for providing benefits?
• Which strategies can lead these stakeholders to take immediate and continuing action?
• How could each experience build more interest in and support for providing your excellent solution?

Part Five

Applying Lessons

Apply your heart to instruction,
And your ears to words of knowledge.

— Proverbs 23:12 (NKJV)

Before starting this book, your experience with making large improvements may have been limited. If so, having learned about so much potential could cause you to feel a bit overwhelmed. Also, you might not be sure where to start. In addition, you may lack confidence that you can achieve the kinds of remarkable results described here. If you lack complete confidence, relax!

While there are some clear guideposts for making breakthroughs involving three different types of processes contained in the lessons you have been studying, remember that none of the guideposts suggest that you should immediately work on all of them. Even if you were to do so over time, you would clearly space out the schedule to match your time, effort, and financial resources. In fact, you might decide to free up more time before beginning any other activities to produce breakthroughs. Lesson One suggests accomplishing that result in Practice Four.

In this part of *Your Breakthroughs*, I provide more detailed directions about how you can personalize what you've just read so that it will be easier, faster, and more effective for you to accomplish what you are called by God to do. We begin in Lesson Twenty-Four by looking at how you can set appropriate goals for applying the first twenty-three lessons. While space does not permit dealing with all the permutations, this lesson can certainly help you see how following the right small, comfortable steps can direct you down a path that will eventually lead to astonishing breakthroughs that will delight one and all.

One reason that such work can seem daunting at first is due to your not yet knowing everything that is needed. Well, realize that you will never know everything that's needed, but you can access lots of help from knowledgeable people who will be excited about the opportunity to do so. If you reach out for such assistance in the right ways, you'll not only be amazed at how rapidly a solution develops, but you'll also be delighted to meet some terrific people who will make your life better in all kinds of unexpected ways unrelated to the solution. This point is so important that I've included Lesson Twenty-Five just to make you more effective in recognizing when you need help and how to get it. As you focus on human help, don't forget that God knows everything that you need and will provide the knowledge to advance His Kingdom through the Holy Spirit when you ask. How can you not get enough help?

After you know what to work on and how to get help when you aren't able to proceed with the people and knowledge then available to you, what else could you need? Well, you must keep up-to-date on the most valuable developments for making breakthroughs. Otherwise, you might be working with some process described in this book that has been superseded by one that is infinitely better. I see this problem occurring all of the time by authors introducing me to "new" concepts that they've just mastered, ones that were outdated in the nineteenth century. But the authors do not know that. So for them, these concepts are brand new. Don't fall behind!

While staying current may seem daunting, I again encourage you to relax. Almost all improvements related to breakthrough methods described in *Your Breakthroughs* were communicated to me within a year of their initial occurrence. I do my best through e-mails, blogging, and publishing new materials to make such information available to all those who sincerely want to make breakthroughs. If you are on the e-mail list (sign up at www.fastforward400.com), you won't miss anything important that I learn.

Well, you might ask, what about all those improvements made to methods not being used by those connected to the breakthrough methods described in this book? I also monitor those and build them into the methods described here where they best fit. The good news is that I don't have to spend much time doing so, simply because such methods are almost always seeking to make "breakthroughs" that are well below the lower level of what 2,000 percent solutions already accomplish. Invariably, I find that the methods involved take hundreds of times more time, resources, and effort compared to the benefits provided by 2,000 percent solutions. With other methods falling further and further behind what you've read here, I suspect that the relative importance of such sources will also decrease. I also pray for the Holy Spirit to point me to whatever human sources I need to supply improvements, and He regularly does.

I hope this part of the book will fill you with encouragement, curiosity, and a desire to experience what it is like to be one of the world's greatest improvers. Think of how proud God will be if you do so in ways that advance His Kingdom and give Him the glory!

Lesson Twenty-Four

Goal Setting

"If anyone desires to come after Me, let him deny himself,
and take up his cross, and follow Me.

"For whoever desires to save his life will lose it,
but whoever loses his life for My sake will find it.

"For what profit is it to a man if he gains the whole world,
and loses his own soul?
Or what will a man give in exchange for his soul?

"For the Son of Man will come in the glory of His Father with His angels,
and then He will reward each according to his works."

— Matthew 16:24-27 (NKJV)

Given that Lesson Twenty-Two went into some detail about how to identify the benefit dimensions to provide when creating an excellent solution, you may be wondering why we are discussing excellent-solution goal setting here. Well, we aren't. We are, instead, discussing your personal goal setting for applying the book's first twenty-three lessons.

I added these words of Jesus that begin this chapter to remind you that following Him is the way to Salvation and also to rewards for what you do to advance His Kingdom. Many Christians are satisfied with the idea of simply being saved, either ignoring or not realizing that they have the command and opportunity to serve Jesus and to be rewarded by Him. Given that saved people will be with Jesus for all eternity, wouldn't it make sense to begin serving Him in more fruitful ways?

Only you can search your heart to learn what Jesus is calling you to do. Hopefully, reading the Bible, praying, listening to the Holy Spirit, worshiping, and reading the material in this book have helped you to notice more of your calling. If not, a good first goal is to better understand what that calling is. You can do so more effectively by repenting any sins as soon as you commit them, asking God to take away the desire to sin, and increasing your time in Bible reading, praying, listening to the Holy Spirit, worshiping, and reading any material that the Holy Spirit directs you to. In such seeking, you may find it helpful to engage in retreats, especially silent ones, during which your attention can be more fully engaged with God. If such approaches don't work, seek counseling from a pastor about how else you should go about finding your calling.

Once you know your calling, it's helpful to then create a sense of what changes are needed to fulfill that calling before setting any personal goals. For instance, if you have no time available to work on the calling, then your priorities and activities are going to have to be adjusted so that you can do so. Almost everyone who reads this book can accomplish more for God by first enhancing personal effectiveness. While Lesson One describes quite an impressive list of potential personal improvements, you may not need to do them all to succeed in fulfilling your calling. In addition, you may be able to work with others whose callings, talents, and skills complement yours so that you do not have to improve in as many areas. In any case, first develop goals for enhancing personal effectiveness. The fourteen practices in Lesson One are a good place to start. Evaluate yourself to see where you need to improve the most. If you think it would be helpful, also ask others for their views.

After that, realize that each of the methods for making break-throughs can be held back by attitudes, opinions, incautious thinking, and habits (what I call stalls) that need to be eliminated. If you will be working with an organization, the organization will also need to do the same kind of mental housecleaning. So before engaging with any method, be sure to do that work.

I find that people vary quite widely in how they like to engage in new tasks. Some favor the A to Z method where first things come first, second things come second, and so forth. Such individuals will find the layout of *Your Breakthroughs* helpful because it shows a logical progression of how to go from increasing personal effectiveness through gaining knowledge and experience in each of the various breakthrough methods described here (for 2,000 percent solutions, complementary 2,000 percent solutions, and excellent solutions). For such people the question will remain of whether to master all three methods or to focus on just one after first increasing personal effectiveness and eliminating stalls.

Here are some observations that might help. If what you are called by God to improve involves few people and an increase in effectiveness that's less than 500 times, you can gain the results you want by simply applying and repeating the 2,000 percent solution process. If, instead, your calling is to affect hundreds or more people and to make effectiveness improve by more than 500 times, the right complementary 2,000 percent solutions will probably take you to your goal a little faster. In the alternative, if your calling will affect many thousands or more people and require increasing effectiveness by at least 3 million times, an excellent solution is probably a faster and more reliable method.

Having picked one or more of these methods, reread the relevant sections of this book and develop an inventory of the skills and knowledge that you are missing in order to employ a given method. Then consider the most effective ways to fill in for whatever is lacking, including:

- Reading more about the methods
- Partnering with people who have the skills or knowledge you lack
- Working with organizations having complementary capabilities
- Conducting new research
- Searching for future best practices to use for filling in your remaining lacks

Next, break down into as many independent tasks as possible the steps you need to take for improving personal effectiveness, eliminating stalls, and implementing the solution method or methods you'll be using. After that, evaluate the best order for performing those tasks so that the amount of work, the elapsed time, and the expense will be minimized.

Once you have those tasks identified, break them down further into specific actions that are needed to accomplish each task. Doing so will help you avoid getting lost in a maze of steps and tasks. Instead, you'll be able to follow a list of actions and check them off as they are taken.

Good goal setting always requires selecting dates for accomplishing the elements of each task. However, since you don't have experience in doing some of these tasks, it will be hard for you to know how long each one will take. So I suggest that you only assign completion dates to what you believe you can finish with the time and resources available over the next sixty days. In doing so, be sure to start taking actions when timely where the tasks will take much longer than sixty days to complete. Then, regularly review the dates and adjust them to reflect your experience. Most people will do so weekly, but feel free to choose any frequency that makes sense to you.

To assess how appropriate your plans are before you actually begin performing any of these actions, review your steps, tasks, and actions with others whom you will be working with or who have more experience. If you cannot find anyone else with whom to do so, I'll be happy to help you with your initial list. Just send me an e-mail to donmitchell@fastforward400.com/.

In providing this explanation, I've been addressing the A to Z people. I know that there are also Z to A people. I'm sometimes one of them. For example, I like to read magazines and newspapers from the back to the front. Does that help you understand what I mean by Z to A?

For such individuals, the planning processes I've been describing would normally be conducted in the opposite order: Begin with a sense of what the result in increased fruitfulness will look like and then work backward in time through the process most likely to develop such a result to identify what impediments will have to be removed in terms of stalls, ignorance, mental baggage of other sorts, and current priorities. Such individuals will develop quite remarkable insights into what actions will make the biggest differences and will eventually establish a list of what to work on that will give those actions a much higher priority. I think the benefits of such thinking are potentially so substantial that the A to Z thinkers should consider testing their thinking in this manner, in addition to what they did with a logical or chronological sequence.

Some few other individuals may also see a sort of connect-the-dots way through what needs to be done. What I mean here is that they link from the beginning of what's missing to make the successful breakthrough to what isn't being done now and then build a simple set of steps to get from one place to the other. This way of planning can also be quite effective. Once again, I commend it as an additional approach to those who normally prefer to use a different planning method.

Of course, many people will just be called to work on certain aspects of making a breakthrough, such as part of its development or perhaps an element of its implementation. For these individuals, it will be valuable to orient any roles that can only begin after the work of others is done to what those other individuals actually do. So there will be a need for these people to monitor key developments that affect the timing and shape of their roles. Naturally, for those who will be involved during the project's inception, the steps involved will be much like what is done by those who will be starting a 2,000 percent or an excellent solution and then continuing with it through an extended period of implementation.

Your Lesson Twenty-Four Assignments

1. What is your calling from God?

2. Which breakthrough method will work best for what you are called to accomplish?

3. What effectiveness improvements do you need to make personally for accomplishing this calling?

4. What stalls do you need to overcome for effectively employing the breakthrough method?

5. What stalls do any organizations you will be working with need to overcome?

6. How will you organize the steps needed to accomplish your calling?

7. How will you manage following those steps?

8. What is your initial schedule for accomplishing tasks in the next sixty days?

Lesson Twenty-Five

Get Help

Let us therefore come boldly to the throne of grace,
that we may obtain mercy and find grace to help in time of need.

— Hebrews 4:16 (NKJV)

Have you ever been alone, lost, hungry, cold, wet, and miserable? If you've ever hiked by yourself in the mountains without a compass or a map during wintry weather, I'm sure you can quickly bring such a memory to mind. Even if you haven't, I'm sure that question strikes your imagination deeply enough that you can easily feel like you are having this experience. In either case, I'm sure that you don't find the recollection or imagined event to be very encouraging.

Needing help to start a big project or to get over a seemingly insurmountable hurdle can feel reasonably similar, minus the hungry, cold, and wet parts. Why? When we don't have an experience with something, we draw a mental blank. Without appropriate questions to steer us to useful memories, resources, and information, being in such a mental state can feel like being totally defeated. Don't let that happen to you!

As a child of our Heavenly Father, a follower of Jesus Christ, and someone who is inhabited by the Holy Spirit, you are never alone, never without access to all the resources in the universe, and never without an ability to gather the exact information that you need at just the right time. So if your mind doesn't immediately tell you that, just remember that the enemy who is in the world tries to make you less fruitful by sowing thoughts of fear, doubt, and disbelief. Don't fall for such attacks. Instead, just repeat aloud the verse above from Hebrews. Doing so will keep you operating in faith, a faith that will illuminate the way to where God wants you to be when He wants you to be there.

After reciting Hebrews 4:16 (NKJV) aloud, an excellent prayer at such times might go something like this:

Dear Heavenly Father,

I confess and repent now all the sins I haven't previously confessed to You. They are [describe]. Please wash me clean in the blood of the Lord, Jesus Christ, who is my Savior. I believe that You have called me to accomplish [the outcome of your calling], and I praise and thank You for directing me to do so. Right now, I'm stuck. I don't know what to do next. Please refill me with Your Holy Spirit and ask Him to show me in unmistakable ways exactly what You want me to do now. If Your direction is to wait, I will wait. If it is to act, I will act. If it is to undo what I have done, I will undo whatever You direct. Improve my ability to sense and appreciate what the Holy Spirit is directing. Please help me to always act according to Your will, not mine. In the name of the Lord, Jesus Christ, I pray. Amen.

Then, be patient and follow the Lord's lead.

Also, keep in mind that there are many people who know exactly what you need, who want to help you, and who are immediately available. Either research to find such people, or ask a good researcher to do so. If you can't do either one, send me an e-mail at donmitchell@fastforward400.com, and I'll suggest where to find the help you need.

Now, let me reverse perspectives by describing a different kind of situation. Have you ever felt highly confident, so confident that you believed you couldn't fail? Such a feeling often follows a streak of success or just being in a very good mood. Did everything always work out on such occasions? I hope so, but perhaps it didn't. If not, the consequences could have been quite painful if you had just risked more than you could afford.

Whenever you are feeling that much confidence, you need help. Someone needs to point out the pros and cons of what you are about to do, especially the costs if it doesn't all work out. Perhaps another person can identify alternatives that will be much less risky and probably deliver better results. Yet another person might be able to help attract people and resources for implementing one of those better alternatives.

Here's a third situation: You have tried everything and accomplishing your calling seems to be moving backwards, rather than advancing. In such a situation, you need to figure out if you are doing something wrong, or if such a circumstance is merely a natural lull along a path of rising improvements. You should get help to figure that out.

Let's look at a fourth circumstance: You would like to have help, but you are confident that no one in the world knows as much as you do. Let me suggest that you may be underestimating the potential resources. I have always been able to find someone who knew more than I did about at least some aspects of what was going on. When I sought out such knowledge, I often gained insights that kept me going more productively for decades. So in such a circumstance, you should also get help.

What about all other circumstances? Get help! Do you understand that you always need help?

If you accept that point, then you should begin as soon as possible to identify the information, people, and organizations that are available to help you with almost any conceivable need. When you combine your needs with world-class expertise, you'll be amazed at how much more you can accomplish.

It's easy to move from being ignorant to making big mistakes by only listening to yourself instead of to the Holy Spirit. A major reason for seeking help in all circumstances is that you don't know what you don't know. Many times the Holy Spirit will lead you to resources rather than changing the circumstances. Be open to that.

By looking for such resources, you will also find quick and easy ways to test your thinking. If you latch onto something that seems better, pray about using it and then follow wherever God leads you.

Lesson Twenty Five Assignments

1. How and when will you pray for God's guidance in accomplishing your calling?

2. How can you arrange in advance to identify the people, information and organizations that can help you to accomplish your calling more rapidly and effectively?

3. How will you overcome the temptation not to get enough help?

4. How can you gain assistance to ensure that you get enough of the right kinds of help?

Lesson Twenty-Six

Update Your Knowledge

The heart of the prudent acquires knowledge,
And the ear of the wise seeks knowledge.

— Proverbs 18:15 (NKJV)

In a sense, your direction from this lesson is the same as that of the prior lesson: Get help. However, the time dimension and perspectives are different. Lesson Twenty-Five told you to get help *now*, regardless of your circumstances, and mental and emotional states. This lesson directs you to get help in the *future* after updating your knowledge shows a better way to gain assistance.

Let me present some reasons for updating your knowledge, illustrated with examples drawn from my own experiences. First, updating knowledge can help with expanding capacity and expediting progress. Correctly interviewing executives and investment managers to derive insights into how to accomplish more is tricky business. Having engaged in such activities for many decades, I was thoroughly impressed by how unlikely it would be that someone else could do the work as effectively as our organization did for the purposes of expanding stakeholder value. Nevertheless, I occasionally tried to work with others, always unsuccessfully. After decades of doing so, yet another vendor wanted to try. I was reluctant. After badgering me unmercifully, I eventually relented. The work was terrific! I had updated my knowledge and formed a valuable new alliance in the process. Unfortunately, the vendor firm was soon sold, and I had to validate that the new ownership operated this activity as effectively as before. Doing so meant again updating my knowledge. Naturally, I also need to keep searching to see if there are still better vendors to help me.

Second, what once worked well will, at some point, cease to be effective. In the early days of Amazon.com, the Web site featured whatever I wrote in extremely flattering ways. I also received significant publicity. I was able to use such implied endorsements to introduce many people to The 400 Year Project. Later, the site's administrators decided that they wanted to encourage a different kind of participation for writing material on the site. This shift didn't match well with my gifts, talents, or interests. As a result, the site was soon burying most of what I produced. I quickly perceived that this channel had closed down, and I stopped working with it. Fortunately, I had already found effective individuals who were strongly called by God to work on activities related to mine. I simply shifted to using the methods those connections enabled. I continue to look for ways to replace my former writing for Amazon.com with something new that will have broad reach and appeal. So far, I haven't found a replacement, but I continue to search. I'm sure God will lead me to one or more through the Holy Spirit when His time is right.

Third, a breakthrough may occur quite unexpectedly. The first method described in *Your Breakthroughs* for making an excellent solution was revealed to me by the Holy Spirit in a few seconds while my daughter was driving me near our house. This method totally shifted the focus of what I did for The 400 Year Project for the following two highly fruitful years. I can now see a possible way to use the two excellent solutions methods to accomplish similar levels of enhanced fruitfulness with a great deal less time and effort, as well as with fewer resources.

Fourth, best practices are always evolving. During The 400 Year Project, successful practitioners of the breakthrough methods have also identified useful practices that no one else had previously applied. I learn about some of what those best practices are by sending queries to those I happen to know are good at providing breakthrough solutions. If I stopped making such inquiries, my knowledge of the best practices related to my own calling would soon become hopelessly out of date.

Fifth, being curious, continually looking at whatever else is happening, and absorbing new examples of excellence are outstanding ways to stimulate your creativity, thus enabling you to use the Holy Spirit's lessons in more fruitful ways. Before writing this lesson, I had just returned from an amazing four days during which I unexpectedly gained deep, new insights into the creative processes of some of the world's most effective artists, authors, choreographers, composers, and performers. While I won't finish absorbing what I learned for some time, I can already discern a major shift in what I notice that is bringing much helpful new information to bear. God had obviously decided that I needed to update my knowledge, and He provided the information to make doing so easy for me.

While I cannot hope to provide you with a substitute for what the Holy Spirit can do in helping you update knowledge, I believe that I can assist by helping you keep your mind more open to what the Holy Spirit intends for you to learn. Here is a list of some questions that may help:

- What do you assume will always work?
- What would you love to have work much better?
- What one change would make the biggest improvement in fulfilling your calling?
- What do you most depend on to work well?
- What do you think will never work better?
- Who haven't you asked?
- Who should know better ways?
- When was the last time you checked?

When you find something that's unexpectedly valuable, please share it with me at donmitchell@fastforward400.com/. I'll be sure to pass along the good word to those who would most benefit.

Many thanks for your thoughtful attention to these twenty-six lessons. I pray that they will assist you in becoming far more fruitful.

Lesson Twenty-Six Assignments

1. When did you last update your knowledge about expanding capacity for and expediting the progress of accomplishing your calling?

2. When did you last check on the effectiveness of what had once worked well for accomplishing your calling?

3. When did you last update your knowledge to learn about any new breakthrough processes for accomplishing your calling?

4. When did you last update your knowledge to learn from anyone who has achieved enormous success in activities that might include useful lessons for accomplishing your calling?

5. When did you last update your knowledge to learn how to use any new best practices for accomplishing your calling?

6. With what frequency should such updates and checks occur?

7. Are you on schedule with the required updates and checks?

Appendix A

Donald Mitchell's Testimony

He will lift you up.

*Humble yourselves
in the sight of the Lord,
and He will lift you up.*

— James 4:10 (NKJV)

Let me share with you how I became a Christian so you'll know where I'm coming from with regard to encouraging you to become a Christian and to be fruitful in Godly contributions for creating and implementing breakthrough solutions.

There has been a long commitment to the Lord in our family. For example, I remember my great-grandmother, Edith Foster, reading the Bible every day. As a youngster, my mother regularly took me to Sunday school. It was my least favorite activity; sleeping was much preferred. I did enjoy listening to sermons, but it was frowned on to take youngsters to the adult services where the sermons were given.

If I pretended to be asleep, mom would sometimes let me stay in bed on Sundays. I was pretty good at pretending, and I soon was the biggest backslider in my Sunday school grade. Fortunately, it was an evangelical church so my classmates were always cooking up schemes to get me to attend again. Because of my high opinion of myself, I would always return if invited to play my clarinet for the congregation.

By the time I turned thirteen, I was pretty full of myself. There wasn't much room for God in there alongside my exaggerated opinion of myself.

One day at home while my family was away for a drive, I felt really sick. By the time they returned, I was delirious. Within an hour, I was in the hospital where I would stay for two weeks as I barely survived a bad case of double pneumonia.

My physician, Dr. Helmsley, was an observant Christian and worried about my soul because my life was in jeopardy. He talked to me about our Heavenly Father, Jesus, and the Holy Spirit twice a day when he stopped by to check on me. These conversations were when I first learned how to become a Christian through being born again. I also came to realize that I couldn't stop sinning on my own. I needed a Savior, Jesus Christ! After I recovered, he took my mom and me to a tent revival meeting.

Having recovered from the illness, I soon pushed God out of my life again. During the next year, I was, instead, very caught up in athletics. When I was in ninth grade, I desperately wanted to make a contribution to our junior high track team, which had a remote chance of winning the big meet. Our coach, Mr. Layman, told each of us exactly what had to be accomplished for the team to win. I was determined to do my part. I had to come in first!

But that wasn't likely to happen. Based on past performances, there were at least two people who could out leap me in the standing broad jump, my main event. To make such a jump, you stand on a slightly raised, forward-tilted board and spring outward as far as you can into a sand-filled pit. After two of the three jumping rounds, I knew it was hopeless. I was in sixth place and four of the competitors' jumps were longer than I had ever gone before. I also didn't like the board we were using.

Remembering that we should call on God when we need help, I thought of praying ... but what I wanted was so trivial in God's terms that I didn't think it was worthy of prayer. So I decided to make God an offer instead: "Dear God, help me win this event, and I'm yours forever." After all, if He came through, any doubts I had about God would be dispelled.

I stepped onto the broad-jump board and felt very calm. I did my routine and took off into the air. Instantly, I felt light as a feather cradled in a large, gentle hand that was lifting me. I was dropped softly at the far end of the pit. I had outleapt everyone and gone more than six inches past my best previous jump. I couldn't believe it. Then I remembered my promise to God, thanked Him, repented my sins, accepted Jesus as my Lord and Savior, and ran off to tell everyone on the team.

Even more remarkable, I was the only person on the team who performed up to the plan. Knowing what had to be done had probably given us performance anxiety, and people underperformed because they didn't believe they could do what the team needed. I also suspect that God wanted to make a point with me that I needed Him.

After a few days, I started to think that perhaps I'd just developed a new broad-jump technique and God didn't have a role at all. God soon dispelled that thought by making sure that my jumps for the rest of my life were much shorter than I had jumped when He lifted me up.

Since then, God has been speaking to me on a regular basis through the Holy Spirit. I've learned to pay attention and to act promptly. When I pursue my own ideas, things don't go so well. When I follow His directions, things work out great. That's my secret to high performance, and I just wanted to share it with you so you could benefit, too. He knows the answers, even when you and I don't ... which is most of the time.

As a management consultant, the Holy Spirit has often filled me with knowledge about what the consequences of one set of actions would be compared to another for my clients. Naturally, I always recommended as the Holy Spirit directed me. Clients often told me that they were impressed by how certain I was of my conclusions and of how persuasive I could be in describing the advantages of whatever recommendations were made. Once again, the explanatory words came from the Holy Spirit, rather than from me.

Unfortunately, I wasn't comfortable in my younger days sharing my faith with clients, and I wrongly gave many people the impression that I was the author of the solutions rather than merely the transmitter.

I wish I had been more faithful in this regard. I apologize to my clients for having missed so many great witnessing opportunities. I didn't always listen as well as I should in making decisions that primarily affected me, but God would always do something to get my attention. Here's an example. I made an investment that I hoped would reduce my taxes in addition to making some money. I didn't have a good feeling from the Holy Spirit at the time, and I shouldn't have invested.

My tax return was later audited by the Internal Revenue Service concerning that investment. It turned out I was in the wrong for the deductions I had taken. Anticipating a big tax bill plus penalties and interest, you can imagine my astonishment when the revised tax return showed me owing no additional money to the government even though I had lost on the audit issues. I knew that result was a gift from God, and I was overwhelmed by His wisdom and power in protecting me. Praise God for His mercy!

I rededicated my life to Jesus in 1995, and I have enjoyed great peace since then. I have also done a lot better in being obedient to the Holy Spirit and to what the Bible tells us to do in all aspects of my life. Many blessings have been mine since then.

After being told by God to start The 400 Year Project (demonstrating how everyone in the world could make improvements 20-times faster and more effectively than normal with no additional resources) in 1995, I continued to receive His instructions. In 2005, for example, God told me to start explaining to people how to live their lives by gaining more joy from what they already have.

In the summer of 2006, I began to see how The 400 Year Project could be brought to a successful conclusion (as I reported in *Adventures of an Optimist*, Mitchell and Company Press, 2007). Realizing that perhaps I had devoted too much of my attention to this one challenge, I began to seek ways to rebalance my life. One of those rebalancing methods was to spend more time communing with God through prayer, Scriptural studies, attending church services and Bible classes, and listening more to the still, small voice within.

For several years I had been enjoying the devotionals sent to me daily over the Internet by evangelist Bill Keller. One of those devotionals speared me like an arrow that summer. The evangelist reminded his readers that our responsibility as believers is to share our faith with others through our example and sharing the Gospel message from the Bible. Not feeling well equipped to do more than try to be a good example, I began to pray about what else I should be doing.

The next day, my answer came: I was to launch a global contest to locate the most effective ways that souls were being saved and be sure that information was shared widely. This sharing would be a blessing for those who wished to fulfill the Great Commission to spread the Good News of Jesus as commanded in Matthew 28:18-20 (NKJV):

And Jesus came and spoke to them, saying, "All authority has been given to Me in heaven and on earth. Go therefore and make disciples of all the nations, baptizing them in the name of the Father and of the Son and of the Holy Spirit, teaching them to observe all things that I have commanded you; and lo, I am with you always, *even* to the end of the age."

The contest winners were Jubilee Worship Center in Hobart, Indiana, and Step by Step Ministries in Porter, Indiana. You can read their experiences to learn amazingly effective ways to help unsaved people choose to accept Salvation in *Witnessing Made Easy: Yes, You Can Make a Difference* (Jubilee Worship Center Step by Step Press, 2010) by Bishop Dale P. Combs, Lisa Combs, Jim Barbarossa, Carla Barbarossa, and me. Six other worthy ideas and practices from the contest for assisting more people to learn about and some to be moved by the Holy Spirit to pledge their lives to Jesus are described in a second book, *Ways You Can Witness: How the Lost Are Found* (Salvation Press, 2010) by Cherie Hill, Roger de Brabant, Drew Dickens, Gael Torcise, Wendy Lobos, Herpha Jane Obod, Gisele Umugiraneza, and me.

Let me tell you another interesting thing about my life with Jesus. When my daughter was about a year old, I suffered what resembled a stroke that caused me to start to become paralyzed. As I could feel my face's muscles freezing, I immediately prayed to Jesus to stop the paralysis and He did. I was left with a lot of pain and numbness on the left side of my body and was very weak for over a year.

Part of that pain continued for the next twenty-two years until, on November 8, 2009, I asked two of my pastors during a communion service to pray in the name of Jesus that the remaining pain be removed. During the prayer, the pain started leaving immediately and was totally gone within a half hour. As I felt the pain leaving me, through some power traveling inch by inch down my body, I was overcome with gratitude and fell on my knees in thanks.

That wasn't the only time He recently healed me. Encouraged by that miraculous experience, I came forward again on December 19, 2010, during another communion service to request prayer for relief from the pain in my wrists that was making it difficult for me to write books to serve Him and to do my other work. Knowing that my mother had been plagued with arthritis, I assumed it was a similar onset for me. My pastors were occupied with prayers for other members of the congregation. This time an elder of the church and his wife anointed me with oil and prayed for me. Almost immediately, my whole body shook violently in a way that I couldn't stop. Gradually, the shaking was reduced until it ceased after about half an hour, and my wrist pain was totally gone. It has not returned. I was even more overwhelmed that He had healed me again. Can anyone appreciate all the goodness that God has in store for us?

Let me share yet another miraculous healing (not the last that I've experienced). I've always been troubled with many respiratory and food allergies and sensitivities. In my sixties, these problems had become worse. I finally reached the point where it was difficult to be in the same room with another person due to my reactions to any deodorants and scents they were using. During still another communion service on January 16, 2012, two pastors again prayed for me to be relieved of these problems so that I could be a better witness for Him. Once again, power filled my body. My allergies and sensitivities were gone in a few minutes. Since then, they haven't returned. It has made a huge improvement in my life and in my witnessing.

I have also been saved by God from what I believed to be certain death on twelve occasions, most recently on July 2, 2013. I won't go into all of these events, but I did want you to be aware that He is always touching all aspects of my life in beneficial ways.

While it's up to God to decide if and when He wants to heal us or to protect us from harm, it's certainly reassuring to know that He has the ability and power to do anything He wants.

Glory be to God! Praise Him always! His miracles, grace, and mercy never end. I am so happy and honored to be His servant and witness to you.

Appendix B

Summary of
The 400 Year Project

Therefore we also pray always for you
that our God would count you worthy of this calling,
and fulfill all the good pleasure of His goodness
and the work of faith with power,
that the name of our Lord Jesus Christ
may be glorified in you, and you in Him,
according to the grace of our God
and the Lord Jesus Christ.

— 2 Thessalonians 1:11-12 (NKJV)

One morning during the summer of 1995 at around 3:45 a.m., I felt a warm presence fill the bedroom. In response, my body temperature seemed to rise and I felt deliriously happy. A voice that I didn't recognize filled my mind and told me in tones that were more resonant and powerful than James Earl Jones on his best day that I should hold a meeting for all of my management consulting clients to celebrate and share their greatest accomplishments on the autumnal e-quinox. At the end of the meeting, I should announce that I would be starting a 20-year project to find ways for the whole world to make 400 years of normal progress in only 20 years, beginning in 2015 and finishing in 2035. For the next few weeks, I could think of little else.

What had happened? I prayed over the experience quite a bit and concluded that God had sent me a message. Why me? I have no idea. Maybe He couldn't find anyone else crazy enough to take on such an impossible task. I certainly felt that only God would know how to do it.

Why that time frame? I don't know, but it later occurred to me that the 2000th anniversary of Jesus' resurrection would occur during 2015–2035. Perhaps that was an important connection. Since then, I've come to appreciate that 20 is a spiritually important number to God: Notice that the dimensions of the Holy of Holies in the Temple were measured in terms of 20 cubits. But who knows, except God?

How would I pursue this project? I had no idea, not even a clue. All I knew was that I was supposed to make this announcement at the autumnal equinox.

I quickly organized the meeting. Clients graciously agreed to fly in to share their triumphs and lessons with one another. Not knowing how anyone else would take the announcement of the new project, I decided to keep it to myself. I also had the impression that I should keep the project private until the announcement. Otherwise, why make the announcement then rather than sooner?

The event went much better than I could have hoped, especially since I wasn't sure what to say during the unexpected announcement. Almost all listeners were encouraging, and many volunteered to help with the project.

A key early focus was to engage in writing a book that Peter Drucker, the founder of the management discipline, had encouraged Carol Coles and me to write encapsulating a problem-solving method that we had been using for many years. We were fortunate to gain the assistance of Robert Metz, a veteran author and journalist, as a coauthor to lead us through the publication twists and turns. That book was *The 2,000 Percent Solution*, still the most widely read publication produced by The 400 Year Project.

Having experienced a warm reception for this book, I was delighted when the Holy Spirit kept providing concepts, processes, or the actual words for many future books, of which eighteen more have been completed with the publication of *Your Breakthroughs*. Through these books, readers and students of mine have created their own breakthroughs by employing The 400 Year Project's methods. I'm aware of successful demonstration projects that have been conducted so far in over 60 countries. There are probably more such successes that I'm unaware of. What a blessing! Praise God!

I have also had the pleasure of conducting several global contests, building experience to supplement the concepts first articulated in *The Ultimate Competitive Advantage* about this way of making rapid advances.

I also established a learning organization, The Billionaire Entrepreneurs' Master Mind, to advance how complementary 2,000 percent solutions could be most effectively developed and combined. I continue to be delighted by the lessons developed by that group, which have richly informed *Business Basics* and the three books in the recently completed Advanced Business series.

Today, The 400 Year Project is ready for prime time. The books, experiences, and networks of breakthrough problem solvers provide a sound foundation for expanding and transforming God's Kingdom in every possible dimension between now and 2035 by far more than 20 times. I'm delighted that you will be part of creating such remarkable transformations.

May God bless you, your family, and all you do in the name of Jesus!

www.ingramcontent.com/pod-product-compliance
Lightning Source LLC
LaVergne TN
LVHW051452080426
835509LV00017B/1750